Collins · *do brilliantly!*

Revision Guide

GCSE Science

■ **Chris Sunley and Mike Smith**

■ **Series editor: Jayne de Courcy**

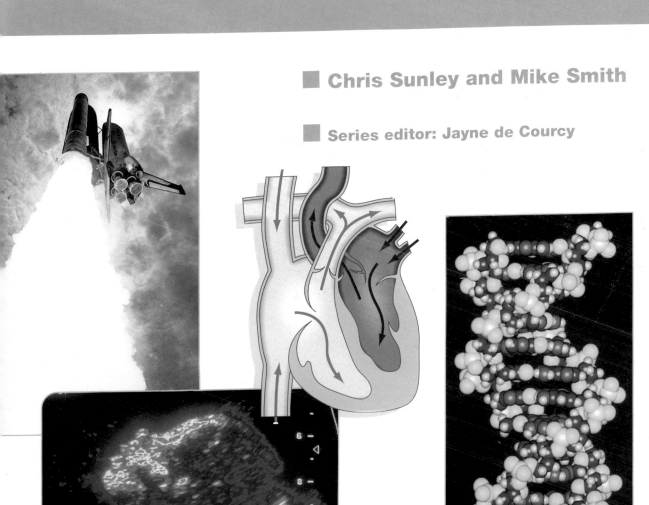

CONTENTS AND REVISION PLANNER

EXAM TIPS

Comments from the most recent Examiners' reports

General

- Candidates should be encouraged to use scientific terminology in their answers wherever possible.

- Candidates cannot be awarded marks for repeating information from the question.

- Many candidates lost marks for careless plotting of graphs. Too many incorrectly joined the points with straight lines rather than drawing a smooth curve through the points.

- When doing calculations, it is important that students quote the equation they are using and show their working out.

- Candidates often lost marks in calculation questions because they did not include a unit with their answer.

- Some candidates did not label or add to diagrams at all, suggesting that they had not read the instructions carefully.

Biology

Life Processes and Cells

- A very large number of candidates in this question [on osmosis] failed to gain a mark because they described water as moving from an area of high concentration to an area of low concentration. However if they stated that water moved from an area of high water concentration to one of low water concentration, this was acceptable...

- Some candidates thought that active transport included movement through transport systems such as vascular tissue in plants.

- ... many candidates explained the idea of oxygen debt but were unable to say why extra oxygen was needed.

- A significant number of candidates seem to have the [incorrect] idea that the biconcave shape [of red blood cells] is important as oxygen is carried in the 'dip'.

(see pp 1-5)

Human Body Systems

- A large proportion of candidates [on the foundation paper] confused physical digestion with chemical digestion.....

- Most candidates knew that the semi-lunar valve prevented backflow.

- Only the best candidates [on the foundation paper] could correctly identify the left atrium.

(see pp 6-20)

Body Maintenance

- Most candidates [incorrectly] thought that the brain was involved in all reflexes.

- Some candidates thought that the kidneys can take water from urine, even when it has been sent to the bladder.

- Unfortunately there are still many candidates stating that blood vessels move closer to the surface of the skin when it becomes redder during exercise.

  - Many candidates think that the release of hormones by the pancreas is controlled by the brain.

    (see pp 21-37)

Ecology and the Environment

- Some candidates confused pesticides with fertilisers.

- Many candidates seemed unfamiliar with leguminous plants [e.g. peas and beans], with some relating the nodules to an increase in surface area.

- Most candidates were able to write down the correct food chain ... although the flow of energy was reversed in some cases.

- A very small minority of candidates appeared to have understood and learnt ... the nitrogen cycle.

    (see pp 49-67)

Plants

- Most candidates were able to name a suitable plant nutrient, though many answers were vague, such as 'minerals' and other substances such as 'protein' and 'glucose' were quite common.

- ...many candidates scored one mark for the correct use of the term flaccid or turgid but only a very few could give an explanation in terms of relative water uptake and loss.

    (see pp 38-48)

Genetics and Evolution

- Some lost the mark by describing male as XX and female as XY.

- Whilst most candidates are now able to display knowledge of the mechanics of genetics, definitions of key terms such as recessive and phenotype are still poor. This would suggest that understanding remains weak.

- The use of the Punnett square almost invariably results in full marks and is the preferred method for showing the possible outcomes of a cross, since it leads to the reduced likelihood of errors.

    (see pp 68-81)

Chemistry

Structure and Bonding

- Many candidates did not appreciate that neutrons have no charge.

- Candidates do not appreciate that an atom must contain the same number of protons and electrons, as it is neutral.

- Very few candidates appeared to realise that water is covalently bonded and contains molecules.

  (see pp 89-97)

Fuels and Energy

- Many candidates identified the components of a hydrocarbon incorrectly, common answers including 'hydro', 'hyroxide' or 'carbon dioxide'.

- The nature of the energy change during the making and breaking of bonds is not well understood.

- Few candidates could explain the parts played by respiration and photosynthesis in the carbon cycle.

- Candidates were frequently unable to explain how carbon monoxide is formed during the combustion of fossil fuels.

  (see pp 98-109)

Rocks and Metals

- Many candidates did not understand how electrolysis can be used to extract reactive metals. Few could correctly give the formulae of the ions involved or state at which electrode the metal formed.

- A common mistake was to confuse 'crust' and 'mantle'.

- Few candidates could write the correct equation for the formation of sodium from sodium ions. The most common mistake was: $Na + e- = Na+$.

- The term 'reduction' was often not used. Instead the incorrect term 'de-oxidation' was used.

- The main confusion shown by candidates was between the description of igneous and metamorphic rocks.

- Candidates were often unable to link the formation of volcanoes with moving tectonic plates. Candidates often confused magma and lava.

  (see pp 110-118)

Chemical Reactions

- Few candidates were able to refer to the fact that a permanent change occurs in a chemical reaction.

- When answering questions about the effect of temperature on the rate of a reaction, only a few candidates referred to successful collisions with many writing about 'particles beginning to move' or 'vibrate' when the temperature is increased.

- When trying to explain the effect of increasing concentration on reaction rate, candidates often simply referred to 'more particles' rather than the idea of 'more crowded particles'.

- In questions on fermentation, few candidates appreciated that yeast contains enzymes and that enzymes make the reaction go faster.

- Candidates were often unclear about the difference between the rate of the reaction [how quickly the product formed] and the yield or conversion rate in a reversible reaction.

  (see pp 119-131)

The Periodic Table

- When comparing hydrogen with the noble gases, many candidates failed to mention the flammability of hydrogen and the inert nature of the noble gases.

- In writing symbol equations, many candidates used Cl for chlorine rather than Cl_2.

  (See pp 132-142)

Chemical Calculations

- Poor layout of the calculation made it difficult to award marks for working when the answer was incorrect.

  (See pp 143-149)

Physics

Electricity

- Candidates often wrote about electricity being 'pollution free', showing a lack of understanding of the environmental issues related to electricity generation.

- Many candidates could not explain that the neutral wire completes the circuit or takes the current away.

- Many candidates did not appreciate that the case of a double insulated device is an insulator itself.

- A common misunderstanding about the function of fuses was 'the fuse prevented too much current from flowing as it was a constriction in the circuit'.

  (See pp 150-163)

Waves

Candidates often confused frequency with loudness, amplitude or wavelength.

A common misconception was that optical fibres have mirrors inside them. Many candidates wrote about 'refraction' of light in the fibre rather than reflection.

- When drawing ray diagrams, candidates often failed to use a ruler.

- Many candidates did not appreciate that UV light and visible light travel at the same speed.

- Many candidates understood that sound was transmitted by air particles but the idea of vibrations was rarely used.

  (see pp 189-199)

Forces and Motion

- Thinking distance is defined in terms of time by many candidates, for example: 'it is the time it takes while you are thinking about stopping'.

- A significant number ... incorrectly described gravity as a 'pushing force'.

- Too many candidates think that there is no gravity on the Moon.

- Candidates often confused force and pressure.

  (See pp 171-179)

Energy

- There was very little evidence of candidates having understanding of the relationship between heat and particle vibration, or how energy is transferred from particle to particle. They often incorrectly referred to 'heat particles'.

- In writing about insulators, many candidates did not appreciate the significance of trapped air in the insulator – that is, it prevents energy transfer by convection.

  (see pp 180-188)

Radioactivity

- Few candidates could explain what a beta particle is.

- Many candidates had failed to grasp the concept of 'half-life'.

  (see pp 204-210)

ABOUT THIS BOOK

Exams are about much more than just repeating memorized facts, so we have planned this book to make your revision as active and effective as possible.

How?

- by breaking down the content into manageable chunks (Revision Sessions)

- by testing your understanding at every step of the way (Check Yourself Questions)

- by providing extra information to help you aim for the very top grade (A* Extras)

- by highlighting Ideas and Evidence topics (Ideas and Evidence)

- by listing the most likely exam questions for each topic (Question Spotters)

- by giving you invaluable examiner's guidance about exam technique (Exam Practice)

REVISION SESSION 1

Revision Sessions

- Each topic is divided into a number of **short revision sessions**. You should be able to read through each of these in no more than 30 minutes. That is the maximum amount of time that you should spend on revising without taking a short break.

- Ask your teacher for a copy of your own exam board's **GCSE Science specification**. Tick off on the Contents list each of the revision sessions that you need to cover. It will probably be most of them.

CHECK YOURSELF QUESTIONS

- At the end of each revision session there are some **Check Yourself Questions**. By trying these questions, you will immediately find out whether you have understood and remembered what you have read in the revision session. **Answers** are at the back of the book, along with **extra hints and guidance**.

- If you manage to answer all the Check Yourself Questions for a session correctly, then you can confidently tick off this topic in the box provided in the Contents list. If not, you will need to tick the 'Revise again' box to remind yourself to return to this topic later in your revision programme.

Exam Practice

- This unit gives you **invaluable guidance on how to answer exam questions well**.

- It contains some sample students' answers to typical exam questions, followed by examiner's comments on them, showing where the students lost and gained marks. Reading through these will help you get a very clear idea of what you need to do in order to score **full marks** when answering questions in your exam.

- There are also some **typical exam questions** for you to try answering. Model answers are given at the back of the book for you to check your own answers against. There are also examiner's hints, highlighting **how to achieve full marks**.

ABOUT YOUR GCSE SCIENCE COURSE

Does this book match my course?

This book has been written to support all the double and single-award Science GCSE specifications produced by the four Exam Boards in England and Wales. These specifications include content from the three main areas of Biology, Chemistry and Physics and are based on the National Curriculum Key Stage 4 Programmes of Study. This means that although different specifications may arrange the content in different ways, they must all cover the same work.

The double-Science courses lead to the award of two GCSE Science grades. The single-Science courses result in a single GCSE grade. The content of the single award specifications taken from the double award. Ask your teacher whether you are following a single or double-award course.

Foundation and Higher Tier papers

In your GCSE science exam you will be entered for either the Foundation Tier exam papers or the Higher Tier exam papers. The Foundation exams allow you to obtain grades from G to C. The Higher exams allow you to obtain grades from D to A*.

Higher Tier							
A*	A	B	C	D	E	F	G
			Foundation Tier				

What will my exam questions be like?

The exam questions will be of a type known as structured questions. Usually these are based on a particular topic and will include related questions. Some of these questions will require short answers involving a single word, phrase or sentence. Other questions will require a longer answer involving extended prose. You will have plenty of practice at both types of questions as you work through this book.

Short answer questions

These are used to test a wide range of knowledge and understanding quite quickly.

They are often worth one mark each.

Extended prose questions

These are used to test how well you can link different ideas together. Usually they ask you to explain ideas in some detail. It is important to use the correct scientific terms and to write clearly.

They may be worth four or five marks and sometimes more.

How should I answer exam questions?

- Look at the number of marks. The marks should tell you how long to spend on a question. A rough guide is a minute for every mark. The number of marks will indicate how many different points are required in the answer.

- Look at the space allocated for the answer. If only one line is given, then only a short answer is required, e.g. a single word, a short phrase or a short sentence. Some questions will require more extended writing and so four or more lines will be allocated.

- Read the question carefully. Students frequently answer the question they would like to answer rather than the one that has actually been set! Circle or underline the key words. Make sure you know what you are being asked to do. Are you choosing from a list? Are you using the Periodic Table? Are you completing a table? Have you been given the formula you will need to use in a calculation? Are you describing or explaining?

UNIT 1: LIFE PROCESSES AND CELLS

REVISION SESSION 1 ▬ ## Characteristics of living things

⬚ What is biology?

■ Biology is the study of living things. An individual living thing is called an **organism**. The two main types of organism are **animals** (which includes us) and **plants**.

■ Although there is a huge variety of organisms, they have many things in common. This includes the way they are built and how they work.

⬚ Cells

■ Most living things are made up of building blocks called **cells**. Most cells are so small that they can only be seen with a microscope.

■ There are many different types of cells, which all have different jobs, such as nerve cells, muscle cells and blood cells. However, most cells have certain features in common.

■ Plant cells have features that are not found in animal cells. The diagrams show a typical animal cell and a typical plant cell.

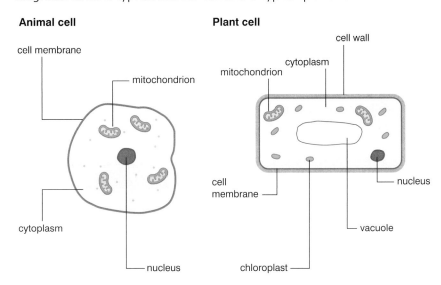

Animal cell
- cell membrane
- mitochondrion
- cytoplasm
- nucleus

Plant cell
- cell wall
- cytoplasm
- mitochondrion
- nucleus
- cell membrane
- vacuole
- chloroplast

⬚ What do the different parts of a cell do?

■ The **cell membrane** holds the cell together and controls substances entering or leaving the cell.

■ The **cytoplasm** is more complicated than it looks. This is where many different chemical processes happen.

■ The **nucleus** contains **chromosomes** and **genes**. These control how a cell grows and works. Genes also control the features that can be passed on to offspring.

■ The **mitochondria** (singular: mitochondrion) are the parts of the cell where energy is released from food in the process known as **respiration**.

⚡ A* EXTRA

The chemical reactions that take place in the cytoplasm are controlled by enzymes (biological catalysts).

> You will often be asked to label the outside layer of a cell.
> Whether it is the cell membrane or the cell wall depends on what type of cell it is.

■ Plants have a **cell wall** as well as a cell membrane. It is much more rigid than the cell membrane and gives the cell shape and support.

■ The plant cell's **vacuole** contains a liquid called cell sap, which is water with various substances dissolved in it. In a healthy plant the vacuole is large and helps support the cell.

■ Plants also contain **chloroplasts**. These contain the green pigment **chlorophyll**, which absorbs the light energy that plants need to make food in the process known as **photosynthesis**.

Similarities	Differences	
Most cells contain	**Animal cells**	**Plant cells**
Cell membrane	No cell wall	Have a cell wall
Cytoplasm	No large vacuole (although there may be small ones)	Usually have a large vacuole
Nucleus	No chloroplasts	Green parts of a plant contain chloroplasts
Mitochondria	Many irregular shapes	Usually have a regular shape

IDEAS AND EVIDENCE

> In 1665 Robert Hooke invented the first useful microscope. He used it to look at thin slices of cork. He saw little box-like shapes that he called cells because he thought they looked like the tiny rooms or cells in which monks lived.
> The invention of the microscope allowed scientists to develop a greater understanding of living organisms.

Organisation of cells

■ Many cells are not 'typical' cells like the ones just described. They are **specialised** – they have special features that allow them to carry out different jobs.

■ Cells of the same type form **tissue**. Different tissues may make up an **organ**. Organs that work together make up an **organ system**.

■ For example, the circulatory system includes the heart organ, which contains muscle tissue and nervous tissue, which are made of muscle cells and nerve cells.

CHECK YOURSELF QUESTIONS

Q1 Look at the diagram of an onion cell.
  a How is the onion cell different from a typical plant cell?
  b Explain the reason for this difference.
  c How is the onion cell different from an animal cell?

Q2 Name which part of a cell does the following:
  a Releases energy from food.
  b Allows oxygen to enter.
  c Contains the genes.
  d Contains cell sap.
  e Stops plant cells swelling if they take in a lot of water.

Q3 For each of the following say whether it is a cell, a tissue, an organ, a system or an organism:
  a oak tree
  b human egg
  c brain, spinal cord and nerves
  d leaf
  e stomach lining
  f kidney.

Answers are on page 232.

Transport into and out of cells

☐ How do substances enter and leave cells?

■ It's not only whole organisms that take in or give out in substances (for example when animals eat and breathe or when they excrete) – each cell in a body has to take in and give out different things. All of these things will have to pass through the **cell membrane**.

■ There are three main ways substances enter and leave cells:

1 diffusion

2 osmosis

3 active transport.

☐ Diffusion

■ Substances like water, oxygen, carbon dioxide and food are made of particles. You will find out more about particles in Unit 8.

■ In liquids and gases the particles are constantly moving around. This means that they will tend to spread themselves out evenly. For example, if you dissolve sugar in a cup of tea, even if you do not stir it, the sugar will eventually spread throughout the tea because the sugar molecules are constantly moving around, colliding with and bouncing off other particles. This is an example of **diffusion**.

> diffusion is net movement from a region of high concentration to a region of low concentration.

 water molecules

 sugar molecules

The sugar molecules are concentrated in one area.

The sugar molecules are spreading out because they are constantly moving and colliding.

The sugar molecules are now evenly concentrated throughout.

SUMMARY OF DIFFUSION

■ Diffusion occurs when there is a difference in concentration. The greater the difference in concentration the faster the rate of diffusion.

■ Particles diffuse from regions of high concentration to regions of low concentration. They move along the **concentration gradient**.

■ Diffusion stops when the particles are evenly concentrated. But this does not mean that the particles themselves stop moving.

■ Diffusion happens because particles are constantly and randomly moving. It does not need an input of energy from a plant or animal.

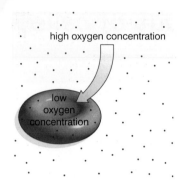

high oxygen concentration

low oxygen concentration

A high concentration gradient leads to diffusion. Red blood cells low in oxygen will soak it up from more oxygen-rich surroundings.

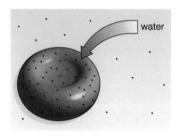

water

A red blood cell in pure water.

water

A red blood cell in in a concentrated solution.

DIFFUSION IN CELLS

- Substances can enter and leave cells by diffusion. If there is a higher concentration on one side of the membrane than the other and the substance can move through the membrane, then it will.

- For example, red blood cells travel to the lungs to collect oxygen. There is a **low** oxygen concentration in the cells (because they have given up their oxygen to other parts of the body) but a **high** oxygen concentration in the air spaces in the lungs. Therefore oxygen diffuses into the red blood cells.

- Other examples of diffusion are oxygen and carbon dioxide moving in and out of plant leaves, and digested food in the small intestine entering the blood. You can read more about diffusion in Unit 8.

Osmosis

- Osmosis is a special example of diffusion where **only water** moves into or out of cells. It occurs because cell membranes are **partially permeable** – they allow some substances (such as water) to move through them but not others.

- Water will diffuse from a place where there is a high concentration of water molecules (such as a dilute sugar solution) to where there is a low concentration of water molecules (such as a concentrated sugar solution).

- Many people confuse the concentration of the solution with the concentration of the water. Remember, it is the **water that is moving**, so we must think of the **concentration of water in the solution** instead of the concentration of substance dissolved in it.
  - A low concentration of dissolved substances means a high concentration of water.
  - A high concentration of dissolved substances means a low concentration of water. So the water is still moving from a high concentration (of water) to a low concentration (of water), even though this is often described as water moving from a low-concentration **solution** to a high-concentration **solution**.

The water is less concentrated on the right and more concentrated on the left. The water diffuses to the right. This sort of diffusion is known as osmosis.

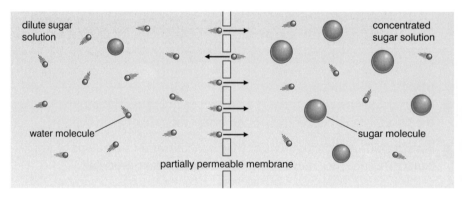

dilute sugar solution

concentrated sugar solution

water molecule

sugar molecule

partially permeable membrane

- One important example of osmosis is water entering the roots of plants.

- If animal cells such as blood cells are placed in different-strength solutions they will shrink or swell up (and even burst) depending on whether they gain or lose water via osmosis.

⌷ Active transport

- Sometimes cells need to absorb substances **against a concentration gradient** – from a region of low concentration to a region of high concentration.

- For example, root hair cells may take in nitrate ions from the soil even though the concentration of these ions is higher in the plant than in the soil. The way that the nitrate ions are absorbed is called **active transport**. Another example of active transport is dissolved ions being actively absorbed back into the blood from kidney tubules.

- Active transport occurs when special **'carrier proteins'** on the surface of a cell pick up particles from one side of the membrane and transport them to the other side. You can see this happening in the diagram below.

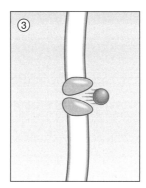

① carrier protein / sugar molecule / membrane ② ③

💡 QUESTION SPOTTER

▸ Examiners will often expect you to know which type of movement is involved in a particular situation.
▸ An example would be: 'By what process do minerals enter plant roots?'

- Active transport uses energy that the cells release during respiration.

❓ CHECK YOURSELF QUESTIONS

Q1 An old-fashioned way of killing slugs in the garden is to sprinkle salt on them. This kills slugs by drying them out. Explain why this would dry them out.

Q2 Which of the following are examples of: diffusion, osmosis or neither?
  a Carbon dioxide entering a leaf when it is photosynthesising.
  b Food entering your stomach when you swallow.
  c Tears leaving your tear ducts when you cry.
  d A dried out piece of celery swelling up when placed in a bowl of water.

Q3 Why would you expect plant root hair cells to contain more mitochondria than other plant cells?

Answers are on page 232.

UNIT 2: HUMAN BODY SYSTEMS

Respiration

A* EXTRA

Energy from respiration is used:
▸ to keep warm
▸ to enable muscles to contract
▸ to build up large molecules from small ones
▸ in the active transport of substances across cell membranes

What is respiration?

■ The energy that our bodies need to keep us alive is released from our food. Releasing the energy is called **respiration** and happens in every cell of our body. The food is usually **glucose** (sugar) but other kinds of food can be used if enough glucose is not available.

■ Respiration usually involves **oxygen**. This kind of respiration is called **aerobic respiration**. Water and carbon dioxide are produced as waste products.

■ Aerobic respiration can be summarised by a word equation:

glucose + oxygen → water + carbon dioxide + energy

■ It can also be written as a chemical equation:

$C_6H_{12}O_6 + 6O_2 \rightarrow 6H_2O + 6CO_2$ + energy

■ The energy released is used for all the processes of life: movement, sensitivity, growth, reproduction, excretion and nutrition (feeding). Eventually most of the energy is lost as heat.

■ Aerobic respiration provides most of the energy we need. If we need to release more, for example if we are exercising, then aerobic respiration increases. For this to happen the cells involved, in this case the muscle cells, need more glucose and oxygen. Breathing gets faster and deeper to take in more oxygen and the heart beats faster to get the oxygen and glucose to the muscles more quickly.

Anaerobic respiration

■ There is a limit to how fast we can breathe and how fast the heart can beat. This means that the muscles might not get enough oxygen. In this case another kind of respiration is used that does not need oxygen. This is called **anaerobic respiration**.

■ Anaerobic respiration is shown by the word equation:

glucose → lactic acid + energy

■ Although anaerobic respiration may be happening to a small extent a lot of the time, it really only happens to a great extent when aerobic respiration can not provide all the energy needed.

- There are other kinds of anaerobic respiration in other organisms that produce different substances. For example, yeast respires anaerobically, converting sugar directly into ethanol and carbon dioxide, releasing energy.

Differences between aerobic and anaerobic respiration	
Aerobic respiration	**Anaerobic respiration**
Uses oxygen	Does not use oxygen
Does not make lactic acid	Makes lactic acid
Makes carbon dioxide	Does not make carbon dioxide
Makes water	Does not make water
Releases a large amount of energy	Releases a small amount of energy

The oxygen debt

- The lactic acid that builds up during anaerobic respiration in humans is poisonous. It causes muscle fatigue (tiredness) and makes muscles ache.

- Lactic acid has to be broken down, and oxygen is needed to do this. This is why you continue to breathe quickly even after you have finished exercising. You are taking in the extra oxygen you need to remove the lactic acid. This is sometimes called **'repaying the oxygen debt'**.

- Only when all the lactic acid has been broken down do your heart rate and breathing return to normal.

QUESTION SPOTTER

▸ You can expect to get at least one question on respiration in your exam.
▸ A key to answering most questions is remembering the equations. For example, you may be asked why your breathing rate increases during exercise. In your answer include the need for an increased oxygen supply so the muscles can release more energy, and the need to get rid of the extra carbon dioxide produced.

? CHECK YOURSELF QUESTIONS

Q1 Why do living things respire?

Q2 Where does respiration happen?

Q3 a Why is aerobic respiration better than anaerobic respiration?

   b If aerobic respiration is better, why does anaerobic respiration sometimes happen?

Answers are on page 233.

Blood and the circulatory system

⭐ **IDEAS AND EVIDENCE**

▸ You need to understand how ideas about science have changed over time.

▸ William Harvey (1578–1657) carried out experiments and after careful observation concluded correctly that blood is pumped around the body by the heart. He demonstrated the existence of valves in veins and predicted the existence of capillaries.

▸ Before Harvey, people believed the ideas of Galen. The ideas of Galen had been recorded 1000 years before Harvey. Galen thought incorrectly that blood just moved from one side of the heart to the other. He did not realise that the blood transported materials all around the body.

⬚ What are the functions of the blood?

■ Blood is the body's **transport system**, carrying materials from one part of the body to another. Some of the substances transported are shown in the table below:

Substance	Carried from	Carried to
Food (glucose, amino acids, fat)	Small intestine	All parts of the body
Water	Intestines	All parts of the body
Oxygen	Lungs	All parts of the body
Carbon dioxide	All parts of the body	Lungs
Urea (waste)	Liver	Kidneys
Hormones	Glands	All parts of the body (different hormones affect different parts)

■ The blood also plays a part in **fighting disease** and in **controlling body temperature**. You can find out more about these in Unit 3.

Parts of the blood	Job
Plasma (pale yellow liquid making up most of the blood)	Transports food, carbon dioxide, urea, hormones, antibodies and other substances all dissolved in water. Heat is also redistributed around the body
Red blood cells	Carry oxygen (and some carbon dioxide)
White blood cells	Defend body against disease. (See Unit 3)
Platelets	Involved in blood clotting

red blood cells

platelets

white blood cells

Blood is mostly water, containing cells and many dissolved substances.

⚡ **A* EXTRA**

▸ In the lungs, haemoglobin combines with oxygen to form oxyhaemoglobin.

▸ In other organs and tissues oxyhaemoglobin splits up into oxygen and haemoglobin.

Red blood cells

■ Red blood cells are specialised to carry oxygen.

Feature of red blood cells	How it helps
'Biconcave' disc shape (flattened with a dimple in each side)	Large surface area for oxygen to enter and leave
No nucleus	More room to carry oxygen
Contains haemoglobin (red pigment)	Haemoglobin combines with oxygen to form oxyhaemoglobin. The oxygen is released when the cells reach tissues that need it.
Small	Can fit inside the smallest blood capillaries. Small cells can quickly 'fill up' with oxygen as it is not far for the oxygen to travel right to the centre.
Flexible	Can squeeze into the smallest capillary
Large number	Can carry a lot of oxygen

In this micrograph you can see the distinctive 'biconcave' shape of red blood cells.

The circulatory system

■ Blood flows around the body through **arteries**, **veins** and **capillaries**. The **heart** pumps to keep the blood flowing.

The heart

- The heart is a muscular bag that pumps blood by expanding in size, filling with blood, and then contracting, forcing the blood on its way.

- The heart is two pumps in one. The right side pumps blood to the lungs to collect oxygen. The left side then pumps the **oxygenated blood** around the rest of the body. The **deoxygenated** (without oxygen) blood then returns to the right side to be sent to the lungs again.

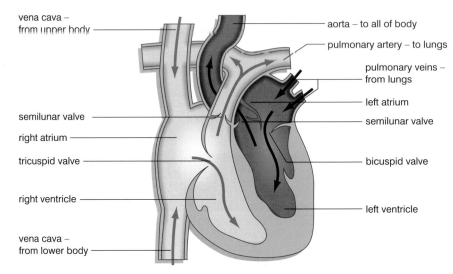

- The heart contains several valves and four chambers, two called atria (singular: atrium) and two called ventricles. The **atria** have thin walls. They collect blood before it enters the ventricles. The **ventricles** have thick muscular walls that contract, forcing the blood out. The **valves** allow the blood to only flow one way, preventing it flowing back the way it has come from.

Blood vessels

- Blood leaves the heart through **arteries** and returns through **veins**. **Capillaries** connect the two. (Remember, **a** for **a**rteries that travel **a**way from the heart. Ve**in**s carry blood **in**to the heart.)

- Arteries, veins and capillaries are adapted to carry out their different jobs.

artery:
thick-walled carrying blood at high pressure

vein:
thin-walled carrying blood at low pressure

capillary:
very small; the walls may be just one cell thick

QUESTION SPOTTER

- Make sure you know the jobs of all the parts of the heart as well as their names.
- You will frequently be asked to explain the differences between arteries, veins and capillaries – i.e. relate their differences to their functions.

Blood vessel	Job	Adaptations	Explanation
Arteries	Carry blood away from heart.	Thick muscular and elastic wall.	Blood leaves the heart under high pressure. The thick wall is needed to withstand and maintain the pressure. The elastic wall gradually reduces the harsh surge of the pumped blood to a steadier flow.
Veins	Carry blood back to the heart.	Thinner walls than arteries.	Blood is now at a lower pressure so there is no need to withstand it.
		Large lumen (space in the middle).	Provides less resistance to blood flow.
		Valves.	Prevent back flow which could happen because of the reduced pressure.
Capillaries	Exchange substances with body tissues.	Thin, permeable wall (may only be one cell thick).	Substances such as oxygen and food can enter and leave the blood through the capillary walls.
		Small size.	Can reach inside body tissues and between cells.

normal blood flow

open

veins have valves to stop the blood flowing backwards

closed

The valves in the veins prevent backflow.

⌂ Double circulation

- In humans (but not all animals) the blood travels through the heart twice on each complete journey around the body. This is a **double circulation**.

- By the time the blood has been pushed through a system of capillaries (in either the lungs or the rest of the body) it is at quite a low pressure. The pressure required to push the blood through the lungs and then the rest of the body in one go would be enormous and could damage the blood vessels. A double circulation system maintains the high blood pressure needed for efficient transport of materials around the body.

- The double circulation also allows for the fact that the pressure needed to push blood through the lungs (a relatively short round trip) is much smaller than the pressure needed to push blood around the rest of the body. This is why the left half of the heart is much more muscular than the right half.

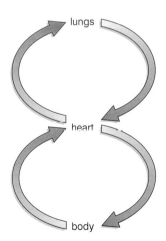

lungs

heart

body

The heart pumps blood to the lungs and back, then to the body and back. This is a double circulation.

CHECK YOURSELF QUESTIONS

Q1 Small organisms, like *Amoeba*, a single-celled animal, do not need a transport system. So why do bigger organisms need them?

Q2 This equation shows the reversible reaction between oxygen and haemoglobin.

oxygen + haemoglobin $\rightleftharpoons$ oxyhaemoglobin

a Where in the body would oxyhaemoglobin form?

b Where in the body would oxyhaemoglobin break down?

c People who live at high altitudes, where there is less oxygen, have more red blood cells per litre of blood than people who live at lower altitudes. Suggest why.

Q3 a In the heart, the ventricles have thicker walls than the atria. Why is this?

b Why does the left ventricle have a thicker wall than the right ventricle?

Q4 a List three ways that veins differ from arteries.

b Substances such as oxygen and food enter and leave the blood through the capillary walls. Why not through the walls of arteries and veins?

Answers are on page 233.

REVISION SESSION 3 ■■ Breathing ■■

Breathing is *not* respiration

■ Breathing is the way that oxygen is taken into our bodies and carbon dioxide removed. Sometimes it is called **ventilation**.

■ Do not confuse breathing with respiration. Respiration is a chemical process that happens in every cell in the body. Unfortunately, the confusion is not helped when you realise that the parts of the body responsible for breathing are known as the **respiratory system**!

How we breathe

■ When we breathe, air is moved into and out of our lungs. This involves different parts of the respiratory system inside the thorax (chest).

■ When we **breathe in**, air enters though the nose and mouth. In the nose the air is moistened and warmed.

■ The air travels down the **trachea** (windpipe) to the lungs. Tiny hairs called **cilia** help to remove dirt and microbes. (You can find out more about the cilia in Unit 3.)

■ The air enters the lungs through the **bronchi** (singular: bronchus), which branch and divide to form a network of **bronchioles**.

■ At the end of the bronchioles are air sacs called **alveoli** (singular: alveolus) which are covered in tiny blood capillaries. This is where oxygen enters the blood and carbon dioxide leaves the blood.

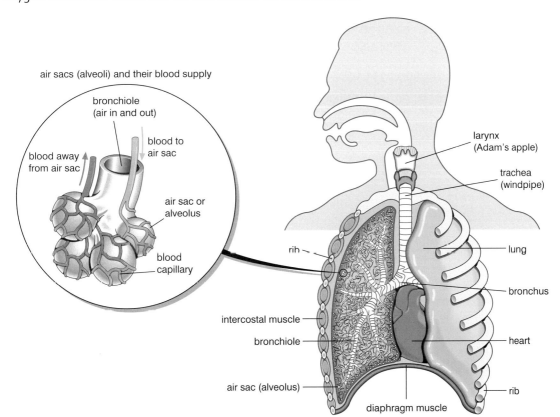

air sacs (alveoli) and their blood supply

bronchiole (air in and out)

blood to air sac

blood away from air sac

air sac or alveolus

blood capillary

larynx (Adam's apple)

trachea (windpipe)

rib

lung

bronchus

intercostal muscle

bronchiole

heart

air sac (alveolus)

rib

diaphragm muscle

Inhalation and exhalation

- Breathing in is known as **inhalation** and breathing out **exhalation** (sometimes they are called inspiration and expiration).

- Both happen because of changes in the volume of the thorax (chest cavity). This causes pressure changes which in turn cause air to enter or leave the lungs.

- The changes in thorax volume are caused by the **diaphragm**, which is a domed sheet of muscle under the lungs, and the **intercostal muscles**, which connect the ribs. There are two sets: the internal intercostal muscles and the external intercostal muscles.

INHALATION

- We breathe in air in this way:

  1 The diaphragm **contracts** and **flattens** in shape.

  2 The external intercostal muscles **contract**, making the ribs move upwards and outwards.

  3 These changes cause the **volume** of the thorax to **increase**.

  4 This causes the air **pressure** inside the thorax to **decrease**.

  5 This causes air to enter the lungs.

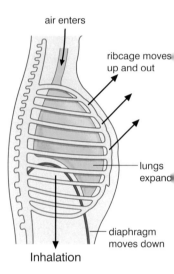

air enters

ribcage moves up and out

lungs expand

diaphragm moves down

Inhalation

- Rings of **cartilage** in the trachea, bronchi and bronchioles keep the air passages open and prevent them from collapsing when the air pressure decreases.

EXHALATION

- Air is breathed out from the lungs as follows:

  1 The diaphragm **relaxes** and returns to its domed shape, pushed up by the liver and stomach. This means **it pushes up on the lungs**.

  2 The external intercostal muscles **relax**, allowing the ribs to drop back down. This also presses on the lungs. If you are breathing hard the internal intercostal muscles also contract, helping the ribs to move down.

  3 These changes cause the **volume** of the thorax to **decrease**.

  4 This causes the **air pressure** inside the thorax to **increase**.

  5 This causes air to leave the lungs.

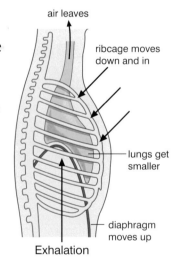

air leaves

ribcage moves down and in

lungs get smaller

diaphragm moves up

Exhalation

Composition of inhaled and exhaled air

■ The air we breathe contains many gases. **Oxygen** is taken into the blood.
Carbon dioxide and **water vapour** are added to the air we breathe out.
The other gases in the air are breathed out almost unchanged, except
for being warmer.

	In inhaled air	In exhaled air
Oxygen	21%	16%
Carbon dioxide	0.03%	4%
Nitrogen and other gases	79%	79%
Water	variable	high
Temperature	variable	high

Alveoli

■ The alveoli are where oxygen and carbon dioxide diffuse into and out of
the blood. For this reason the alveoli are described as the site of **gaseous
exchange** or as the **respiratory surface**.

■ The alveoli are adapted (have special features) to make them efficient at
gaseous exchange:
  • **Thin, permeable walls** to allow a short pathway for diffusion.
  • **Moist lining** in which oxygen dissolves first before it diffuses through.
  • **Large surface area.** Lots of alveoli means a very large surface area.
  • **Good supply of oxygen** and **good blood supply.** This means that a
    concentration gradient is maintained ensuring that oxygen and
    carbon dioxide rapidly diffuse across.

QUESTION SPOTTER

You will often be asked to explain how alveoli are adapted for efficient gas exchange.

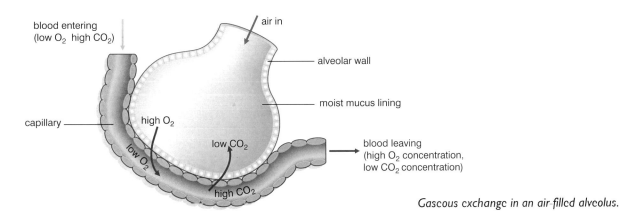

Gaseous exchange in an air-filled alveolus.

CHECK YOURSELF QUESTIONS

Q1 a How many cells does oxygen pass
through on its way from the alveoli to
the red blood cells?

  b Why is it important for oxygen to have
a large concentration gradient between
the inside of the alveoli and the blood?

Q2 When you breathe in, how do the positions
of the diaphragm and ribcage change?

Q3 Why do we need rings of cartilage in the
walls of the air passages?

Answers are on page 234.

▣ Digestion ▣

▢ Why *do* we need to digest food?

- If the food we eat is to be of any use it must enter the blood so that it can travel to every part of the body.

- Many of the foods we eat are made up of **large insoluble molecules,** which would not easily enter the blood. This means they have to be **broken down into small soluble molecules,** which can easily enter and be carried dissolved in the blood. Breaking down the molecules is called **digestion**.

- There are two stages of digestion:

  1 **Physical digestion** occurs mainly in the mouth, where food is broken down into smaller pieces by the teeth and tongue.

  2 **Chemical digestion** is the breakdown of large food molecules into smaller ones.

- Some molecules, like glucose, vitamins, minerals and water are already small enough to pass through the gut wall and do not need to be digested.

Breaking down food for absorption.

starch (a carbohydrate)   + water ⟶   single sugars (e.g. glucose)

sucrose, maltose (both carbohydrates)   + water ⟶

proteins   + water ⟶   amino acids

fats   + water ⟶   glycerol / fatty acids

▢ Enzymes

- Chemical digestion happens because of chemicals called **enzymes.** Enzymes are a type of catalyst found in living things. (You can find out more about catalysts in Unit 11.)

FEATURES OF ENZYMES

- Enzymes are proteins.

- They are produced by cells.

- They change chemical substances into new products.

- Enzymes are **specific**, which means that each enzyme only works on one substance.

- Enzymes work best at a particular temperature (around 35–40°C for digestive enzymes) called their **optimum temperature**. At temperatures that are too high the structure of an enzyme will be changed so that it will not work. This is irreversible and the enzyme is said to be **denatured**.

- They work best at a particular pH, called their **optimum pH**. Extremes of pH can also denature enzymes.

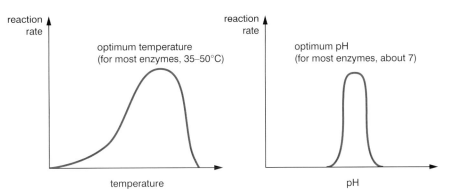

Enzymes work best at an optimum temperature and pH.

GROUPS OF DIGESTIVE ENZYMES

- Every cell contains many enzymes, which control the many chemical reactions that happen inside it. Digestive enzymes are only one kind. They are produced in the cells lining parts of the digestive system and are secreted to mix with the food.

- There are different groups of digestive enzymes, such as:
  - **proteases**, which break down proteins
  - **lipases**, which break down fats
  - **amylase**, which breaks down starch
  - **maltase**, **sucrase** and **lactase**, which break down the different sugars maltose, sucrose and lactose.

Substances that help digestion

- **Hydrochloric acid** is secreted in the stomach. This is important to **kill bacteria** in food. Also, the enzymes in the stomach work best at a low pH.

- **Sodium hydrogencarbonate** is secreted from the pancreas to **neutralise the acid** leaving the stomach so that the enzymes in the small intestine can work.

- **Bile** is produced in the liver, stored in the gall bladder, and passes along the bile duct into the duodenum. Bile **emulsifies fats**. It breaks down large fat droplets into smaller ones, which means that a larger surface area is exposed for the enzymes to work on.

large fat droplet   small fat droplets

Bile lowers the surface tension of large droplets of fat so that they break up. This part of the digestive process is called emulsification.

☐ The digestive system

- Eating food involves several different processes:
  - **ingestion** – taking food into the body
  - **digestion** of food into small molecules
  - **absorption** of digested food into the blood
  - **egestion** – removal of indigestible material (**faeces**) from the body. Note that egestion is not the same as excretion, which is the removal of waste substances that have been made in the body.

- All these different processes take place in different parts of the digestive system (the **alimentary canal**).

Part of digestive system	What happens there
Mouth	Teeth and tongue break down food into smaller pieces. Saliva from salivary glands moistens food so it is easily swallowed and contains amylase to begin breakdown of starch.
Oesophagus or gullet	Each lump of swallowed food, called a **bolus**, is moved along by waves of muscle contraction called **peristalsis**.
Stomach	Food enters through a ring of muscle known as a **sphincter**. Acid and protease are secreted to start protein digestion. Movements of the muscular wall churn up food into a liquid known as **chyme** (pronounced 'kime'). The bulk of the food is stored while a little of the partly digested food at a time passes through another sphincter into the duodenum.
Gall bladder	Stores bile. The bile is passed along the bile duct into the duodenum.
Pancreas	Secretes amylase, lipase and protease as well as sodium hydrogencarbonate into the duodenum.
Small intestine (made up of duodenum and ileum)	Secretions from the gall bladder and pancreas as well as sucrase, maltase, lactase, protease and lipase from the wall of the duodenum complete digestion. Digested food is absorbed into the blood through the **villi**.
Large intestine or colon	Water is absorbed from the remaining material.
Rectum	The remaining material (**faeces**), made up of indigestible food, dead cells from the lining of the alimentary canal and bacteria, is compacted and stored.
Anus	Faeces is egested through a sphincter.

The distance from mouth to anus is about nine metres.

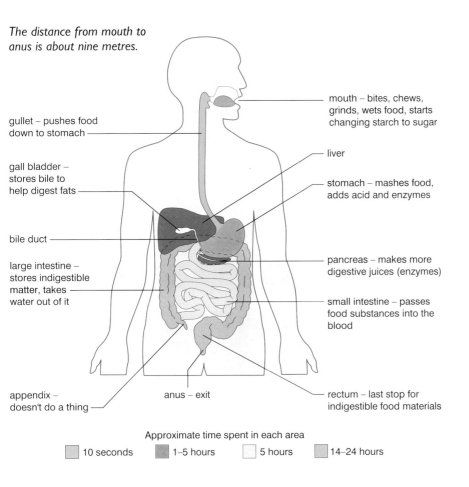

mouth – bites, chews, grinds, wets food, starts changing starch to sugar

gullet – pushes food down to stomach

liver

gall bladder – stores bile to help digest fats

stomach – mashes food, adds acid and enzymes

bile duct

pancreas – makes more digestive juices (enzymes)

large intestine – stores indigestible matter, takes water out of it

small intestine – passes food substances into the blood

appendix – doesn't do a thing

anus – exit

rectum – last stop for indigestible food materials

Approximate time spent in each area

| | 10 seconds | | 1–5 hours | | 5 hours | | 14–24 hours |

QUESTION SPOTTER

Make sure you know the name of each part of the digestive system as well as what happens there.

■ Food moves along the digestive system because of the contractions of the muscles in the walls of the alimentary canal. This is called **peristalsis**.

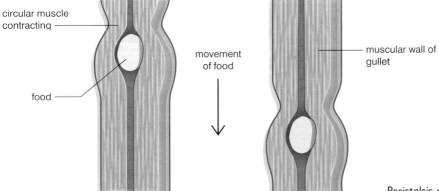

circular muscle contracting

movement of food

muscular wall of gullet

food

Peristalsis moves food along the digestive system.

Absorption of food

- After food has been digested it can enter the blood. This happens in the main part of the small intestine, known as the **ileum**. To help this process, the lining of the ileum is covered in millions of small finger-like projections called **villi** (singular: villus).

- The ileum is adapted for efficient absorption of food by having a large surface area. This is because:
  - it is **long** (6–7 metres in an adult)
  - the inside is covered with villi
  - the villi are covered in **microvilli**.

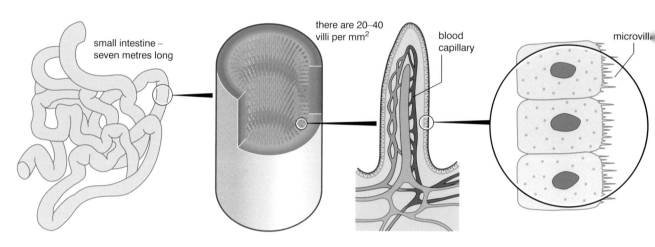

small intestine – seven metres long

there are 20–40 villi per mm^2

blood capillary

microvilli

The structure of the ileum.

- The villi themselves have features that also help absorption:
  - **thin, permeable walls**
  - **good blood supply**, which maintains a concentration gradient that aids diffusion
  - they contain **lymph vessels** (or lacteals), which absorb some of the fat. The lymph vessels eventually drain into the blood system.

CHECK YOURSELF QUESTIONS

Q1 a Protein molecules are long chains of amino acid molecules joined together. Why do proteins need to be digested?

b What is the difference between physical and chemical digestion?

c What happens to enzymes at high temperatures?

d Why is the alkaline sodium hydrogencarbonate secreted into the duodenum?

Q2 a What is the difference between ingestion, egestion and excretion?

b Where do ingestion and egestion happen?

Q3 The villi are adapted to absorb food and the alveoli in the lungs are adapted to absorb oxygen. In what ways are they similar?

Answers are on page 234.

UNIT 3: BODY MAINTENANCE

The nervous system

⟦⟧ What does the nervous system do?

■ The nervous system collects information about changes inside or outside the body, decides how the body should respond and controls that response.

⟦⟧ Receptors

■ Information is collected by **receptor cells** that are usually grouped together in **sense organs**, also known as **receptors**.

■ Each type of receptor is sensitive to a different kind of change or **stimulus**.

Sense organ	Sense	Stimulus
Skin	Touch	Pressure, pain, hot/cold temperatures
Tongue	Taste	Chemicals in food and drink
Nose	Smell	Chemicals in the air
Eyes	Sight	Light
Ears	Hearing	Sound
	Balance	Movement/position of head

⟦⟧ The eye

■ The eye is the receptor that detects light.

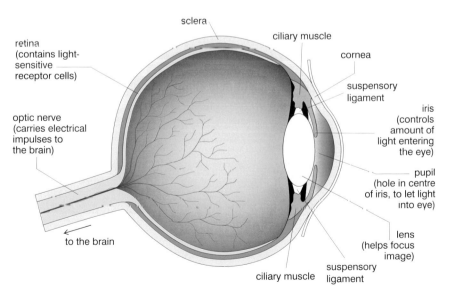

Part of eye	Job
Ciliary muscles	Contract or relax to alter the shape of the lens
Cornea	Transparent cover that does most of the bending of light
Iris	Alters the size of the pupil to control the amount of light entering the eye
Lens	Changes shape to focus light on to the retina
Humour	Clear jelly that fills the inside of the eye
Retina	Contains light-sensitive receptor cells, which change the light image into electrical impulses. There are two types of receptor cells: **rods**, which are sensitive in dim light but can only sense 'black and white', and **cones**, which are sensitive in bright light and can detect colour
Sclera	Tough outer layer
Suspensory ligaments	Hold the lens in position
Optic nerve	Carries electrical impulses to the brain

■ The **iris** (the ring shaped, coloured part of the eye) controls the amount of light entering the eye by controlling the size of the hole in the centre, the **pupil**. The iris contains **circular** and **radial** muscles. In bright light the circular muscles contract and the radial muscles relax, making the pupil smaller. This reduces the amount of light entering the eye, as too much could do damage. The reverse happens in dim light when the eye has to collect as much light as possible to see clearly.

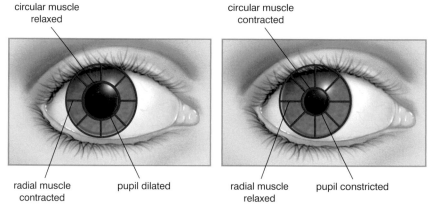

circular muscle relaxed — radial muscle contracted — pupil dilated

circular muscle contracted — radial muscle relaxed — pupil constricted

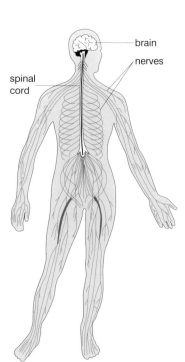

brain
nerves
spinal cord

The nervous system.

■ The lens changes shape in order to focus light from objects which are distant or near. You can find out how glass lenses form images in Unit 17.

⟳ Nerves

■ The sense organs are connected to the rest of the nervous system, which is made up of the **brain**, **spinal cord** and **peripheral nerves**.

■ In the brain and spinal cord information is processed and decisions made. The brain and spinal cord together are called the **central nervous system** (CNS).

■ Signals are sent through the nervous system in the form of electro-chemical **impulses**.

TYPES OF NERVE CELLS (OR NEURONES)

- **Sensory neurones** carry signals to the CNS.

- **Motor neurones** carry signals from the CNS, controlling how we respond.

- **Relay** (intermediate or connecting) **neurones** connect other neurones together.

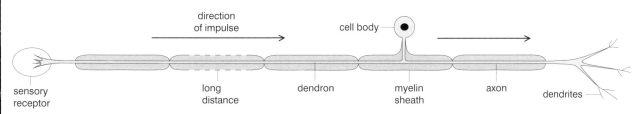

direction of impulse   cell body

sensory receptor   long distance   dendron   myelin sheath   axon   dendrites

Sensory neurone

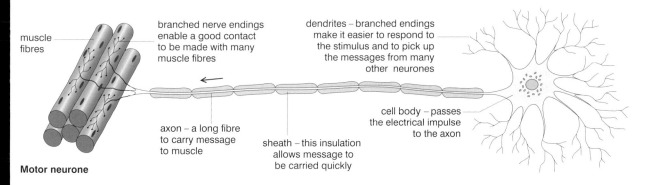

muscle fibres

branched nerve endings enable a good contact to be made with many muscle fibres

dendrites – branched endings make it easier to respond to the stimulus and to pick up the messages from many other neurones

axon – a long fibre to carry message to muscle

sheath – this insulation allows message to be carried quickly

cell body – passes the electrical impulse to the axon

Motor neurone

A relay neurone

NEURONES ARE SPECIALISED

- They can be **very long** to carry signals from one part of the body to another.

- They have many branched nerve endings or **dendrites** to collect and pass on signals.

- Many neurones are wrapped in a layer of fat and protein, the **myelin sheath**, which insulates cells from each other and allows the impulses to travel faster.

- Neurones are usually grouped together in bundles called **nerves**.

neurones

nerve

Cross-section of a nerve.

⌂ Reflexes

- The different parts of the nervous system may all be involved when we respond to a stimulus. The simplest type of response is a **reflex**. Reflexes are rapid, automatic responses which often act to protect us in some way – for example, blinking if something gets in your eye or sneezing if you breathe in dust.

- The pathway that signals travel along during a reflex is called a **reflex arc**:

stimulus → receptor → sensory neurone → CNS → motor neurone → effector → response

- Simple reflexes are usually **spinal reflexes**, which means that the signals are processed by the spinal cord, not the brain. The spine sends a signal back to the **effector**. Effectors are the parts of the body that respond – either muscles or glands. Examples of spinal reflexes include standing on a pin or touching a hot object.

stand on pin → nerve endings → sensory neurone → spinal cord → motor neurone → leg muscles → leg moves

- When the spine sends a signal to the effector, other signals are sent on to the brain so that it is aware of what is happening.

- There are also reflexes in which the signals are sent straight to the brain. These are called **cranial reflexes**. Examples include blinking when dirt lands in your eye, or salivating at the smell of food.

smell of food → nose → sensory neurone → brain → motor neurone → salivary glands → mouth waters

The flow of information from stimulus to response.

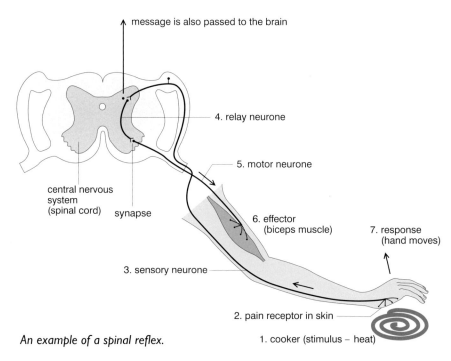

An example of a spinal reflex.

⭑ IDEAS AND EVIDENCE

▸ The scientist Ivan Pavlov lived in the early 1900s. His observations led to the understanding of conditioned (learnt) reflexes.

▸ During his experiments on dogs, Pavlov rang a bell before feeding his dogs. After many months the dogs would produce saliva just on hearing a bell, even when food was not provided.

Synapses

- Between nerve endings there are very small gaps called **synapses,** where signals are passed from one neurone to another even though the cells do not touch.

- Signals can be passed across synapses because when an electrical impulse reaches a synapse, chemicals called **transmitter substances** are released from the membrane of one nerve ending and travel across to special **receptor sites** on the membrane of the next nerve ending, triggering off another nerve impulse.

- Sometimes signals are not passed across synapses, which stops us from responding to every single stimulus. You can find out more about synapses in the section about drugs on pages 35-36.

QUESTION SPOTTER

You will often be asked to analyse a reflex in terms of stimulus, receptor, CNS or co-ordinator, effector and response.

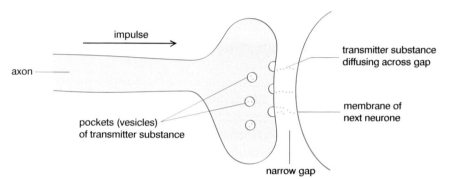

A synapse.

? CHECK YOURSELF QUESTIONS

Q1 a What is a stimulus?
   b What is the difference between a receptor and an effector?

Q2 a What are the two parts of the CNS?
   b What is the difference between a nerve and a neurone?
   c Describe three features that neurones have in common with other cells.
   d Describe two features that neurones have which make them different from other cells.

Q3 a Which of the following are reflexes?
    A Coughing when something 'goes down the wrong way'.
    B Changing channels on the TV when a programme ends.
    C Jumping up when you sit on something sharp.
    D Always buying the same brand of soft drink.
   b Why are reflexes important?

Answers are on page 235.

The endocrine system

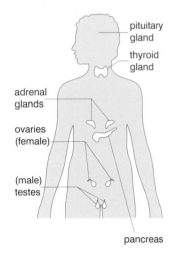

The endocrine system.

pituitary gland
thyroid gland
adrenal glands
ovaries (female)
(male) testes
pancreas

Hormones

- **Hormones** are chemical messengers. They are made in **endocrine glands**.

- Endocrine glands do not have ducts (tubes) to carry away the hormones they make – the hormones are **secreted directly into the blood** to be carried around the body. (There are other types of glands, called exocrine glands, such as salivary or sweat glands, that *do* have ducts.)

- Most hormones affect several parts of the body, others only affect one part of the body, which is termed the **target organ**.

- The changes caused by hormones are usually slower and longer-lived than the changes brought about by the nervous system.

What hormones are made where?

ADRENAL GLANDS

- The adrenal glands produce **adrenaline**. This is released in times of excitement, anger, fright or stress and prepares the body for 'flight or fight' – the crucial moments when an animal must instantly decide whether to attack or run for its life.

- Effects of adrenaline:
  - increases heart rate
  - increases depth of breathing and breathing rate
  - increases sweating
  - makes hair stand on end (this makes a furry animal look larger but only gives humans goose bumps)
  - releases glucose from liver and muscles
  - makes pupils dilate
  - makes skin go pale as blood is redirected to muscles.

PITUITARY GLAND

- Among other hormones, the pituitary gland produces **growth hormone**.

- Growth hormone encourages mental and physical development in children.

- The pituitary gland also controls many other glands.

THYROID GLAND

- The thyroid gland produces **thyroxine**.

- Thyroxine encourages mental and physical development in children.

PANCREAS

- The pancreas secretes **insulin** and **glucagon**. (It also secretes digestive enzymes through the pancreatic duct into the duodenum.)

- Insulin controls **glucose levels** in the blood. It is important that the blood glucose level remains as steady as possible. If it rises or falls too much you can become very ill.

- After a meal, the level of glucose in the blood tends to rise. This causes the pancreas to release **insulin**, which travels in the blood to the liver. Here it causes any excess glucose to be converted to another carbohydrate, **glycogen**, which is insoluble and is stored in the liver.

- Between meals, glucose in the blood is constantly being used up, so the level of glucose in the blood falls. When a low level of glucose is detected, the pancreas stops secreting insulin and secretes the hormone **glucagon** instead. Glucagon converts some of the stored glycogen back into glucose, which is released into the blood to raise the blood glucose level back to normal.

QUESTION SPOTTER

- In exams you will not only be asked about the effects of hormones. Often you will also be required to explain these effects.
- An example would be: 'Why is it important that adrenaline increases heart rate in times of stress?'

TESTES (MALES ONLY)

- **Testosterone** (male sex hormone) is secreted from the testes. Testosterone causes secondary sexual characteristics in boys:
  - growth spurt
  - hair grows on face and body
  - penis, testes and scrotum grow and develop
  - sperm is produced
  - voice breaks
  - body becomes broader and more muscular
  - sexual 'drive' develops.

The male reproductive system.

OVARIES (FEMALES ONLY)

- The ovaries produce the female sex hormones **progesterone** and **oestrogen**. These hormones cause secondary sexual characteristics in girls:
  - growth spurt
  - breasts develop
  - vagina, oviducts and uterus develop
  - menstrual cycle (periods) start
  - hips widen
  - pubic hair and hair under the arms grows
  - sexual 'drive' develops.

The female reproductive system.

- These hormones also control the changes that occur during the menstrual cycle:
  - oestrogen encourages the repair of the uterus lining after bleeding
  - progesterone maintains the lining
  - oestrogen and progesterone control ovulation (egg release).

The menstrual cycle.

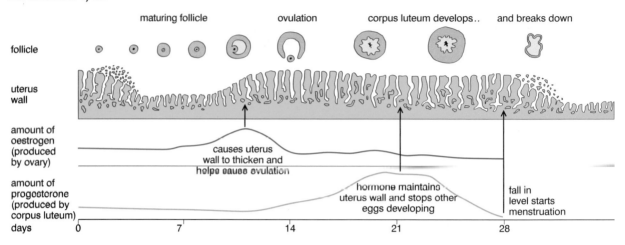

maturing follicle   ovulation   corpus luteum develops..   and breaks down

follicle

uterus
wall

amount of
oestrogen
(produced
by ovary)

causes uterus
wall to thicken and
helps cause ovulation

amount of
progesterone
(produced by
corpus luteum)

hormone maintains
uterus wall and stops other
eggs developing

fall in
level starts
menstruation

days   0   7   14   21   28

The menstrual cycle

- About every 28 days an egg is released from one of a woman's ovaries.
(The egg develops from one of the thousands of **follicles** present in the
ovaries.) The egg travels down the oviduct to the uterus (womb) where,
if it has been fertilised, it can implant and grow into a baby.

- To prepare for this the lining of the uterus thickens – controlled by the
release of progesterone from the **corpus luteum**, the remains of the
follicle left behind in the ovary. If the egg has not been fertilised then
the lining breaks down and is released (**menstruation**). Oestrogen from
the ovary will encourage the uterus lining to grow again for the next
released egg.

- If the egg has been fertilised then progesterone continues to be released
from the corpus luteum, which maintains the uterus lining during
pregnancy and prevents further ovulation.

OTHER HORMONES INVOLVED IN THE MENSTRUAL CYCLE

- **FSH (follicle–stimulating hormone)** is secreted by the pituitary gland. It
causes eggs to mature in the ovaries and stimulates the ovaries to
produce hormones such as oestrogen.

- **LH (luteinising hormone)** is also secreted by the pituitary gland. It
stimulates ovulation.

- The release of FSH and LH is partially controlled by oestrogen, which
inhibits FSH production and stimulates LH production.

Medical uses of hormones

- Hormones can be used to treat various medical conditions – for example in illnesses caused by the hormone not being made naturally in the correct quantities.

INSULIN

- There are different types of diabetes, but in **diabetes mellitus** the body is unable to make enough of the hormone insulin. Insulin controls the level of glucose in the blood. Someone with diabetes cannot store the excess glucose from their blood and it is excreted in urine instead. Other symptoms of diabetes include thirst, weakness, weight loss, coma.

- Some people can control their diabetes with their diet and activity. For example, they make sure they do not go a long time without a meal, eat snacks between meals and make sure that they eat some high-glucose food before any energetic activity.

- Another way of controlling diabetes is to inject insulin before a meal.

- Insulin can be extracted from animals' blood, but is now produced by genetically engineered bacteria.

CONTROLLING FERTILITY

- **Contraceptive pills** contain oestrogen and progesterone. They inhibit FSH production, so no eggs mature to be released.

- FSH is used as a **fertility drug** to stimulate eggs to mature.

GROWTH HORMONE

- Injections of growth hormone can be given during childhood to ensure that growth is normal.

Illegal uses of hormones

- Some drugs containing hormones, or chemicals similar to them, have been used by some athletes to enhance their performance. This is not only illegal but can have harmful side effects.

CHECK YOURSELF QUESTIONS

Q1 Signals can be sent round the body by the nervous system and the endocrine system. How are the two systems different?

Q2 a How do the changes that adrenaline causes help the body react to a stressful situation (fight or flight)?
   b After it has been released, adrenaline is broken down fairly quickly. Why is this important?

Q3 Explain the differences between glucose, glycogen and glucagon.

Answers are on page 236.

Homeostasis

What is homeostasis?

■ For our cells to stay alive and work properly they need the conditions in and around them, such as their temperature and the amount of water and other substances, to stay within acceptable limits. Keeping conditions inside these limits is called **homeostasis**.

Temperature control

■ The temperature inside your body is about 37°C, regardless of how hot or cold you may feel on the outside. This **core temperature** may naturally vary a little, but it is never very different unless you are ill.

■ Heat is constantly being released by respiration and other chemical reactions in the body, and is transferred to the surroundings outside the body. To maintain a constant body temperature these two processes have to balance. If the core temperature rises above or falls below 37°C various changes happen, mostly in the skin, to restore normal temperature.

Too cold?	Too hot?
Vasoconstriction: blood capillaries in the skin become narrower so they carry less blood close to the surface. Heat is kept inside the body.	**Vasodilation:** blood capillaries in the skin widen so they carry more blood close to the surface. Heat is transferred from the blood to the skin by **conduction**, then to the environment by **radiation**.
Sweating is reduced.	Sweating: sweat is released onto the skin surface and as it evaporates heat is taken away.
Hair erection: muscles make the hairs stand up, trapping a layer of air as insulation (air is a poor conductor of heat). This is more beneficial in animals but still occurs in humans (goose bumps).	Hairs lay flat so less air is trapped and more heat is transferred from the skin.
Shivering: muscle action releases extra heat from the increased respiration.	No shivering.
A layer of fat under the skin acts as insulation.	

Section through skin.

a cold day

air trapped between hairs – insulation layer

blood vessels close to the skin surface become narrower

blood vessels further from the surface widen

a hot day

less air between hairs – heat escapes from the body

blood vessels close to the skin surface widen

blood vessels further from the surface get narrower

- The core temperature is monitored by the **hypothalamus** – a part of the brain that monitors the temperature of the blood passing through it.

Water balance

- Our bodies are about two-thirds water. The average person loses and gains about three litres of water a day under normal conditions.

- Water is constantly being **lost** from the body:
  - in the air we breathe out
  - in sweat (sweat also contains mineral salts)
  - in urine
  - in faeces.

- Water is **gained** by the body:
  - in food and drink
  - from respiration and other chemical reactions.

The water balance for an average person.

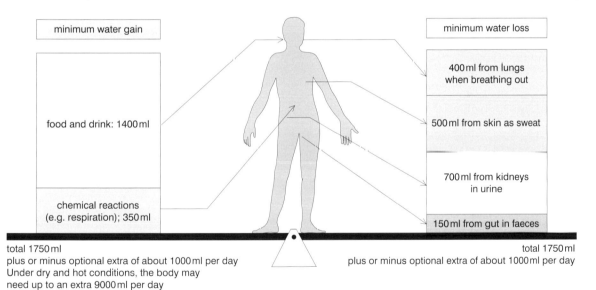

minimum water gain

food and drink: 1400 ml

chemical reactions (e.g. respiration); 350 ml

minimum water loss

400 ml from lungs when breathing out

500 ml from skin as sweat

700 ml from kidneys in urine

150 ml from gut in faeces

total 1750 ml
plus or minus optional extra of about 1000 ml per day
Under dry and hot conditions, the body may
need up to an extra 9000 ml per day

total 1750 ml
plus or minus optional extra of about 1000 ml per day

- **The water lost cannot be much more or less than the water gained.** So on a hot day, when you sweat more, you lose less water as urine, producing a smaller amount of more concentrated (darker) urine than normal.

THE ROLE OF THE KIDNEYS

■ The amount of water that is lost as urine is controlled by the **kidneys**.

■ The kidneys regulate the amounts of water and salt in the body by controlling the amounts in the blood.

■ The kidneys remove waste products such as **urea** from the blood. Urea is formed in the liver from the breakdown of excess amino acids in the body. This is an example of **excretion**.

■ As blood flows around the body it passes through the kidneys, which remove urea, excess water and salt from the blood:

1 Blood enters the kidneys through the **renal arteries**, which divide to form many tiny capillaries.

2 A lot of the blood plasma (water, urea and other substances) is forced under great pressure into tiny tubules called **nephrons**.

3 Further along each nephron, useful contents (such as sugar) and some water are reabsorbed into the blood, leaving urea, excess water and excess salt. This mixture is called **urine**.

4 The capillaries join up to form the **renal veins**, which carry blood away from the kidneys.

5 The nephrons join up to form a **ureter**, which carries the urine to the bladder where it is stored until you go to the toilet when the urine leaves the body through the **urethra**.

Human urinary system

renal vein
kidney
vena cava
ureter
bladder
ring of muscle
urethra

aorta
renal artery

blood from renal artery
capillaries
blood to vein
joins other nephron and ureter
nephron
Movement of wastes

Section through human kidney

pelvis
cortex
renal artery
renal vein
ureter
medulla

MONITORING WATER BALANCE

■ Like temperature, the water content of the blood is monitored by the **hypothalamus**.

■ If there is too little water in the blood – if you have been sweating a lot, for example – then the hypothalamus is stimulated and sends a hormone (called **ADH**) to the kidneys, making them reabsorb more water back into the blood so less is lost in urine.

■ If your blood water level is high – if you have been drinking a lot, for example – the hypothalamus is much less stimulated so less hormone is released, less water is reabsorbed and more water is lost as urine.

Monitoring water level.

less water in blood

more water in blood

receptors in hypothalamus highly stimulated

normal water level in blood

receptors in hypothalamus less stimulated

lots of hormone released by pituitary gland

less urine highly concentrated

more urine very dilute

less of hormone released by pituitary gland

more hormone in blood

less hormone in blood

more water re-absorbed into blood from kidney tubes

less water re-absorbed into blood from kidney tubes

Negative feedback

- The body maintains a constant internal environment by monitoring changes and reacting to reduce these changes. This process is an example of **negative feedback**. It is 'negative' because the body attempts to **reduce** changes that occur.

EXAMPLES OF NEGATIVE FEEDBACK

- If the amount of glucose in your blood increases after a meal insulin is released to reduce the amount.

- If your body temperature falls then shivering and vasoconstriction will increase the temperature

- If you drink a lot, increasing the amount of water in your blood, the kidneys will remove more water in urine.

- When you exercise you breathe faster. Muscles respiring more than usual use up oxygen faster. Faster breathing increases the amount of oxygen in the blood. These two processes counter each other, producing a steady oxygen level. The faster breathing also removes the extra carbon dioxide that has been produced by the muscles respiring. In fact, it is mainly the carbon dioxide levels in the blood that the brain monitors to control the rate of breathing. This is because high levels of carbon dioxide in the blood are toxic and have to be reduced quickly.

> ## ⚡ A* EXTRA
>
> ▸ Homeostasis and negative feedback do not mean exactly the same thing.
> ▸ Homeostasis means keeping the conditions inside the body constant.
> ▸ Negative feedback is the way this happens.

? CHECK YOURSELF QUESTIONS

Q1 A farmer who has been working outside all day on a hot summer's day produces a much smaller amount of urine than normal. It is also a much darker yellow colour than normal. Explain these points.

Q2 Why are the lungs organs of excretion?

Q3 How would the blood in the renal arteries be different from the blood in the renal veins?

Answers are on page 236.

Good health

Virus

protein coat

genes

Bacterium cell

cell wall

cytoplasm

genes
(not in a nucleus)

The two diagrams are not to scale. Viruses are much smaller than bacteria. They can reproduce only inside living cells.

cilia   mucus being released

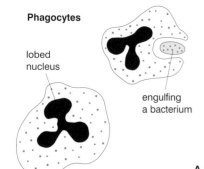

Cells lining the air passages in the trachea, bronchi and bronchioles.

⟳ Preventing microbial attack

■ One main cause of disease is the presence of foreign organisms – **micro-organisms,** or **microbes,** in the body. Most of the time our bodies are able to prevent microbes, such as **viruses** or **bacteria,** from getting in or from spreading.

Barriers to infection	How they work
Skin	The skin provides a barrier that micro-organisms cannot penetrate unless through a wound or a natural opening.
Mucus and ciliated cells in lining of respiratory tract	The lining of the nasal passages, and the trachea, bronchi and bronchioles in the lungs are covered with a slimy mucus which traps air-borne micro-organisms as well as dirt. Tiny hair-like cilia use a waving motion to move the mucus upwards where it usually ends up going down the oesophagus.
Acid in the stomach	Stomach acid kills micro-organisms present in food or drink.
Blood clots	At the site of a wound, blood platelets break open, triggering off a series of chemical changes that result in the formation of a network of threads at the wound. This network traps red blood cells, forming a clot. The clot prevents blood escaping and provides a barrier to infection.

⟳ The immune system

■ If micro-organisms do manage to enter the body they can cause harm by either damaging the cells around them or by releasing toxins (poisons) that make us ill. In either case they are attacked by **white blood cells,** which are part of our **immune system.**

■ There are two main types of white blood cells:
  • **Phagocytes,** because of their flexible shape, can engulf and then digest micro-organisms. This is called phagocytosis.
  • **Lymphocytes** produce chemicals called **antibodies.** Antibodies destroy the micro-organisms in various ways, for example by making them clump together so that they are more easily engulfed by phagocytes, by killing the micro-organisms themselves or by destroying the toxins they release (acting as **anti-toxins**).

Phagocytes

lobed nucleus

engulfing a bacterium

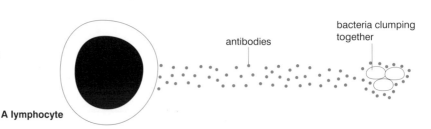

antibodies

bacteria clumping together

A lymphocyte

DEVELOPING IMMUNITY TO A DISEASE

- On the surface of all cells are chemicals called **antigens**. Each different type of micro-organism has its own **specific** antigens, which can only be attacked by the right type of antibody.

- When micro-organisms first invade the body, the white blood cells start to make the antibody to destroy these micro-organisms. This may take a while, and this is usually when you show the symptoms of the disease. When the white blood cells have made enough antibodies to attack the micro-organisms you (hopefully) recover from the disease.

- If you are ever invaded by the same type of micro-organism, your white blood cells 'remember' the antigen and can make the right type of antibody to quickly destroy the micro-organisms before the symptoms of the disease appear. You are then said to be **immune** to the disease.

- You can be artificially **immunised** against a disease by being injected with the antigen in the form of dead or harmless forms of the micro-organism or a harmless form of the toxin they release. The harmless foreign antigens stimulate your white blood cells to produce antibodies against them in the normal way but you won't be as ill as if you had the disease. Your white cells will 'remember' how to do this in the future and you will be protected if you ever catch the real disease-causing micro-organisms. Sometimes this immunity will last for the rest of your life but you may need 'booster' injections for some diseases.

QUESTION SPOTTER

You will gain marks for correctly using terms like antibody and antigen.

IDEAS AND EVIDENCE

- ▸ Edward Jenner produced the world's first vaccine in 1796.

- ▸ Jenner noticed that milkmaids with cowpox never caught smallpox. He infected a young boy with cowpox. A few weeks later he injected the boy with smallpox. The boy did not develop smallpox.

- ▸ The results of Jenner's experimentation have saved many lives.

IDEAS AND EVIDENCE

- ▸ Louis Pasteur developed a vaccine against rabies. He developed a weakened form of the virus.

- ▸ He injected the virus into an animal then took a tissue sample and allowed it to dry out. He then injected some of the tissue into another animal.

- ▸ He repeated this process until the virus was weak enough to inject into a person. After a few weeks he injected the person with a virulent form of the rabies virus, and the person did not develop rabies.

- ▸ Louis Pasteur's work has saved the lives of many people.

ORGAN TRANSPLANTATION

- The reason that organ transplants are ideally taken from a close relative is that their organs are more likely to have antigens similar to the patient's own cells, and are therefore less likely to be attacked by the patient's immune system.

- When the immune system attacks a transplanted organ, the organ is said to be **rejected**. If the donor is not a close relative, **immunosuppressant drugs** have to be used to stop the transplant being rejected.

Drugs

- The various drugs, both illegal and otherwise, that people may take can also cause health problems. ('Drugs' in this case are defined as substances that affect the way our bodies behave. The effects may be useful but many can be dangerous.)

A* EXTRA

Many drugs work by stimulating or inhibiting the synapses between nerve cells.

▸ Dirty hypodermic needles used by drug addicts are thought to increase the spread of diseases such as HIV (see Unit 9).

▸ Some people believe that drug addicts should be provided with clean hypodermic needles. Other people think this may encourage more people to take drugs.

▸ You need to think about issues such as these before your exam, so that you can write about them with understanding.

- **Stimulants** (e.g. caffeine, nicotine, ecstasy, cocaine, amphetamines) **increase nervous activity** – they can speed up your heart rate, keep you awake or help depression. Stimulants affect synapses so nervous impulses cross them more readily.

- **Depressants** (e.g. alcohol, painkillers, tranquillisers, solvents, heroin) **decrease nervous activity** – they can slow your heart rate or reaction times, deaden pain or relax you. They do this by restricting the passage of nervous impulses across synapses.

- **Hallucinogens** (e.g. LSD, marijuana) affect the way we **perceive things** so people see or hear things that are not there or perceive things more vividly.

- Some drugs can be **addictive** – if you stop taking the drug you will show various **withdrawal** symptoms, which may include cravings for the drug, nausea and sickness.

- Another danger with drugs is that you build up a **tolerance** to them. This means that your body gets used to them and you have to take larger amounts of the drug for it to have the same effect.

TOBACCO

- Contains **nicotine**, which is a stimulant, increases blood pressure and is addictive. Nicotine can also lead to the formation of blood clots, increasing the chances of heart disease.

- Tobacco smoke contains **tar**, which irritates the lining of the air passages in the lungs, making them inflamed and causing **bronchitis**. Tar can cause the lining cells to multiply, leading to **lung cancer**. Tar also damages the cilia lining the air passages and causes **extra mucus** to be made, which trickles down into the lungs as the cilia can no longer remove it. Bacteria can breed in the mucus so you are more likely to get chest infections and **smokers' cough** as you try to get rid of the mucus. The **alveoli** are also damaged, so it is more difficult to absorb oxygen into the blood. This condition is known as **emphysema**.

- Tobacco smoke contains **carbon monoxide**, which stops red blood cells from carrying oxygen by combining irreversibly with the haemoglobin in the cells. This could also seriously affect the development of the fetus in the womb of a pregnant smoker, leading to a baby with low birth weight.

ALCOHOL

- Long-term alcohol use can cause **liver damage** (because the liver has the job of breaking down the alcohol), **heart disease**, **brain damage** and other dangerous conditions.

- Alcohol is a **depressant**. Short-term effects include:
  - making you more relaxed – which is why in small amounts it can be pleasant
  - slower reactions and impaired judgement – which is why drinking and driving is so dangerous.

- Larger amounts of alcohol can cause lack of co-ordination, slurred speech, unconsciousness and even death.

QUESTION
SPOTTER

If you are asked to describe the effects of alcohol, make sure you are clear whether the question is about its short-term or long-term effects.

SOLVENTS

- Solvents are **depressants** and slow down brain activity.

- The effects last for a much shorter time than alcohol but can include dizziness, loss of co-ordination and sometimes unconsciousness.

- Solvents can cause damage to the lungs, liver and brain.

THREAT OF HEART DISEASE

- Drinking large amounts of alcohol and smoking, combined with a diet containing a lot of fatty foods, little exercise and stress, can increase the chance of **coronary heart disease** – the main cause of death in Britain today.

- This disease affects the **coronary arteries**, which are the blood vessels that supply the heart muscle itself. Fatty substances such as **cholesterol** can build up on the inside of the vessels, narrowing them and restricting the blood flow. If a blood clot gets stuck in an artery the blood flow may be stopped altogether, so no oxygen or food can be supplied to part of the heart. If this stops the heart beating then the result is a **heart attack**.

Normal artery.

Artery affected by build up of cholesterol.

A* EXTRA

Don't confuse the coronary arteries with the large blood vessels carrying blood to and from the atria and ventricles. The coronary arteries are much smaller and take blood to the muscular walls of the heart.

CHECK YOURSELF QUESTIONS

Q1 a Most of the time there are very few white blood cells in the blood compared with the red blood cells. Explain why.

b When would you expect the numbers of white blood cells to increase?

Q2 If you have had measles once why are you unlikely to catch it again?

Q3 Why is it dangerous to drive after drinking alcohol?

Answers are on page 236.

UNIT 4: PLANTS

Photosynthesis

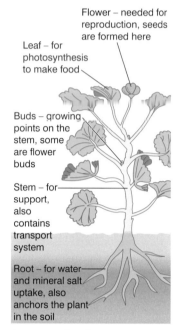

Flower – needed for reproduction, seeds are formed here

Leaf – for photosynthesis to make food

Buds – growing points on the stem, some are flower buds

Stem – for support, also contains transport system

Root – for water and mineral salt uptake, also anchors the plant in the soil

Anatomy of a plant.

⌷ What is photosynthesis?

■ Plants need and use the same types of foods as animals (carbohydrates, proteins and fats) but while animals have to eat other things to get their food, plants **make it themselves**. The way they do this is called **photosynthesis**. The other ways that plants are different from animals, such as having leaves and roots, or being green, are all linked with photosynthesis.

■ In photosynthesis, plants take **carbon dioxide** from the air and **water** from the soil, and use the energy from **sunlight** to convert them into food. The first food they make is **glucose** but that can later be changed into other food types.

■ **Oxygen** is also produced in photosynthesis and, although some is used inside the plant for respiration (releasing energy from food), most is not needed and is given out as a **waste product** (although it is obviously vital for other living things).

■ The sunlight is absorbed by the green pigment **chlorophyll**.

■ The process of photosynthesis can be summarised in a **word equation**:

$$\text{carbon dioxide} + \text{water} \xrightarrow[\text{light}]{\text{chlorophyll}} \text{glucose} + \text{oxygen}$$

■ It can also be written as a balanced **chemical equation**:

$$6CO_2 + 6H_2O \xrightarrow[\text{light}]{\text{chlorophyll}} C_6H_{12}O_6 + 6O_2$$

■ Much of the glucose is converted in to other substances such as **starch**. Starch molecules are made of lots of glucose molecules joined together. Starch is insoluble and so can be stored in the leaf without affecting water movement into and out of cells by **osmosis**.

■ Some glucose is converted to **sucrose** (a type of sugar consisting of two glucose molecules joined together), which is still soluble, but not as reactive as glucose, so it is easily carried around the plant in solution.

■ The energy needed to build up sugars into larger molecules comes from respiration.

☀ QUESTION SPOTTER

▶ You will almost certainly be set at least one question on photosynthesis in your exams.
▶ The key to answering many questions about photosynthesis is remembering the equation.

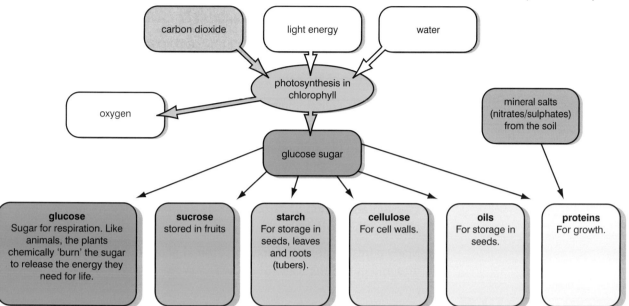

glucose	sucrose	starch	cellulose	oils	proteins
Sugar for respiration. Like animals, the plants chemically 'burn' the sugar to release the energy they need for life.	stored in fruits	For storage in seeds, leaves and roots (tubers).	For cell walls.	For storage in seeds.	For growth.

⌷ Where does photosynthesis occur?

- Photosynthesis takes place mainly in the **leaves**, although it can occur in any cells that contain green chlorophyll. Leaves are adapted to make them very efficient at photosynthesis.

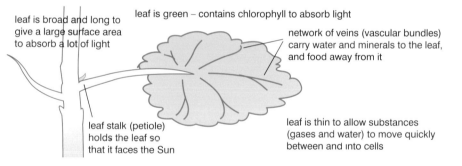

leaf is broad and long to give a large surface area to absorb a lot of light

leaf is green – contains chlorophyll to absorb light

network of veins (vascular bundles) carry water and minerals to the leaf, and food away from it

leaf stalk (petiole) holds the leaf so that it faces the Sun

leaf is thin to allow substances (gases and water) to move quickly between and into cells

- Leaves are **broad**, so as much light as possible can be absorbed.

- A leaf is **thin**, so it is easy for carbon dioxide to diffuse in to reach the cells in the centre of the leaf.

- Leaves contain green **chlorophyll**, in the **chloroplasts**, which absorbs the light energy.

- Leaves have **veins** to bring up water from the roots and carry food to other parts of the plant.

- A leaf has a stalk, or **petiole**, that holds the leaf up so it can absorb as much light as possible.

INSIDE LEAVES

■ The leaf has a transparent **epidermis** to allow light to penetrate.

■ There are many **palisade cells**, tightly packed together in the top half of the leaf so as many as possible collect sunlight. Most photosynthesis takes place in these cells.

■ **Chloroplasts** containing chlorophyll are concentrated in the top half of the leaf to absorb as much sunlight as possible.

■ Air spaces in the **spongy mesophyll** layer allow the movement of gases (carbon dioxide and oxygen) through the leaf to and from cells.

■ The leaf has a **large internal surface area to volume ratio** to allow the efficient absorption of carbon dioxide and removal of oxygen by the photosynthesising cells.

■ Many pores or **stomata** (singular: stoma) allow the movement of gases into and out of the leaf.

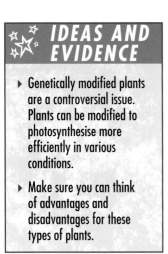

IDEAS AND EVIDENCE

▸ Genetically modified plants are a controversial issue. Plants can be modified to photosynthesise more efficiently in various conditions.

▸ Make sure you can think of advantages and disadvantages for these types of plants.

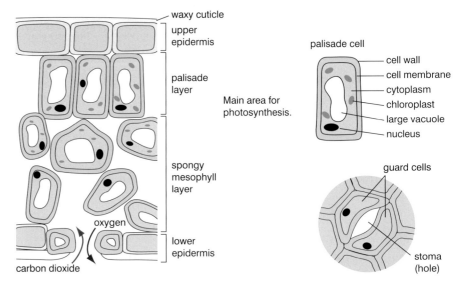

waxy cuticle
upper epidermis
palisade layer
Main area for photosynthesis.
spongy mesophyll layer
oxygen
lower epidermis
carbon dioxide

palisade cell
cell wall
cell membrane
cytoplasm
chloroplast
large vacuole
nucleus

guard cells
stoma (hole)

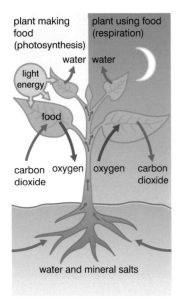

plant making food (photosynthesis)
plant using food (respiration)
water   water
light energy
food
carbon dioxide   oxygen   oxygen   carbon dioxide
water and mineral salts

Photosynthesis and respiration

■ Once plants have made food using sunlight, they will at some stage need to release the energy in the food. They do this in the same way that humans and other animals do – **respiration**.

■ During the day, plants respire 'slower' than they photosynthesise so we only detect carbon dioxide entering and oxygen leaving the plant. During the night, photosynthesis stops and then we can detect oxygen entering and carbon dioxide leaving during respiration.

■ At dawn and dusk, the rates of photosynthesis and respiration are the same and **no gases enter or leave** the plant because any oxygen produced by photosynthesis is immediately used up in respiration and any carbon dioxide produced is used up in photosynthesis. These occasions are known as **compensation points**.

☐ Limiting factors

- If a plant gets more light, carbon dioxide, water or a higher temperature, then it might be able to photosynthesise at a faster rate. However, the rate of photosynthesis will eventually reach a maximum because there is not enough of one of the factors needed – one of them becomes a **limiting factor**.

- For example, if a farmer pumps extra carbon dioxide into a greenhouse the rate of photosynthesis might increase so the crop will grow faster. But if the light is not bright enough to allow the plants to use the carbon dioxide as quickly as it is supplied, the light intensity would be the limiting factor. The graphs show how the rate of photosynthesis is affected by limiting factors.

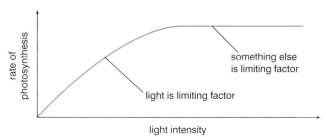

Increasing the levels of light and carbon dioxide, two of the factors necessary for photosynthesis, will increase the rate of photosynthesis until the rate is halted by some other limiting factor.

- If the limiting factor in the first graph was the amount of carbon dioxide and the plants were then given more carbon dioxide, the graph would look like this:

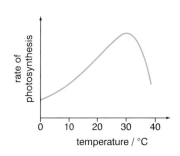

- **Temperature** is also a limiting factor. Temperature affects the enzymes that control the chemical reactions of photosynthesis. Compare the shape of the graph on the right with the graph showing the effect of temperature on enzyme activity on page 17.

CHECK YOURSELF QUESTIONS

Q1 How does a plant get the raw materials it needs for photosynthesis?

Q2 Why isn't the food that is made in the leaves transported around the plant as starch?

Q3 Why are leaves usually broad and thin?

Answers are on page 237.

Transport in plants

📋 How are materials carried round a plant?

■ In humans and many other animals, substances are transported around the body in the blood through blood vessels. In plants, water and dissolved substances are also transported through a series of tubes or vessels. There are two types of transport vessel, called **xylem** and **phloem**.

■ **Xylem vessels** are long tubes made of the hollow remains of cells that are now dead. They carry **water** and **dissolved minerals** up from the roots, through the stem, to the leaves. They also give **support** to the plant.

■ **Phloem vessels** are living cells. They carry **dissolved food** materials, mainly sucrose, from the leaves to other parts of the plant such as growing roots or shoots, or storage areas such as fruit. This movement of food materials is called **translocation**.

■ In roots the xylem and phloem vessels are usually grouped together separately, but in the stem and leaves they are found together as **vascular bundles** or 'veins'.

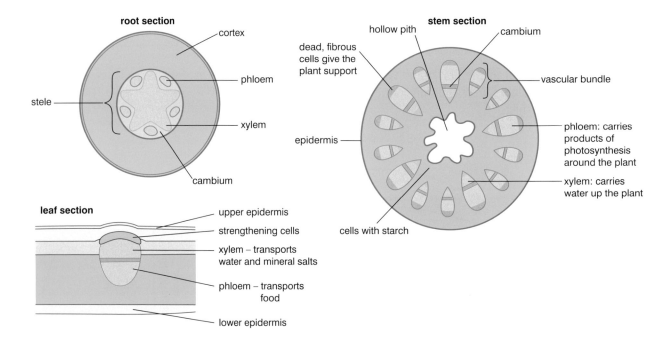

root section
- cortex
- phloem
- xylem
- stele
- cambium

stem section
- hollow pith
- cambium
- dead, fibrous cells give the plant support
- vascular bundle
- epidermis
- phloem: carries products of photosynthesis around the plant
- xylem: carries water up the plant
- cells with starch

leaf section
- upper epidermis
- strengthening cells
- xylem – transports water and mineral salts
- phloem – transports food
- lower epidermis

How do plants gain water?

- Roots are covered in tiny **root hair cells**, which increase the surface area for absorption. Water enters by **osmosis** because the solution inside the cells is more concentrated than the water in the soil.

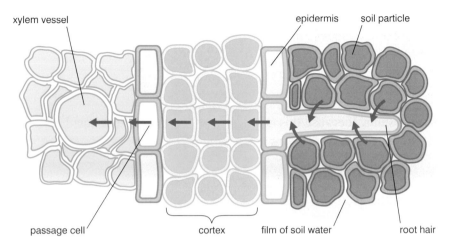

- Water continues to move between cells by osmosis until it reaches the xylem vessels, which carry it up to the leaves.

How do plants lose water?

- In the **leaves**, water moves out of the xylem and enters the leaf cells by osmosis (as they contain many dissolved substances). Water **evaporates** from the surface of the cells inside the leaf and then **diffuses** out through the open stomata. The evaporation of water causes more water to rise up the xylem from the roots rather like a drink flows up a straw when you suck at the top.

- Water loss from the leaves is known as **transpiration**. The flow of water through the plant from the roots to the leaves is known as the **transpiration stream**.

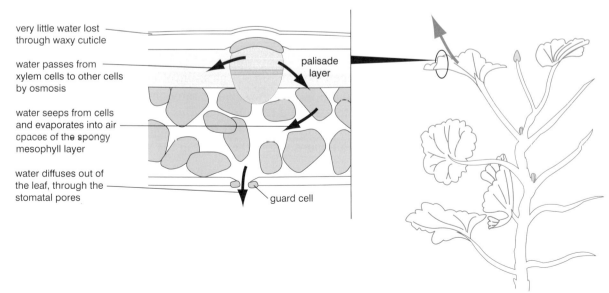

How water leaves a plant.

USES OF TRANSPIRATION TO PLANTS

- It brings up **water and minerals** from the soil.

- As the water evaporates it **cools** the plant. (You can find out more about the cooling effect of evaporation in Unit 17.)

SPEEDING UP TRANSPIRATION

- Transpiration happens faster in conditions that encourage evaporation, when it is:
  - warm
  - windy
  - dry
  - very sunny (because this is when the stomata are most open)
  - and when the plant has a good water supply.

Water balance

- In a healthy plant the cells are full of water and the cytoplasm presses hard against the inelastic cell wall, making the cell rigid. The cell is **turgid** or has **turgor**.

- Most plants do not have wood to hold them up: they are only upright because of cell turgor. If cells lose water, the vacuole shrinks and the cytoplasm stops pressing against the cell wall. The cell loses its rigidity and becomes **flaccid**. The plant will start to droop, or **wilt**.

- If water loss continues the cytoplasm can shrink so much that it starts to come away from the cell wall. This process is known as **plasmolysis**.

> ### ⚡ A* EXTRA
>
> It is the effect of the pressure inside a turgid plant cell acting against the inelastic cell wall that makes it rigid.

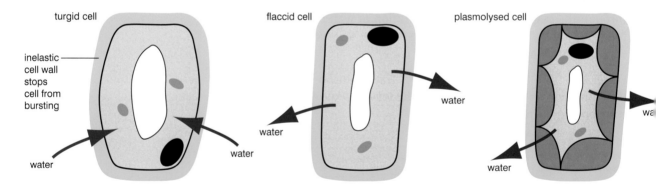

turgid cell

inelastic cell wall stops cell from bursting

water

water

flaccid cell

water

water

plasmolysed cell

water

water

wa

Water plays a key role in the structure of plant cells.

- Plants need open stomata for the gases involved in photosynthesis to move in and out – but they lose water through the stomata, and losing too much water can be a real problem. This is particularly important to plants living in places where water is not readily available, such as dry deserts or cold regions where the water in the soil is frozen.

WAYS OF REDUCING WATER LOSSES

- The leaf has a **waxy cuticle** – so water can not evaporate from epidermal cells.

- Stomata are located mostly on the **underside** of leaves – where it is cooler and evaporation is less.

- Some stomata are **sunk** below the surface of the leaf so they are less exposed.

- In some conditions the plant will **close** its stomata.

- Some plants have leaves covered with **hairs** – this creates a thin layer of still, moist air close to the leaf surface, which reduces evaporation.

- Plants in areas where water is very scarce reduce their leaves to **spines** – e.g. cactus spines or pine needles – so they have **less surface area**.

QUESTION SPOTTER

Examiners will often ask you to describe several of the ways water loss from leaves can be reduced.

GUARD CELLS

- Around each stoma there are two **guard cells**.

- In **daylight** these cells absorb water by osmosis, which makes them **swell**. The inner walls are thickened and can not stretch, unlike the outer ones. As the cells swell they curve and the gap between them opens up. During **darkness** the guard cells lose water by osmosis and the stomata **close**.

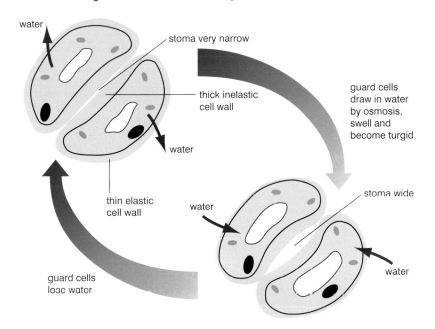

water

stoma very narrow

thick inelastic cell wall

water

guard cells draw in water by osmosis, swell and become turgid

thin elastic cell wall

water

stoma wide

water

guard cells lose water

The cell walls in guard cells are designed to open the stoma when the cell swells.

? CHECK YOURSELF QUESTIONS

Q1 What are the differences between xylem and phloem?

Q2 Why does transpiration happen faster on a hot sunny day than on a cool dull day?

Q3 What is the difference between a turgid cell and a plasmolysed cell?

Answers are on page 238.

Minerals

Why do plants need minerals?

- To grow properly, plants need **minerals**, which they get from the **soil**. Some minerals are more important than others as they may be needed in larger amounts.

Mineral	Element	Use in plant	Problems caused by deficiency
Nitrates	Nitrogen	To make proteins, which are needed to make new cells	• poor growth • pale or yellow leaves
Phosphates	Phosphorus	Involved in respiration and photosynthesis	• poor growth of roots and stems • low fruit yield • small purple leaves
Potassium salts	Potassium	To control salt balance in cells. Helps enzymes involved in respiration and photosynthesis	• mottled leaves • low fruit yield • low disease resistance
Magnesium salts	Magnesium	The chlorophyll molecule contains magnesium	• yellow patches between leaf veins

Absorption

- Minerals may only be present in the soil in low concentrations and so may need to be absorbed by the root hairs against a concentration gradient. This means that they have to be absorbed by **active transport** (see Unit 1).

- They enter the roots in solution (dissolved in water) and are carried in the **transpiration stream** through the xylem up the plant.

- Although minerals are constantly being taken from the soil by plants they are restored when animal and plant materials decay. You will find out more about this and artificial fertilisers in Unit 5.

CHECK YOURSELF QUESTIONS

Q1 a Plants make proteins from carbohydrates. What extra elements do they need to do this?
   b Why do plants need proteins?

Q2 Suggest why a lack of magnesium can cause yellow leaves.

Q3 Root hair cells contain many mitochondria. Suggest why.

Answers are on page 238.

Plant hormones

Controlling plant growth and development

- Many of the ways that plants grow and develop are controlled by chemicals called **plant hormones** or **plant growth regulators**.

- Like animal hormones they are made in one part of the organism and travel to other parts where they have their effects. They are different from animal hormones in that they are not made in glands and obviously do not travel through blood – they **diffuse** through the plant.

What plant hormones control

- Growth of roots, shoots and buds.
- flowering time.
- Formation and ripening of fruit.
- Germination.
- Leaf fall.
- Healing of wounds.

Commercial uses of hormones

- **Selective weedkillers** kill the weeds in a lawn without harming the grass. The hormones make the weeds grow very quickly, which usually results in death through a number of causes (e.g. a weighty structure the plant can't support, constricted veins).

- **Rooting powder**, which is applied to cuttings to make them grow roots.

- Keeping potatoes and cereals **dormant** so that they do not germinate during transport or storage.

- **Delaying the ripening** of soft fruit and vegetables so that they are not damaged during transport.

- Making crops such as apples **ripen at the same time** to make picking them less time-consuming.

Tropisms

- Tropisms are **directional growth** responses to stimuli.

- Examples include shoots growing towards the light and against the force of gravity or roots growing downwards away from the light but towards moisture and in the direction of the force of gravity. Growth in response to the direction of light is called **phototropism**. Growth in response to gravity is called **geotropism**.

- Tropisms are controlled by a hormone called **auxin**. Auxin is made in the tips of shoots and roots and diffuses away from the tip before it affects growth. One effect of auxin is to inhibit the growth of side shoots. This is why a gardener who wants a plant to stop growing taller and become more bushy will pinch off the shoot tip – removing a source of auxin.

QUESTION SPOTTER

Examiners will often ask you to explain why particular plant hormones are put to particular uses by humans.

A* EXTRA

Auxin causes curvature in shoots by causing elongation of existing cells, not by the production of more cells.

PLANTS ○ ○ ○ ○ ○ ○ ○ ○ ○ 47 ○ ○ ○ ○ ○ ○ ○ ○ ○ UNIT 4

■ The growth of **shoots** towards light can be explained by the behaviour of auxin. Auxin moves **away** from the light side of a plant to the dark side. Here it encourages growth by increasing cell elongation. The dark side then grows more than the light side, and the shoot bends towards the light source.

■ In **roots**, gravity causes the auxin to collect on the **lower** side. Here it **stops** the cells elongating, which causes the root to bend downwards.

CHECK YOURSELF QUESTIONS

Q1 How are plant hormones different from animal hormones?

Q2 Which are the following are controlled by plant hormones?
  A flowering
  B pollination
  C germination
  D leaf fall.

Q3 Once a plant shoot has changed direction so it is growing towards the light why does it stop bending?

Answers are on page 238.

UNIT 5: ECOLOGY AND THE ENVIRONMENT

▰▰ The study of ecology ▰▰

⬚ Some ecological terms

- **Ecology** is the study of how living things affect and are affected by other living things as well as by other factors in the environment.

- An **ecosystem** is a community and its environment – e.g. a pond.

- **Environment** is a term often used to refer only to the physical features of an area, but can include living creatures.

- A **community** means the different species in an area – e.g. the grassland community.

- A **species** is one type of organism, e.g. a robin. Only members of the same species can breed successfully with each other.

- **Population** means the numbers of a particular species in an area or ecosystem.

- An organism's **niche** is its way of life or part it plays in an ecosystem.

- An organism's **habitat** is where an organism lives.

⬚ Competition

- Animals and plants are always trying to survive and reproduce. However, there is always a 'struggle' for survival for various reasons.

- **Animals** struggle:
  - for food
  - for water
  - for protection against the weather
  - against being eaten by predators
  - against disease
  - against accidents.

- Survival of **plants** is affected by:
  - lack of water
  - lack of light
  - lack of minerals in the soil
  - weather
  - disease
  - being eaten.

▶ In 1759 Thomas Austin introduced rabbits into Australia. He imported 24 rabbits from England and set them free on his property.

▶ The rabbits had very little competition and very few predators. The rabbit population increased quickly and they soon became a pest.

▶ In 1919 Dr Aragao realised the rabbits were a problem and suggested using the myxoma virus. The virus was tested for thirty years. In 1950 the virus was released into the environment in order to kill the rabbits.

▶ You need to be aware of the balance within an ecosystem. You should understand that when people change one organism in an ecosystem this has an effect on other

⚡ A* EXTRA

▶ Most predators and their prey don't show such a clear link as the lynx and hares because usually predators have more than one type of prey and animals are preyed on by more than one predator.

▶ This means that if the population size of one predator, or prey, falls then their place is taken by another.

■ Animals and plants generally produce many young but their population sizes usually **do not vary significantly** from year to year because most of the young do not survive to adulthood. One reason for this is that they are having to **compete** for the resources they need, such as food, as there is not enough to go around.

■ To help them survive, animals and plants are **adapted** to the environments in which they live. You will find out more about adaptations in Unit 6.

▢ Predation

■ One of the factors affecting a population of animals is the number of animals trying to eat them – their **predators**. The numbers of predators and **prey** are very closely connected.

■ A famous example is that of snowshoe hares and lynxes in northern Canada. Both animals were hunted for their fur and the fur company kept records of how many animals were caught, so we can estimate the sizes of the populations over nearly a hundred years. This is such a vivid example because when a predator's prey reduces in number, the predators usually eat something else instead. In this case the lynx did not.

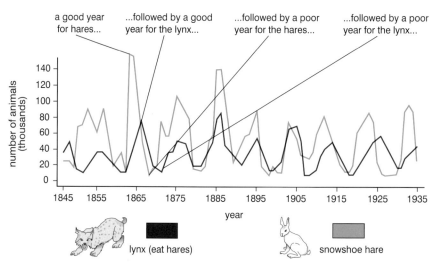

Predators follow prey! Use this phrase to remember how the population graphs relate to each other.

▢ Human population

■ The human population is very rapidly increasing in size. The graph of human population growth is getting steeper and steeper. Not only is the population increasing but the rate of increase is also increasing. This is an **exponential** increase.

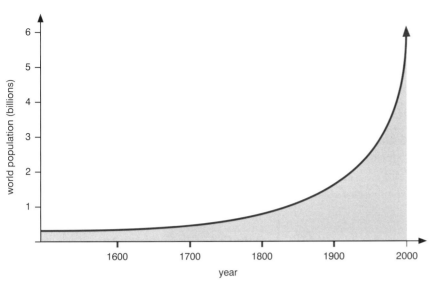

Reasons for this increase include:
- an increase in food production (through farming techniques)
- advances in medicine such as immunisations and antibiotics
- improved living conditions.

Associations

- **Parasitism** – **parasites** live in or on other organisms (their **hosts**) and harm the host. Examples are fleas living and feeding on a cat or tapeworms living inside a cow's gut.

- **Mutualism** – organisms of some species live together very closely, to the benefit of both. For example, **nitrogen-fixing bacteria** live in the root nodules of plants like peas, beans and clover. The bacteria gain sugars, vitamins and a sheltered habitat. The bacteria provide the plants with the nitrogen-containing compounds they need to make proteins (see the nitrogen cycle on page 57).

QUESTION SPOTTER

- You will often be asked to predict how the size of a population may change if other conditions change.
- Expect to be asked to explain your answer.

These root nodules contain nitrogen-fixing bacteria

CHECK YOURSELF QUESTIONS

Q1 In dense woodland there may not be many small plants growing on the ground. Suggest why.

Q2 In this country foxes eat rabbits. However, a graph of the two populations would not show the same oscillating (up and down) pattern as the lynxes and snowshoe hares on page 50. Why not?

Q3 In some summers there are much greater numbers of ladybirds than usual.
  a How would this affect the numbers of greenfly, their prey?
  b Why don't the high numbers of ladybirds persist year after year?

Answers are on page 238.

Relationships between organisms in an ecosystem

☐ Food chains

- **Food chains** show how living things get their food. They also show how they get their **energy**. This is why they are sometimes written to include the Sun.

| Sun | grass | grasshoppers | voles | owls |

An example of a food chain.

- Food chains can be written going up or down a page, or even from right to left. All are correct, as long as the arrows always point **towards** the living thing that is taking in the food or energy.

STAGES OF A FOOD CHAIN

- **Producers** are the green plants (e.g. grass). They make their own food by **photosynthesis**, using energy from the Sun. (There is more about photosynthesis in Unit 4.)

- **Primary consumers** (e.g. grasshoppers) are animals that **eat plants** or parts of plants such as fruit. They are also called **herbivores**.

- **Secondary consumers** (e.g. voles) eat other animals. They may be called **carnivores** or predators.

- **Tertiary consumers** (such as owls) are animals that eat some secondary consumers. They are also called carnivores or predators.

- The animals hunted and eaten by predators are called prey.

- Animals that eat both plants and animals are called **omnivores**.

- The different stages of a food chain are sometimes called **trophic levels** (trophic means 'feeding'). So, for example, producers make up the first trophic level, primary consumers make up the second trophic level and so on.

- **Most food chains are not very long**. They usually end with a secondary consumer or a tertiary consumer but occasionally there is an animal that feeds on tertiary consumers. This would be called a **quaternary consumer**.

Food webs

- Food webs are different food chains joined together. It would be unusual to find a food chain that was not part of a larger food web. Here is part of a food web:

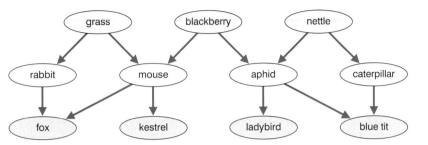

- Food webs show how different animals feed, and they can help us see what might happen if the food web is disturbed in some way.

- For example, what might happen if there was a disease that killed many, if not all, of the rabbits? From the food web above you can see that the foxes would have to eat more of the other animals – which might result in fewer mice. On the other hand, there would be more grass for the mice to eat, which might mean there are more mice.

- It is not possible to say for sure what would happen to all the organisms in a food web because there are so many living things involved.

Pyramids

- **Pyramids of numbers** show the **relative numbers** of each type of living thing in a food chain or web by trophic level. Sometimes pyramids of numbers can be 'inverted' – if, for example, the producers are much larger than the consumers.

A pyramid of numbers.   An 'inverted' pyramid of numbers.

- **Pyramids of biomass** show the mass of living material at each stage in the chain or web, so this shows what you would have if you could weigh all the producers together, then all the primary consumers and so on. Pyramids of biomass are almost **never** inverted.

- Pyramids either show organisms on a single food chain or trophic levels in a food web. If they show trophic levels, **each stage of the pyramid may be labelled** with all the living things at a particular trophic level, for example producers or primary consumers.

blue tits
caterpillars
oak tree

A pyramid of biomass.

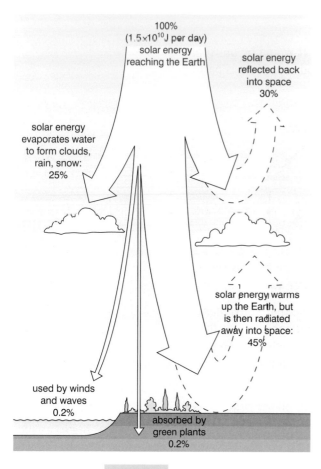

100%
(1.5×10¹⁰J per day)
solar energy
reaching the Earth

solar energy
reflected back
into space
30%

solar energy
evaporates water
to form clouds,
rain, snow:
25%

solar energy warms
up the Earth, but
is then radiated
away into space:
45%

used by winds
and waves
0.2%

absorbed by
green plants
0.2%

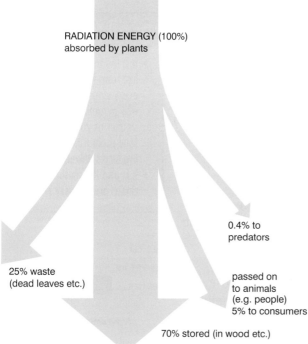

RADIATION ENERGY (100%)
absorbed by plants

0.4% to
predators

25% waste
(dead leaves etc.)

passed on
to animals
(e.g. people)
5% to consumers

70% stored (in wood etc.)

Energy flow in plants.

⌶ Energy flow

■ The arrows in food chains and webs show the **transfer of energy**. Not all the energy that enters an animal or plant is available to the next trophic level. Only energy that has resulted in an organism's growth will be available to the animal that eats it.

Example: cows feeding on grass in a field

> Sun → grass → cow

■ Only a **small proportion** of the energy in the sunlight falling on a field is used by the grass in photosynthesis.
  • Some may be **absorbed** or **reflected** by **clouds** or **dust** in the air.
  • Some may be absorbed or reflected by **trees** or **other plants**.
  • Some may **miss** the grass and hit the ground.
  • Some will be **reflected** by the **grass** (grass reflects the green part of the spectrum and absorbs the red and blue wavelengths).
  • Some will enter the grass but will **pass through** the leaves.

■ The remainder of the energy can be used in photosynthesis.

■ Some of the food made by the grass will be used for respiration to provide the grass's energy requirements, but some will be used for growth and will be available for a future consumer.

■ However, not all the energy in the grass will be available to the cows:
  • Some grass may be eaten by **other animals** (the farmer would probably call these pests).
  • The cows will **not eat all** of the grass (e.g. the roots remain).

■ Of the energy available in the grass the cows **ingest** (eat) they will use only a small proportion for growth. The diagram on page 55 shows what happens to the energy in an animal's food.

HOW ANIMALS LOSE ENERGY

- Energy is lost from animals in two main ways:

  1 **Egestion** – the removal from the body, in faeces, of material that may contain energy but has not been digested.

  2 **Respiration** – the release of energy from food is necessary for all the processes that go on in living things. Most of this energy is eventually lost as heat. (There is more about respiration in Unit 2.)

- Because **energy is lost** from the chain **at each stage** you almost always get a pyramid shape with a pyramid of biomass.

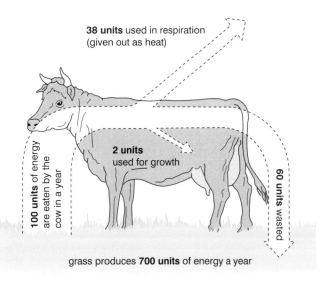

38 **units** used in respiration (given out as heat)

100 **units** of energy are eaten by the cow in a year

2 units used for growth

60 **units** wasted

grass produces **700 units** of energy a year

The energy flow in a young cow.

⊡ Farming

- A farmer raising plant or animal crops will get a greater yield by reducing energy losses from the food chain.

- For a **plant** crop this can be done by:
  - removing plants that are **competing** for light (e.g. weeds)
  - removing other organisms that might **damage** the plant crop (pests)
  - ensuring the plants have sufficient **water** and **minerals** to be able to photosynthesise and grow efficiently.

- The farmer could keep **animals indoors** so they do not have to use as much energy to stay warm or keep them **penned up** to reduce their movement and so lower the heat losses from respiration. This is sometimes known as **battery farming** and some people disagree with it on moral grounds.

QUESTION SPOTTER

You will often be required to describe some of the ways energy is lost from food chains.

CHECK YOURSELF QUESTIONS

Q1 Look at this food chain in a garden:

rose bushes → aphids → ladybirds

  a Draw and label a pyramid of numbers for this food chain.

  b Draw and label a pyramid of biomass for this food chain.

Q2 Which is more energy efficient, to grow crops that we eat ourselves or to use those crops to feed animals which we then eat?

Q3 Why are there usually not more than five stages in a food chain?

Answers are on page 239.

Natural recycling

⬚ Supplies are limited

■ The minerals that plants need from the soil are mostly released from the decayed remains of animals and plants and their waste. This is one example of natural recycling. There is only a limited amount (on Earth) of the elements that living things need and use.

■ Four of the most important elements in living things are **carbon** (C), **hydrogen** (H), **oxygen** (O) and **nitrogen** (N). Important substances such as carbohydrates, fats and proteins are made up of carbon, hydrogen and oxygen. Proteins also contain nitrogen.

■ The only way that animals and plants can continue to take in and use substances containing these elements is if the substances are constantly cycled around the ecosystem for reuse.

⬚ The carbon cycle

QUESTION SPOTTER

You may be given part of the carbon cycle or the nitrogen cycle and asked to add in the missing parts.

■ Plants take in carbon dioxide because they need the carbon (and oxygen) to use in photosynthesis to make carbohydrates and then other substances such as protein.

■ When animals eat plants they use some of the carbon-containing compounds to grow and some to release energy in respiration.

■ As a waste product of respiration animals breathe out carbon as carbon dioxide, which is then available for plants to use. (Don't forget that plants also respire producing carbon dioxide.)

■ Carbon dioxide is also released when animal and plant remains decay (**decomposition**) and when wood, peat or fossil fuels are burnt (**combustion**).

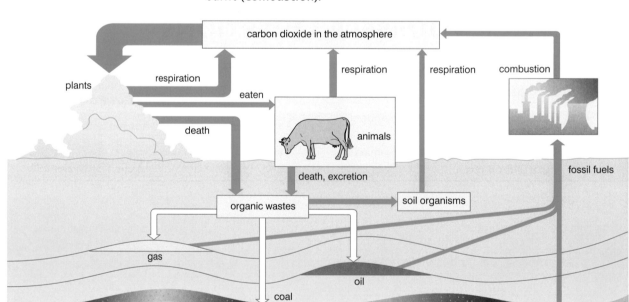

⌷ The nitrogen cycle

- Living things need nitrogen to make proteins – which are needed, for example, to make new cells for growth.

- The air is 79% nitrogen gas (N_2), but nitrogen gas is very unreactive and cannot be used by plants or animals. Instead plants use nitrogen in the form of **nitrates** (NO_3^- ions).

- The process of getting nitrogen into this useful form is called **nitrogen fixation**.

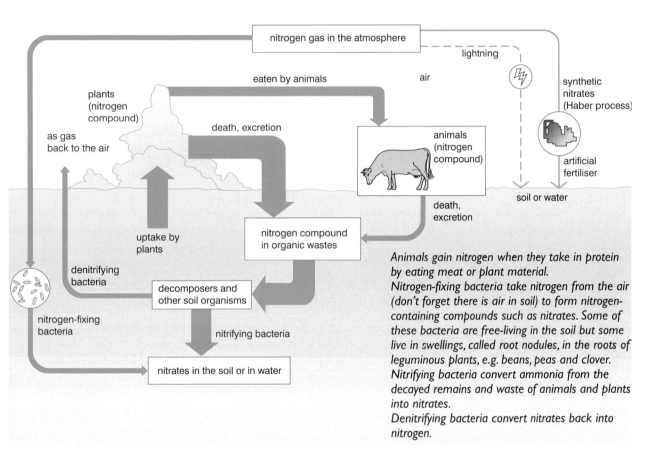

Animals gain nitrogen when they take in protein by eating meat or plant material.
Nitrogen-fixing bacteria take nitrogen from the air (don't forget there is air in soil) to form nitrogen-containing compounds such as nitrates. Some of these bacteria are free-living in the soil but some live in swellings, called root nodules, in the roots of leguminous plants, e.g. beans, peas and clover.
Nitrifying bacteria convert ammonia from the decayed remains and waste of animals and plants into nitrates.
Denitrifying bacteria convert nitrates back into nitrogen.

⊡ Decomposers

■ The decay of dead animal and plant remains is an important part of biological recycling. Decay happens because of the action of **bacteria** and **fungi**. These are known as **decomposers**.

■ Conditions that allow decomposers to thrive are conditions that will help decay:
  • **warm** (but not too hot to kill the micro-organisms)
  • **moist**
  • the presence of **oxygen**.

■ Other organisms, known as **detritivores** (such as worms or woodlice), feed on and break down dead remains (known as **detritus**). This exposes a greater surface area for the decomposers to act upon.

■ Materials that can decompose are known as **biodegradable**.

■ Micro-organisms that cause decay are used by humans – for example:
  • in **sewage works** to break down human waste
  • in **compost heaps** to break down waste plant material.

CHECK YOURSELF QUESTIONS

Q1 a In the carbon cycle, which main process removes carbon dioxide from the atmosphere?

b How is carbon dioxide put back into the atmosphere?

Q2 Nitrogen-fixing bacteria cannot live in waterlogged soil but denitrifying bacteria can, which is why this kind of soil is low in nitrates. Some plants that live in these conditions are carnivorous, trapping and digesting insects. Suggest why you often find carnivorous plants in bogs.

Q3 What is the difference between nitrifying and denitrifying bacteria?

Answers are on page 239.

Human influences on the environment

☐ Why is the effect of humans on the environment increasing?

- An **increasing population** means that more **resources** are needed and used (e.g. land, raw materials for industry, sources of energy and food).

- **Technological advances** and an overall increase in the standard of living also mean that more resources are used.

- Following on from this there is an increase in waste production – **pollution**.

- These problems are caused particularly by the developed countries of the world.

☐ Consequences of misuse of the environment

- The use of some resources like minerals and fossil fuels cannot continue forever – there is only a limited amount of them (they are **finite**). Once they have been used they cannot be replaced. In the future we will have to recycle these materials or find replacements that are renewable.

- Pollution caused by putting waste into the environment is causing changes that may be irreversible.

WAYS OF TACKLING THESE PROBLEMS

- **Reducing the amount** of raw materials we use (e.g. by using less packaging on products).

- **Recycling** more materials, so reducing the need for, and energy cost of, extracting more raw materials.

- Being more **energy efficient** (e.g. by reducing heat losses from buildings or turning off lights when not needed).

- Using **renewable energy sources** that will not run out and which cause little pollution (e.g. solar, wind or wave power).

- Using **sustainable** or renewable **raw materials** that can be produced again (such as wood).

☐ Farming and use of agrochemicals

- **Insecticides** are chemicals which kill insects that damage the crops. They can cause unwanted effects by killing animals that are not pests.

- Some insecticides can enter the food chain. The animals that ingest them cannot break them down or excrete them, so they remain in the animals' bodies. Such substances are described as being **persistent**. This means that predators can contain much higher levels of the substance than the animals below them in a food chain.

⭐ IDEAS AND EVIDENCE

▸ The increasing human population is encouraging farmers to produce as much food as possible from a reduced amount of land. This is called intensive farming. The amount of food produced is called productivity.

▸ There is an increasing interest in organic farming. This farming method does not rely on chemicals for fertilisers or pest control. You need to be able to explain why organic food is becoming more popular.

⭐ IDEAS AND EVIDENCE

▸ You need to be aware of how science is used in our environment.

▸ Environment agencies try to make people aware of the need for conservation of the world's resources. Their policies emphasise the '3 Rs': Reduce, Re-use, Recycle.

▸ Everyone can take an active part by following the 3 Rs. You should be able to apply this policy to examples given in your exams.

- Use of the insecticide DDT is the reason why many birds of prey in Britain, like sparrowhawks and peregrine falcons, suffered in the 1950s and 1960s. DDT is now banned in many countries. Most modern insecticides are not persistent and break down naturally in the environment after a short while.

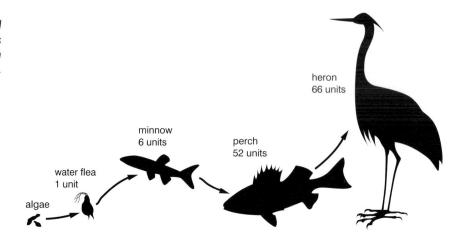

DDT affected many food chains. In this one, the figures give the relative concentration of DDT at each stage.

heron
66 units

minnow
6 units

perch
52 units

water flea
1 unit

algae

- **Biological control,** introducing another organism that will kill the pests, is an alternative to using chemical insecticides. This does not cause pollution and pests cannot become resistant to it (as they can to chemical insecticides). However, biological control can have unwanted effects – for instance the introduced predators might also attack harmless or even useful animals.

- **Fungicides** are chemicals that kill the fungi responsible for many plant diseases. Insecticides and fungicides together are often known as **pesticides**.

- **Herbicides**, or weedkillers, are chemicals which kill plants that would otherwise grow among the crop and compete with them for light, water and minerals. These other plants might also be the home of pests. However, such plants could be used by other animals. Also, by increasing the crop, any pests that normally feed on it will have plenty of food, may rapidly increase in numbers and could become a bigger problem.

- **Fertilisers** are added to improve the growth of crops. **Organic** (natural) fertilisers include compost or manure. **Inorganic** (artificial) fertilisers are mined or manufactured to contain the necessary minerals. Artificial fertilisers come in powdered or liquid form so they are easy to spread, but they can cause pollution.

EUTROPHICATION

- When it rains, the soluble fertiliser dissolves in the water and is carried away into lakes and rivers – it is **leached** from the soil.

- The fertiliser causes excessive growth of plants in rivers and lakes – especially **algae**. The plant overgrowth makes the water murky and blocks much of the light, and plants under the surface die and decay. The bacteria that cause the decay use up the oxygen in the water, so fish and other water animals die.

This river is blocked with algae because of excess nitrates washed in from nearby fields.

- This whole process is called **eutrophication**.

- Eutrophication can be reduced by using **less fertiliser**. This may actually help the farmer because there is a point beyond which adding more fertiliser will not help, and may even hinder, crop growth.

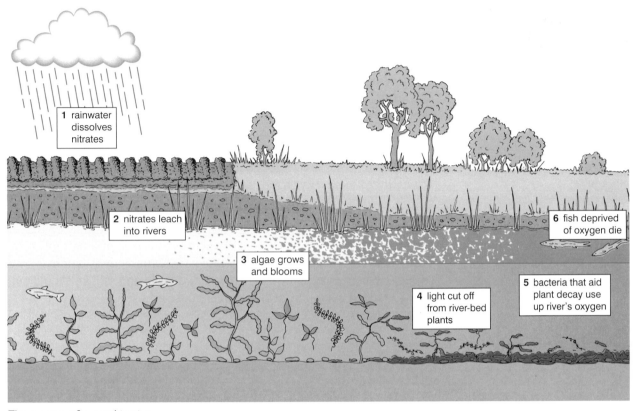

1 rainwater dissolves nitrates

2 nitrates leach into rivers

3 algae grows and blooms

4 light cut off from river-bed plants

5 bacteria that aid plant decay use up river's oxygen

6 fish deprived of oxygen die

The process of eutrophication.

⭐ IDEAS AND EVIDENCE

The increasing use of fertilisers is a key issue in modern farming world-wide.
▸ The advantage of using more fertiliser needs to be set against the environmental damage it causes (eutrophication).
▸ Water contaminated with fertilisers reaches reservoirs and, without suitable treatment, tap water will contain fertilisers that can affect human health.

OTHER WAYS OF MAINTAINING SOIL FERTILITY

- Using **organic fertilisers**, which release minerals into the soil at a slower rate. This also helps to improve soil structure, making it easier to plough for example.

- Using **crop rotation**, which includes growing crops that contain nitrogen-fixing bacteria in their root nodules. This restores soil fertility when the crops or their roots are ploughed back into the soil.

The greenhouse effect

■ Carbon dioxide, methane and CFCs are known as **greenhouse gases**. The levels of these gases in the atmosphere are increasing due to the burning of fossil fuels, pollution from farm animals and the use of CFCs in aerosols and refrigerators.

■ Short-wave radiation from the Sun warms the ground and the warm Earth gives off heat as long-wave radiation. Much of this radiation is stopped from escaping from the Earth by the greenhouse gases. This is known as the **greenhouse effect**.

■ The greenhouse effect is responsible for keeping the Earth warmer than it otherwise would be. The greenhouse effect is normal – and important for life on Earth. However, it is thought that increasing levels of greenhouse gases are stopping even more heat escaping and the Earth is slowly warming up. This is known as **global warming**. If global warming continues the Earth's climate may change and sea levels rise as polar ice melts.

■ The temperature of the Earth *is* gradually increasing, but we do not know for certain if the greenhouse effect is responsible. It may be that the observed rise in recent global temperatures is part of a natural cycle – there have been Ice Ages and intermediate warm periods before. Many people are concerned that it is not part of a cycle and say we should act now to reduce emissions of these greenhouse gases.

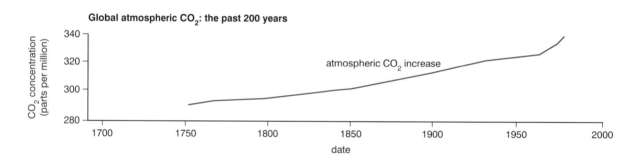

Global atmospheric CO_2: the past 200 years

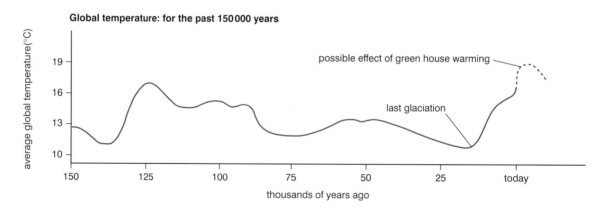

Global temperature: for the past 150 000 years

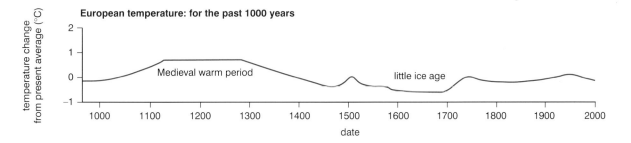

European temperature: for the past 1000 years

⬚ Acid rain

- Burning fossil fuels gives off many gases, including **sulphur dioxide** and various **nitrogen oxides**.

- Sulphur dioxide combines with water to form sulphuric acid. Nitrogen oxide combines with water to form nitric acid. These substances can make the rain acidic (called **acid rain**).

- Acid rain **harms plants** that take in the acidic water and the **animals** that live in the affected rivers and lakes. Acid rain also washes ions such as calcium and magnesium out of the soil, **depleting the minerals available to plants**. It also washes **aluminium**, which is poisonous to fish, out of the soil and into rivers and lakes.

- Reducing emission of the gases causing acid rain is expensive, and part of the problem is that the acid rain usually falls a long way from the places where the gases were given off.

- Fitting **catalytic converters** stops the emission of these gases from cars.

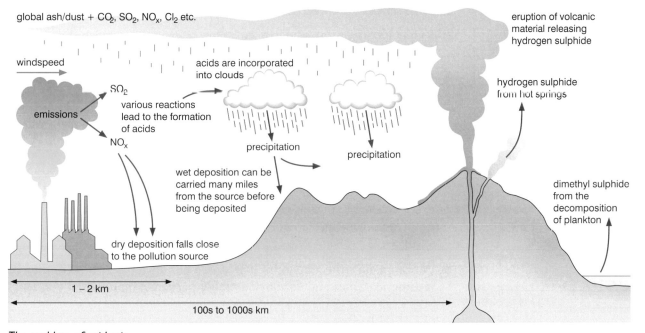

The problem of acid rain.

Depletion of the ozone layer

- High in the atmosphere there is a layer of a gas called **ozone**, a form of oxygen in which the molecules contain three oxygen atoms (O_3). Ozone in the atmosphere is continually being broken down and reformed:

ozone formation	ozone breakdown
$O_2 \xrightarrow{\text{UV light}} O + O$ $O_2 + O \rightarrow O_3$	$O_3 \rightarrow O_2 + O$ $O_3 + O \rightarrow 2O_2$

- The ozone layer reduces the amount of **ultraviolet radiation** (UV) that reaches the Earth's surface. This is important because UV radiation can cause skin cancer.

- Normally the rates at which the ozone forms and breaks down are about the same. **CFCs**, which are gases used as aerosol propellants and in refrigerator cooling systems, **speed up** the rate of ozone breakdown without affecting how quickly it reforms. This means that there is **less ozone** in the atmosphere and that **more UV radiation** will be reaching the Earth's surface. This could cause an increase in skin cancer in people who are exposed to a lot of sunlight.

- We can reduce the damage to the ozone layer by finding alternatives to CFCs, but many of these seem to contribute to other problems, such as the greenhouse effect.

- Even if all CFC emissions stopped today it will still take around a hundred years for all the CFCs presently in the atmosphere to break down.

Household waste

- People produce a lot of waste, including sewage and rubbish they simply throw away.

- **Sewage** has to be treated to remove disease organisms and the nutrients that cause eutrophication, before it can be discharged into the sea.

- Some **household rubbish** is burnt, causing acid gas pollution and acid rain. Rubbish tips create their own problems:
  - they are ugly and can smell
  - they can encourage rats and other pests
  - methane gas produced by rotting material may build up in tips that are covered with soil – this gas is explosive
  - covered-over tips can not be used for building on because the ground settles.

- We can reduce the amount of material in our dustbins by **recycling** or **reusing** materials and not buying **highly packaged** materials.

☐ Habitat destruction

- Many natural habitats are being **destroyed** to create land for farming or building on. The rainforests are being cut down for their wood and to create farming or grazing land. Many species of animals and plants are only found in wetland areas, which are being drained to 'reclaim' the land.

- Destruction of habitats **reduces species diversity**.

- Removing plants exposes the soil to rain, which **washes the soil away**, blocking rivers and causing flooding.

- Habitat destruction can also **alter the climate** – less water is transpired into the atmosphere.

☐ Endangered species

- Many species of animals and plants are in danger of **extinction** because of habitat destruction and hunting.

- Endangered species can be protected by:
  - making some areas protected
  - legal protection (e.g. laws against hunting)
  - educating people so that they are aware of species that are endangered and know how to protect them.

☐ Sustainable development

- One way of reducing the impact of human activity on the environment is to **replace** materials or crops we use.

- For example, quotas on fishing mean that fish stocks do not drop so far that the fish disappear altogether.

- Another example is to replant woodland after trees have been cut down.

QUESTION SPOTTER

Questions about environmental damage may use examples that you have not studied in detail. You will be given enough information to be able to answer them.

? CHECK YOURSELF QUESTIONS

Q1 Why are some pesticides described as 'persistent'?

Q2 What is the difference between the greenhouse effect and global warming?

Q3 Acid rain can be reduced by passing waste gases through lime to remove sulphur dioxide. Why don't all factories automatically do this?

Answers are on page 239.

Sampling techniques

Ecological surveys

- You may have already carried out an **ecological survey** of an area such as your school grounds. This involves finding out what organisms live there, where they live, and the sizes of their populations. To do this you can use different equipment and techniques.

Pooter

- The end of the short tube is placed over the animal and you suck on the other tube, collecting the animal in the bottle. This is suitable for collecting small **insects** or **spiders**, which would otherwise quickly move away.

A simple pooter

Pitfall trap

The standard way of using a pitfall trap.

- The trap can be left overnight. It is useful for collecting insects such as **beetles** that are more active at night and are too heavy to climb out. A lid or drainage holes will prevent water collecting and drowning the animals.

Tullgren funnel

- Soil contains many **small animals**. One way of extracting these from the soil is to put a soil sample inside the funnel. The heat from the lamp makes the animals go deeper until they fall through the sieve inside the funnel and can be collected in a pot underneath. The collecting pot can be filled with ethanol if you wish to preserve the animals.

The apparatus used to make a Tullgren funnel.

Sweep net

- A sweep net can be waved or brushed over grass or other vegetation to collect any insects there.

Beating tray

- The tray is held under a bush or branch, which is then shaken to dislodge any small animals – which can then be caught using a pooter.

Quadrat

- A quadrat can be used to carry out a **plant survey**, for example to compare the plant life in two different areas. You would randomly place the quadrat a number of times in each area, each time identifying and counting the plants within the quadrat. Then you would pool the results to find the average for the two areas.

- If the area of the region being investigated and the area of the quadrat are both known, then an estimate can be made of the total numbers of each species. Using quadrats in this way is called **sampling**, because only a sample of the region is inspected. Inspecting every plant throughout the region would take too long.

- Sampling using a quadrat works best if:
  - the quadrat is placed **randomly**
  - a reasonable **number of samples** is taken, so any 'odd' results will be 'evened out' when averages are taken
  - the plants being investigated are reasonably **evenly spread** throughout the area.

- You could also place a quadrat at regular intervals **along a line** to see how the habitat changes. This is called a **transect**.

- Quadrats can also be used to investigate the numbers or distribution of **animals** in a habitat – as long as they are evenly distributed and not constantly moving around the area.

❓ CHECK YOURSELF QUESTIONS

Q1 What equipment would be best to use to collect:
   a tiny insects living in the soil
   b large ground beetles that come out at night
   c small insects living in a thick bush
   d ants.

Q2 A pupil wanted to estimate the number of dandelions in a field. She used a large quadrat that was 1 m² and the field was 200 m². She used the quadrat 10 times and counted a total of 25 dandelions. Estimate the number of dandelions in the field.

Q3 Why is it important that quadrats are placed randomly?

Answers are on page 240.

UNIT 6: GENETICS AND EVOLUTION

Variation

▶ The 'double-helix' structure of DNA was discovered by James Watson and Francis Crick working in Cambridge in 1953. Rosalind Franklin, working in London, contributed important work on DNA's structure.

Types of variation

■ No two people are the same. Similarly, no two oak trees will be exactly the same in every way – they will be different heights, have different trunk widths and different numbers of leaves.

■ There are two types of variation:

1 **Discontinuous variation** – a characteristic can have one of a certain number of specific alternatives. Examples would be gender, where you are either male or female, or blood groups where you are either A, B, AB or O. This is sometimes referred to as discrete variation.

2 **Continuous variation** – a characteristic can have any value in a range. Examples would be body weight or length of hair.

Causes of variation

■ **Environmental causes.** Your diet, the climate you live in, accidents, your surroundings, the way you have been brought up or your lifestyle all influence your characteristics.

■ **Genetic causes** – the characteristic is controlled by your genes. Genes are inherited from your parents. Examples of characteristics in humans purely influenced by genes are eye colour and gender.

■ Many characteristics are influenced by environment **and** genes. For instance people in your family might tend to be tall, but unless you eat correctly when you are growing you will not become tall even though genetically you have the tendency to be tall. Other examples are more controversial, such as human intelligence, where it is unclear whether the environment or genes is more influential.

Genes

■ Genes are **instructions** that direct the processes going on inside cells. They affect the way cells grow and work and so can affect features of your body such as the shape of your face or the colour of your eyes. All the information needed to make a fertilised egg grow into an adult is contained in its genes.

■ Inside virtually every cell in the body is a **nucleus**, which contains long threads called **chromosomes**. These threads are usually spread throughout the nucleus, but when the cell splits they gather into bundles that can be seen through a microscope. The chromosomes are made of a chemical called deoxyribonucleic acid (**DNA**).

■ DNA is a very long molecule that contains a series of chemicals called **bases**. There are four different types of base in DNA: thymine (T), adenine (A), guanine (G) and cytosine (C). The order in which the bases occur is a **genetic code**. The code spells out instructions that control how the cell works. Each length of DNA that spells out a different instruction is known as a **gene**. Each chromosome contains thousands of genes.

■ All the genes in a particular living thing are known as its **genome**.

■ Genes tell cells how to make different **proteins**. Many proteins are enzymes that control the chemical processes inside cells.

■ Most of our features that are controlled genetically are affected by several genes.

A* EXTRA

Only some of the full set of genes are used in any one cell.

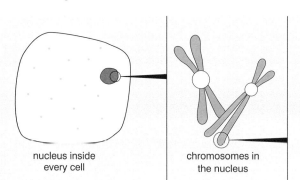

nucleus inside every cell   chromosomes in the nucleus   genes are sections of the chromosomes

QUESTION SPOTTER

You will often be asked about the difference between genes and chromosomes and where they are located in a cell.

Mutations

■ Sometimes genes can be altered so that their message becomes meaningless or a different instruction. This is known as a **mutation**. Mutations can be caused by:
- radiation
- certain chemicals, called **mutagens**
- spontaneous changes.

■ Mutations that occur in **sex cells** can be passed on to offspring, who may develop abnormally or may die at an early stage of development.

■ If mutations occur in **body cells** they may multiply uncontrollably. This is **cancer**.

A* EXTRA

▸ DNA is made of very long strings of four different chemical bases.
▸ Each group of three bases codes for a particular amino acid, so the sequence of bases in a gene codes for the sequence of amino acids in a protein.

DNA is found in the nucleus of cells.

a cell

chromosomes in the nucleus

nucleus

DNA carries a code made from bases

GTAGCTG
CATCGAC

DNA

a strand of chromosomes is a long coil of DNA

A spider plant forms new plants at the end of stalks ('runners'). These new plants eventually grow independently of the parent plant. This is an example of asexual reproduction.

Cell division

■ Cells grow by splitting in two. This is called **cell division**, and is part of normal body growth. It is also the way that single-celled organisms reproduce and is the only type of cell division involved during **asexual reproduction** (reproduction that does not involve sex cells).

■ Before a cell splits, its chromosomes **duplicate** themselves. The new cells formed, sometimes called the **daughter cells**, contain chromosomes identical with the original cell. This type of cell division, in which the new cells are genetically identical to the original, is known as **mitosis**. Cells or organisms that are genetically identical to each other are known as **clones**.

Stage 1. The chromosomes get fatter and become visible.

Stage 2. Each chromosome makes an exact copy of itself

Stage 3. The chromosomes line up in the middle of the cell

Stage 4. The colour chromosomes part and move to opposite halves of the cell.

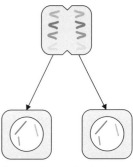

Stage 5. The cell splits in two.

The process of mitosis.

■ There is another type of reproduction in which the new individuals have been formed by two special cells, called **sex cells** or **gametes**, usually one from each parent. This type of reproduction is called **sexual reproduction**.

■ A different type of cell division called **meiosis** ensures that the gametes only have half the number of chromosomes that body cells have. In humans the gametes are sperm cells and egg cells. In flowering plants the gametes are the pollen cells and the female 'egg' cells or ovules.

■ The gametes contain half the normal number of chromosomes so that when they join together (at **fertilisation**) the normal number is restored. For example, human cells normally contain 23 pairs of chromosomes: 46 in total. Human egg and sperm cells contain only 23 chromosomes, so when they join together the new cell formed has the normal 46. (The number of chromosomes depends on an organism's species.)

■ The offspring produced by sexual reproduction are genetically **different** from their parents.

The 23 pairs of chromosomes in a human cell, including the X and tiny Y.

Stage 1. A normal cell in the sex organs. It has the usual number of chromosomes, which fatten and become visible.

Stage 2. Each chromosome makes a copy of itself

Stage 3. Remember that each chromosome has its own 'partner'. They carry similar 'blueprints' – one from the original father and one from the mother. These partner chromosomes get together and line up across the middle of the cell.

Stage 6. In each new cell, the chromosomes part and move to opposite halves of their cells.

Stage 4. The chromosome pairs swap genes, split up and move to opposite halves of the cell.

Stage 5. The cell splits into two new cells. These special cells have half the usual number of chromosomes.

Stage 7. The two new cells split once more to make four new cells. Each has half the usual number of chromosomes.

The process of meiosis.

■ Every gamete formed has one of each pair of chromosomes. However, which one of each chromosome pair ends up in a particular gamete is purely random. An individual human can produce gametes with billions of different combinations of chromosomes.

■ Add this to the fact that when chromosome pairs are lying next to each other they swap lengths of DNA (this is called **crossing over**), altering the combination of genes on a chromosome. It is not surprising that, even with the same parents, we can look very different from our brothers and sisters.

? CHECK YOURSELF QUESTIONS

Q1 Which of the following are examples of (a) continuous and (b) discontinuous variation?
  A Hair colour
  B Blood group
  C Foot size
  D Gender
  E Hair length.

Q2 Bob and Dave are identical twins. Dave emigrates to Australia, where he works outside on building sites. Bob stays in England and works in an office. Suggest how they might look (a) similar and (b) different. Explain your answers.

Q3 Put the following in order of size, starting with the smallest: cell nucleus, chromosome, gene, cell, chemical base.

Answers are on page 240.

How features are passed on

- Some features, such as the colour of your eyes, are passed on, or **inherited**, from your parents, but other features may not be passed on. Sometimes features appear to miss a generation – for instance you and your grandmother might both have ginger hair, but neither of your parents do.

DOMINANT AND RECESSIVE ALLELES

- Leopards occasionally have a cub that has completely black fur instead of the usual spotted pattern. It is known as a black panther but is still the same species as the ordinary leopard.

- Just as in humans, leopard chromosomes occur in **pairs**. One pair carries a gene for fur colour. There are two copies of the gene in a normal body cell (one on each chromosome). Both copies of the gene may be identical but sometimes they are different, one being for a spotted coat and the other for a black coat. Different versions of a gene are called **alleles**.

- Leopard cubs receive half their genes from each parent. Eggs and sperm cells only contain half the normal number of chromosomes as normal body cells. This means that egg and sperm cells contain only one of each pair of alleles. When an egg and sperm join together at fertilisation the new cell formed, the **zygote**, which will develop into the new individual, now has two alleles of each gene.

- **Different combinations** of alleles will produce different fur colour:

  spotted coat allele + spotted coat allele = spotted coat

  spotted coat allele + black coat allele = spotted coat

  black coat allele + black coat allele = black coat

- The black coat only appears when **both** of the alleles for the black coat are present. As long as there is at least one allele for a spotted coat, the coat will be spotted because the allele for a spotted coat overrides the allele for a black coat. It is the **dominant allele**. Alleles like the one for the black coat are described as **recessive**.

- Having two identical alleles is described as being **homozygous**. Animals that have two different alleles are **heterozygous**.

MONOHYBRID CROSSES

- An individual's combination of genes is their **genotype**. An individual's combination of physical features is called their **phenotype**. Your genotype influences your phenotype.

- We can show the influence of the genotype in a **genetic diagram**. In a genetic diagram we use a **capital letter** for the **dominant** allele and a **lower case** letter for the **recessive** allele.

✪ IDEAS AND EVIDENCE

▸ You need to be aware of major scientific developments.

▸ The Human Genome Project was an international project lead by John Sulston of Cambridge University. Scientists all over the world took part in the project to map the genes of human DNA. The project was completed in 2001.

▸ You will need to consider how this project can be useful to various people, for example whether life insurance companies should have access to the data to see whether someone has inherited a genetic disorder. You also need to consider if this information should be made available to everyone.

- Using the example of the leopards, the letter S stands for the dominant allele for a spotted coat and letter s will stand for the recessive allele for the black coat. Two spotted parents who have a black cub must each be carrying an S and an s. The genetic diagram below shows the different offspring that may be born.

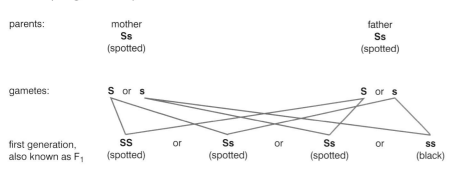

parents: mother **Ss** (spotted)   father **Ss** (spotted)

gametes: **S** or **s**   **S** or **s**

first generation, also known as F₁: **SS** (spotted) or **Ss** (spotted) or **Ss** (spotted) or **ss** (black)

- Because we are looking at only one characteristic (fur colour), this is an example of a **monohybrid cross**. 'Mono' means one, and a 'hybrid' is produced when two different types breed, or cross.

- Another type of genetic diagram is known as a **Punnett square**. The example above can be shown in a Punnett square:

		male gametes	
		S	**s**
female gametes	**S**	**SS** (spotted)	**Ss** (spotted)
	s	**Ss** (spotted)	**ss** (black)

- When two heterozygous parents are crossed, the offspring that have the feature controlled by the dominant allele and those showing the feature controlled by the recessive allele appear in a **3:1 ratio**. This is because of the random way that gametes combine. The 3:1 ratio refers to the **probabilities** of particular combinations of alleles – there is a 1 in 4 chance of a leopard cub being black, for example.

- With a large number of offspring you would expect something near the 3:1 ratio of spotted to black cubs. However, because it does refer only to probabilities you would not be too surprised if in a litter of four two of the cubs were black or none were black.

- How genes are inherited was first worked out in the nineteenth century by an Austrian monk, **Gregor Mendel**, who did lots of breeding experiments using pea plants.

IDEAS AND EVIDENCE

▸ By ten weeks into a pregnancy, it is possible for doctors to predict whether a pregnant woman is carrying a baby with Down's syndrome. If the baby has Down's syndrome, the mother is offered a termination.

▸ The mother is then left in a moral dilemma in trying to decide whether to have the pregnancy terminated.

🗂 Inherited diseases

■ Some diseases or disorders can be inherited. Examples include:
  • **cystic fibrosis** – in which the lungs become clogged up with mucus
  • **haemophilia** – in which blood does not clot as normal
  • **diabetes** – in which insulin is not made in the pancreas (see Unit 3)
  • **sickle–cell anaemia** – in which the red blood cells are misshapen and do not carry oxygen properly
  • **Huntington's disease** – a disorder of the nervous system.

■ Most inherited diseases are caused by **faulty genes**. For example, one form of diabetes is caused by a fault in the gene carrying the instructions telling the pancreas cells how to make insulin.

■ Most of these faulty alleles are **recessive**, which means that you have to have two copies of the faulty allele to show the disorder. Many people will be **carriers**, having one normal allele as well as the faulty version. The diagram below shows how two carrier parents could have a child with a disorder.

		male gametes	
		D	**d**
female gametes	**D**	**DD** (makes insulin)	**Dd** (makes insulin)
	d	**Dd** (makes insulin)	**dd** (has diabetes)

🗂 Sex determination

■ Whether a baby is a boy or a girl is decided by one pair of chromosomes called the **sex chromosomes**. There are two sex chromosomes, the **X chromosome** and the **Y chromosome**. Boys have one of each and girls have two X chromosomes.

■ **Egg** cells always contain **one X chromosome** but **sperm** cells have an equal chance of containing **either** an X chromosome **or** a Y chromosome. This means that a baby has an equal chance of being either a boy or a girl. This is shown in the diagram below.

		male gametes	
		X	**Y**
female gametes	**X**	**XX** (girl)	**XY** (boy)
	X	**XX** (girl)	**XY** (boy)

⊡ Sex-linked inheritance

■ Some genetic disorders such as red–green colour blindness are more common in men than women. The recessive allele causing the disorder is found on the X chromosome, on a part for which there is no equivalent on the Y chromosome as it is smaller (see photograph on page 70). This means that males only need to have one copy of the recessive allele to show the disorder while females would need two copies.

? CHECK YOURSELF QUESTIONS

Q1 In humans, the gene that allows you to roll your tongue is a dominant allele. Use a genetic diagram to show how two 'roller' parents could have a child who is a 'non-roller'.

Q2 In leopards the allele for being spotted, S, is dominant to the allele for being black, s. How could you tell whether a spotted leopard was Ss or SS, given that you have black leopards that you know are ss?

Q3 John and Mary have a little girl who has cystic fibrosis. Cystic fibrosis is caused by a recessive allele. What is the probability of their next child also having cystic fibrosis? Neither John nor Mary have the condition.

Answers are on page 240.

▬ Applications ▬

⊡ Selective breeding

- Selective breeding (also known as **artificial selection**) has been used by farmers for hundreds of years to change and improve the features of the animals or plants they grow. Examples would be breeding:
  - apples that are bigger and more tasty
  - sheep that produce more or better quality wool
  - cows that produce more milk or meat
  - wheat that can be planted earlier so giving an extra crop
  - plants that are more resistant to disease.

- In every case the principle is the same. You select two individuals with the features closest to those you want and breed them together. From the next generation you again select the best offspring and use these for breeding. Repeat this over many generations.

- For example, if you wanted to produce dogs that had short tails, you would breed the male and female with the shortest tails from the dogs you had available. From their offspring you would select those with the shortest tails to use for breeding. After repeating this over many generations you would find that you almost always produced short-tailed dogs – they would be **breeding true**.

- Simply selecting for different features such as size or shape has produced all the breeds of dogs we have today, which are all descended from wolves that were domesticated thousands of years ago.

⚡ A* EXTRA

- Selective breeding usually causes a reduction in variation.
- It may also lead to an accumulation of harmful recessive characteristics. This is the danger of inbreeding.

The power of selection. Selective breeding has produced an enormous variety of dog breeds from wild wolf stock (right).

⟲ Cloning

- If you have an animal or plant with features that you want, its offspring might not show those features. A simple way of producing new **plants** that are genetically identical to the original is by taking **cuttings**. A cutting is a shoot or branch that is removed from the original and planted in soil to grow on its own. Some plants do this easily, others may need rooting hormones (see Unit 4) to encourage them to grow roots.

A small cutting from a geranium that has been encouraged to grow fresh roots.

- A more modern version of taking cuttings is **tissue culture**. This is used to grow large numbers of plants quickly as only a **tiny part** of the original is needed to grow a new plant. Special procedures have to be followed:

  1. Cut many small pieces from the chosen plant. These are called **explants**.

  2. **Sterilise** the pieces by washing them in mild bleach to kill any microbes.

  3. In sterile conditions transfer the explants on to a jelly-like growth medium that contains nutrients as well as plant hormones to encourage growth.

  4. The explants should develop roots and shoots and leaves.

  5. When the plants are large enough they can be transferred to other growth media and eventually to a normal growth medium like compost.

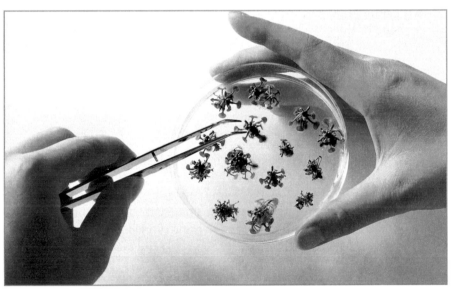

These tiny sundew plants have all grown from tiny cuttings of a single plant.

- Cloning can also now be used with **animals**. For example, cells from a developing **embryo** (such as from a cow) can be split apart before they become specialised and then transplanted, as identical embryos, into **host mothers**.

- Another way of cloning animals involves making ordinary **body cells** grow into new animals. Dolly the sheep was the first mammal clone grown from the cell of a fully grown organism – in Dolly's case a cell from the udder of a sheep.

✦ IDEAS AND EVIDENCE

▸ You need to consider the power and limitations of science in addressing ethical issues.

▸ The main advantage of selective breeding and cloning is to develop features in plants and animals that we want.

▸ Many people are concerned about ethical issues, such as whether this is a natural process and whether we are meant to control nature.

▸ The main concern of other people is that we don't reduce genetic variation.

☐ Genetic engineering

■ Selective breeding works by trying to bring together desirable combinations of genes. **Genetic engineering** allows this to be done quickly and directly. It involves taking genes from **one organism** and **inserting** them into cells of **another**. For example, genes have been inserted into crop plants to make them more resistant to attack by pests.

■ The gene that carries the instructions for making the human hormone insulin has been inserted into bacteria, which now produce insulin. This is where much of the insulin to treat diabetes comes from. The gene was originally from a human cell so the insulin is identical to that made normally in the human pancreas.

STEPS INVOLVED IN GENETIC ENGINEERING

1 **Find** the part of the DNA that contains the gene you want.

2 **Remove the gene** using special enzymes that cut the DNA either side of the gene.

3 **Insert the gene** into the cells of the organism you want to change.

■ Step 3 may be done directly but it often involves using **other organisms**, such as bacteria or viruses, to act as **vectors**. This means the gene is first inserted in the vectors, which transfer the gene to the host when they infect it.

■ Inserting the gene into bacteria means that many copies can be made of the gene because bacteria reproduce asexually, producing new cells that are genetically identical to the original.

DANGERS OF GENETIC ENGINEERING

■ Although genetic engineering promises many benefits for the future, such as curing genetic diseases or changing crops to make them disease resistant, there are possible dangers.

■ For example, the **wrong genes** could accidentally be transferred or viral infection could transfer inserted genes to other unintended organisms. Imagine the problems if, instead of crops becoming resistant to disease, weeds became immediately resistant to herbicides or if harmful bacteria became immediately resistant to medicines like antibiotics.

? CHECK YOURSELF QUESTIONS

Q1 A farmer wants to produce sheep with finer wool. How could this be done by selective breeding?

Q2 What are the advantages and disadvantages of producing new roses by tissue culture (cloning)?

Q3 Both genetic engineering and selective breeding are ways of producing new combinations of genes in an organism. What are the advantages of genetic engineering?

Answers are on page 241.

■ Evolution ■

⊡ Evidence for evolution

- Animal and plant species can change over long periods of time. This change is called **evolution**.

- We cannot **prove** that evolution has happened as we can't go back in time and watch. However, there is a lot of evidence that evolution has happened.

THE FOSSIL RECORD

- **Fossils** show that very different animals and plants existed in the past. In some cases we can see steady **progressive changes** over time. In other cases there is no evidence of a particular organism's ancestors or descendants.

- The likelihood of a fossil forming in the first place is very rare. Fossils may form in various ways:
  - from **hard body parts** that do not decay easily
  - from body parts that have not decayed because of the **conditions** the body was left in
  - when part of the animal or plant decays and is **replaced** by other materials
  - as **traces** – e.g. footprints or burrows.

- Even if fossils did form they might not be discovered or could be destroyed by erosion. If evolution happened relatively quickly there would be less chance of finding fossils of the intermediate stages. Even when fossils are found they usually only provide a record of the hard tissues like bone.

AFFINITIES

- **Affinities** are similarities that exist between different species. For example, humans, dolphins and rats have much the same number and basic arrangement of bones in their skeletons. The easiest explanation is that they are similar because they are related, in other words they have evolved from a common ancestor.

⊡ Accepting the idea of evolution

- It was only after 1859, when **Charles Darwin** published his famous book *On the Origin of Species*, that ideas about evolution were widely discussed. (The scientist **Alfred Russell Wallace** also came up with the same ideas as Darwin, but he did not publish them first.)

A* EXTRA

▸ Most mutations are harmful or neutral in their effects.
▸ Only a minority of mutations are beneficial and able to be spread by natural selection.

■ Many people were angered by Darwin's ideas as they believed they went against the Christian Church's teachings that God had created the world and all the living things in it. Many newspaper cartoons and articles ridiculed Darwin's ideas. Some of these were based on the mistaken idea that Darwin had said that humans had evolved from apes like those present today such as chimpanzees.

■ The idea of evolution is not that the animals and plants we see around us evolved from each other, but that some have similar features because they evolved from some **common ancestor**. The diagram below illustrates how humans and apes may have evolved from a common ancestor. Humans and chimpanzees share more similarities than the other types of apes, which means that they probably share a more recent ancestor than do the others.

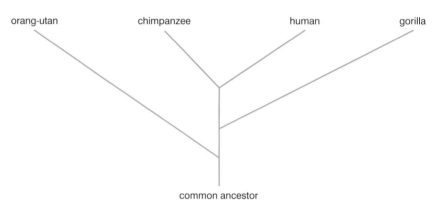

orang-utan   chimpanzee   human   gorilla

common ancestor

IDEAS AND EVIDENCE

▸ The theory of natural selection helps us to explain many scientific observations.

▸ An example is the issue of increased use of antibiotics and how this has led to the evolution of resistant bacteria.

■ Today there are still people who do not believe in the idea of evolution.

Natural selection

■ Darwin suggested how evolution could have happened. He called his theory **natural selection**. He based his ideas on his observations of the wildlife he found on several lengthy sea voyages. He also used his knowledge of selective breeding.

■ Natural selection is the same basic idea as selective breeding, except it is 'nature' rather than the breeder that determines which animals or plants are able to reproduce and pass on their features.

THE IDEAS OF NATURAL SELECTION

1 Animals and plants produce more offspring than will ever survive. This means that if some individuals are slightly better **adapted** they will have a better chance of surviving than the others. For example, a zebra that could run faster than the others would be less likely to be caught by lions, or a cactus with slightly sharper spines would be less likely to be eaten. This idea is sometimes known as the **'survival of the fittest'**.

The cactus is well adapted to dry desert conditions.
● *Long roots reach water far below ground.*
● *Swollen stem stores water.*
● *Leaves are small spines, which deter animals and reduce water loss by having a small surface area.*
● *Rounded shape reduces surface area and therefore water loss.*

2 The animals and plants that are more likely to survive are more likely to **reproduce**. If the features that helped them survive are genetically controlled they may be passed onto their offspring. Offspring who inherit those good features are in turn more likely to survive and reproduce than offspring that do not inherit the best features.

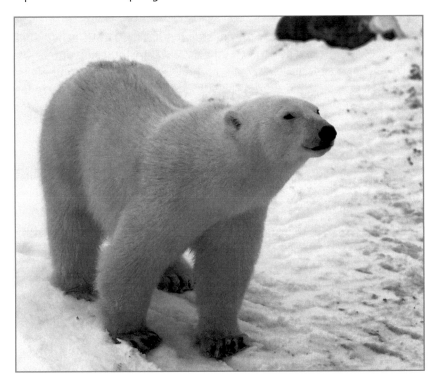

The polar bear is well adapted to its environment.
- *Eyes on front of head for good judgement of size and distance.*
- *Sharp teeth for killing prey and tearing through flesh.*
- *White fur is good camouflage to hide from prey.*
- *Thick fur to trap heat to keep warm.*
- *Lots of fat to act as a food store and to keep warm.*
- *Strong legs for walking and swimming long distances.*
- *Sharp claws to grip ice.*
- *Hair on the soles of the feet provides a grip on icy surfaces.*

3 As this process continues over many generations, organisms with the **best** features will make up a **larger proportion** of the population and those with features that are **not as helpful** will gradually **disappear**. For example, if the fastest zebras in every generation survive, then over many generations zebras will get faster and faster.

■ Natural selection explains why animals and plants are adapted to their surroundings. If the environment changes, the organisms that do not evolve and adapt may become **extinct**.

QUESTION SPOTTER

▸ In questions about natural selection you will often be asked to describe the steps in the process.
▸ Although the examples you are given will vary, the steps themselves will be the same.

CHECK YOURSELF QUESTIONS

Q1 a Why do we have a clearer idea of how vertebrate animals like mammals, birds and reptiles evolved than of how invertebrates like worms and slugs evolved?

 b Why are there many gaps in the fossil record even for animals with skeletons?

Q2 The long necks of giraffes are an adaptation allowing them to feed on the high branches of trees where many other animals cannot reach. Use the theory of natural selection to explain how giraffes could have evolved long necks from shorter-necked ancestors.

Answers are on page 241.

UNIT 7: CHEMICAL FORMULAE AND EQUATIONS

How are chemical formulae calculated?

⬚ Chemical symbols and formulae

■ All substances are made up from simple building blocks called **elements**. Each element has a unique **chemical symbol**, containing one or two letters. Elements discovered a long time ago often have symbols that don't seem to match their name. For example, sodium has the chemical symbol Na. This is derived from the Latin name for sodium – 'nadium'.

■ When elements chemically combine they form **compounds**. A compound can be represented by a **chemical formula**.

⬚ Simple compounds

■ Many compounds contain just two elements. For example, when magnesium burns in oxygen a white ash of magnesium oxide is formed. To work out the chemical formula of magnesium oxide:

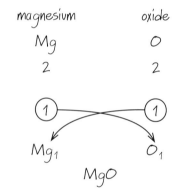

1 Write down the name of the compound.

2 Write down the chemical symbols for the elements in the compound.

3 Use the periodic table to find the 'combining power' of each element. Write the combining power of each element under its symbol.

4 If the numbers can be cancelled down do so.

5 Swap over the combining powers. Write them after the symbol, slightly below the line (as a 'subscript').

6 If any of the numbers are 1 you do not need to write them.

■ Magnesium oxide has the chemical formula you would have probably guessed. What about calcium chloride?

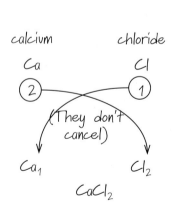

1 Write down the name of the compound.

2 Write down the chemical symbols for the elements in the compound.

3 Use the periodic table to find the 'combining power' of each element. Write the combining power of each element under its symbol.

4 If the numbers can be cancelled down do so.

5 Swap over the combining powers. Write them after the symbol, slightly below the line (as a subscript).

6 If any of the numbers are one there is no need to write them.

■ The chemical formula of a compound is not always immediately obvious, but if you follow these rules you will have no problems.

⬚ 'Combining powers' of elements

- There is a simple relationship between an element's **group number** in the periodic table and its combining power. Groups are the vertical columns in the periodic table.

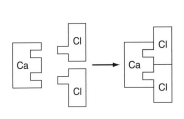

Group number	I	2	3	4	5	6	7	8(or 0)
Combining power	I	2	3	4	3	2	I	0

RULES FOR DETERMINING COMBINING POWER

- Groups 1–4: combining power = group number.

- Groups 5–8: combining power = 8 − (group number).

- If an element is not in one of the main groups, its combining power will be included in the name of the compound containing it. For example, copper is a transition metal and is in the middle block of the periodic table. In copper(II) oxide, copper has a combining power of 2.

- Sometimes an element does not have the combining power you would predict from its position in the periodic table. The combining power of these elements is also included in the name of the compound containing it. For example, phosphorus is in group 5, so you would expect it to have a combining power of 3, but in phosphorus(V) oxide its combining power is 5.

- **The only exception is hydrogen.** Hydrogen is often not included in a group, nor is its combining power given in the name of compounds containing hydrogen. It has a combining power of 1.

- The combining power is linked to the **number of electrons** in the atom of the element.

⬚ Compounds containing more than two elements

- Some elements exist bonded together in what is called a **radical**. For example, in copper(II) sulphate, the sulphate part of the compound is a radical.

- There are a number of common radicals, each having its own combining power. You cannot work out these combining powers easily from the periodic table – you have to learn them. The shaded ones in the table are the ones you are most likely to encounter at GCSE.

☀ QUESTION SPOTTER

▸ Questions will often expect you to write the formulae of simple compounds, usually as part of writing a fully balanced equation.

▸ To do this you will need to remember the formulae of the radicals shown in the table – they cannot easily be worked out from the periodic table.

combining power = I		combining power = 2		combining power = 3	
hydroxide	OH	carbonate	CO_3	phosphate	PO_4
hydrogen carbonate	HCO_3	sulphate	SO_4		
nitrate	NO_3				
ammonium	NH_4				

■ The same rules apply to radicals as to elements. For example:

copper(II) sulphate	potassium nitrate
Cu SO$_4$	K NO$_3$
2 2	I I
CuSO$_4$	KNO$_3$

■ If the formula contains **more than one radical** unit the radical must be put in brackets. For example:

calcium hydroxide	ammonium carbonate
Ca OH	NH$_4$ CO$_3$
2 I	I 2
Ca(OH)$_2$	(NH$_4$)$_2$CO$_3$

A* EXTRA

▶ In a formula containing more than one radical unit the radical should be put in a bracket.
▶ The combining power of a radical is equal to the charge on the radical, e.g. the sulphate ion has a combining power of 2 and its formula is SO$_4^{2-}$.

■ The brackets are used just as they are used in maths – the number outside the bracket multiplies everything inside it. Be careful how you use the brackets – for example, do not be tempted to write calcium hydroxide as CaOH$_2$ rather than Ca(OH)$_2$. This is incorrect.

CaOH$_2$ contains one Ca, one O, two H ✗

Ca(OH)$_2$ contains one Ca, two O, two H ✓

CHECK YOURSELF QUESTIONS

Q1 Work out the chemical formulae of the following compounds:
  a sodium chloride
  b magnesium fluoride
  c aluminium nitride
  d lithium oxide
  e carbon oxide (carbon dioxide).

Q2 Work out the chemical formulae of the following compounds:
  a iron(III) oxide
  b phosphorus(V) chloride
  c chromium(III) bromide
  d sulphur(VI) oxide (sulphur trioxide)
  e sulphur(IV) oxide (sulphur dioxide).

Q3 Work out the chemical formulae of the following compounds:
  a potassium carbonate
  b ammonium chloride
  c sulphuric acid (hydrogen sulphate)
  d magnesium hydroxide
  e ammonium sulphate.

Answers are on page 242.

▬ Chemical equations ▬

⌂ Writing chemical equations

- In a **chemical equation** the starting chemicals are called the **reactants** and the finishing chemicals are called the **products**.

- Follow these simple rules to write the chemical equation.

  1 Write down the **word equation**.

  2 Write down the **symbols** (for elements) and **formulae** (for compounds).

  3 **Balance the equation** (to make sure there are the same number of each type of atom on each side of the equation).

- Many elements are **diatomic**. They exist as molecules containing two atoms.

Element	Form in which it exists
hydrogen	H_2
oxygen	O_2
nitrogen	N_2
chlorine	Cl_2
bromine	Br_2
iodine	I_2

The reaction between hydrogen and oxygen produces a lot of energy as well as water – enough to launch a rocket.

WORKED EXAMPLES

1 When a lighted splint is put into a test tube of hydrogen the hydrogen burns with a 'pop'. In fact the hydrogen reacts with oxygen in the air (the reactants) to form water (the product). Write the chemical equation for this reaction.

Word equation:	hydrogen + oxygen → water
Symbols and formulae:	$H_2 + O_2 → H_2O$
Balance the equation:	$2H_2 + O_2 → 2H_2O$

For every two molecules of hydrogen that react, one molecule of oxygen is needed and two molecules of water are formed.

$2H_2$	+	O_2	→	$2H_2O$
two molecules		one molecule		two molecules

2 What is the equation when natural gas (methane) burns in air to form carbon dioxide and water?

Word equation:	methane + oxygen → carbon dioxide + water
Symbols and formulae:	$CH_4 + O_2 → CO_2 + H_2O$
Balance the equation:	$CH_4 + 2O_2 → CO_2 + 2H_2O$

Methane is burning in the oxygen in the air to form carbon dioxide and water.

☐ Balancing equations

- Balancing equations can be quite tricky. Basically it is done by trial and error. However, the golden rule is that **balancing numbers can only be put in front of the formulae**.

- For example, to balance the equation for the reaction between methane and oxygen:

	Reactants	Products
Start with the unbalanced equation.	$CH_4 + O_2$	$CO_2 + H_2O$
Count the number of atoms on each side of the equation.	1C ✓, 4H, 2O	1C ✓, 2H, 3O
There is a need to increase the number of H atoms on the products side of the equation. Put a '2' in front of the H_2O.	$CH_4 + O_2$	$CO_2 + 2H_2O$
Count the number of atoms on each side of the equation again.	1C ✓, 4H ✓, 2O	1C ✓, 4H ✓, 4O
There is a need to increase the number of O atoms on the reactant side of the equation. Put a '2' in front of the O_2.	$CH_4 + 2O_2$	$CO_2 + 2H_2O$
Count the atoms on each side of the equation again.	1C ✓, 4H ✓, 4O ✓	1C ✓, 4H ✓, 4O ✓

No atoms have been created or destroyed in the reaction. The equation is balanced!

The number of each type of atom is the same on the left and right sides of the equation.

$$CH_4 \quad + \quad 2O_2 \quad \rightarrow \quad CO_2 \quad + \quad 2H_2O$$

- In balancing equations involving **radicals** you can use the same procedure. For example, if lead(II) nitrate solution is mixed with potassium iodide solution, lead(II) iodide and potassium nitrate are produced.

1 Words:
   lead(II) nitrate + potassium iodide → lead(II) iodide + potassium nitrate

2 Symbols:
   $Pb(NO_3)_2$ + KI → PbI_2 + KNO_3

3 Balance the nitrates:
   $Pb(NO_3)_2$ + KI → PbI_2 + $2KNO_3$

   Balance the iodides:
   $Pb(NO_3)_2$ + 2KI → PbI_2 + $2KNO_3$

This reaction occurs simply on mixing the solutions of lead(II) nitrate and potassium iodide. Lead iodide is an insoluble yellow compound.

⌷ Ionic equations

- **Ionic equations** show reactions involving **ions** (charged atoms or molecules). The size of the charge on an ion is the same as the combining power – whether it is positive or negative depends on which part of the periodic table the element is placed in. (If you have not come across ions before you will need to look at Unit 8. You will get further practice using ionic equations in Unit 12.)

- In many ionic reactions some of the ions play no part in the reaction. These ions are called **spectator ions**. A simplified ionic equation can therefore be written, using only the important ions. In these equations **state symbols** are often used.

- The equation must **balance** in terms of chemical symbols and charges.

State	State symbol
solid	s
liquid	l
gas	g
solution	aq

States and their symbols

QUESTION SPOTTER

▸ You are most likely to be asked to write equations including the four common state symbols.
▸ Questions may ask you to explain what a particular state symbol represents.

WORKED EXAMPLES

1   In the reaction given to produce lead(II) iodide, the potassium and nitrate ions are spectators – the important ions are the lead(II) ions and the iodide ions.

The simplified ionic equation is:

$$Pb^{2+}(aq) + 2I^-(aq) \rightarrow PbI_2(s)$$

Balance the equation:

	Reactants	Products
	$Pb^{2+}(aq) + 2I^-(aq)$	$PbI_2(s)$
symbols	1 Pb ✓, 2 I ✓	1 Pb ✓, 2 I ✓
charges	2^+ and $2^- = 0$ ✓	0 ✓

The equation shows that any solution containing lead(II) ions will react with any solution containing iodide ions to form lead(II) iodide.

2   Any solution containing copper(II) ions and any solution containing hydroxide ions can be used to make copper(II) hydroxide, which appears as a solid:

$$Cu^{2+}(aq) + 2OH^-(aq) \rightarrow Cu(OH)_2(s)$$

	Reactants	Products
	$Cu^{2+}(aq) + 2OH^-(aq)$	$Cu(OH)_2(s)$
symbols	1 Cu ✓, 2 O ✓, 2 H ✓	1 Cu ✓, 2 O ✓, 2 H ✓
charges	2^+ and $2^- = 0$ ✓	0 ✓

⚡ A* EXTRA

▸ An ionic equation only shows the ions that change in some way during the reaction – the spectator ions are not shown.
▸ The reaction between copper(II) sulphate solution and sodium hydroxide solution will have the same ionic equation as the reaction between copper(II) nitrate solution and potassium hydroxide solution.

⬚ Half equations

■ In electrolysis, the reactions at the electrodes can be shown as **half equations**.

■ For example, when copper is deposited at the **cathode** the half equation can be written as:

$$Cu^{2+}(aq) + 2e^- \rightarrow Cu(s)$$

The symbol e^- stands for an **electron**. At the cathode positive ions gain electrons and become neutral. The equation must **balance** in terms of symbols and charges.

■ A typical reaction at the **anode** during electrolysis would be:

$$2Cl^-(aq) \rightarrow Cl_2(g) + 2e^-$$

In this reaction two chloride ions combine to form one molecule of chlorine, releasing two electrons.

■ Further examples of half equations are given in Unit 10.

CHECK YOURSELF QUESTIONS

Q1 Write symbol equations from the following word equations:
- **a** carbon + oxygen → carbon dioxide
- **b** iron + oxygen → iron(III) oxide
- **c** iron(III) oxide + carbon → iron + carbon dioxide
- **d** calcium carbonate + hydrochloric acid → calcium chloride + carbon dioxide + water.

Q2 Write ionic equations for the following reactions:
- **a** calcium ions and carbonate ions form calcium carbonate
- **b** iron(II) ions and hydroxide ions form iron(II) hydroxide
- **c** silver(I) ions and bromide ions form silver(I) bromide.

Q3 Write half equations for the following reactions:
- **a** the formation of aluminium atoms from aluminium ions
- **b** the formation of sodium ions from sodium atoms
- **c** the formation of oxygen from oxide ions
- **d** the formation of bromine from bromide ions.

Answers are on page 243.

UNIT 8: STRUCTURE AND BONDING

How are atoms put together?

☐ Sub-atomic articles

■ The smallest amount of an element that still behaves like that element is an **atom**. Each element has its own unique type of atom. Atoms are made up of smaller 'sub-atomic' particles. There are three main sub-atomic particles: **protons**, **neutrons** and **electrons**.

■ These particles are very small and have very little mass. However, it is possible to compare their masses using a **relative** scale. Their charges can also be compared in a similar way. The proton and neutron have the **same** mass, and the proton and electron have **opposite** charges.

Sub-atomic particle	Relative mass	Relative charge
proton	1	+1
neutron	1	0
electron	$\frac{1}{2000}$	−1

■ Protons and neutrons are found in the centre of the atom, in a cluster called the **nucleus**. The electrons form a series of 'shells' around the nucleus.

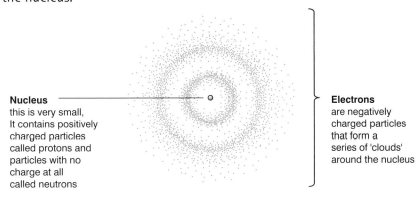

Nucleus
this is very small,
It contains positively
charged particles
called protons and
particles with no
charge at all
called neutrons

Electrons
are negatively
charged particles
that form a
series of 'clouds'
around the nucleus

☐ What are atomic number and mass number?

■ In order to describe the numbers of protons, neutrons and electrons in an atom, scientists use two numbers. These are called the **atomic number** and the **mass number**.

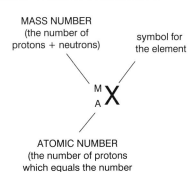

MASS NUMBER
(the number of
protons + neutrons)

symbol for
the element

$$_A^M X$$

ATOMIC NUMBER
(the number of protons
which equals the number
of electrons)

✩ IDEAS AND EVIDENCE

The modern model of the atom came from experiments done by English scientists:

▸ In 1897, J.J. Thompson showed that negative particles – **electrons** – are present in all elements. Atoms are neutral, so they must also have a positive part – containing protons.

▸ In 1911, Ernest Rutherford showed that the atom has a positive central part – the **nucleus**. Electrons move round the nucleus like the planets round the Sun.

▸ In 1932, James Chadwick showed that the nucleus has another type of particle in it. This particle has the same mass as the proton, but no charge. It was named the **neutron**.

- The atomic number is used to order the elements in the periodic table. The atomic structures of the first ten elements are shown in the table.

Element	Atomic number	Mass number	Number of protons	Number of neutrons	Number of electrons
Hydrogen	1	1	1	0	1
Helium	2	4	2	2	2
Lithium	3	7	3	4	3
Beryllium	4	9	4	5	4
Boron	5	10	5	5	5
Carbon	6	12	6	6	6
Nitrogen	7	14	7	7	7
Oxygen	8	16	8	8	8
Fluorine	9	19	9	10	9
Neon	10	20	10	10	10

- **Hydrogen** is the only atom that has **no neutrons**.

Isotopes

- Atoms of the same element with the **same number** of protons and electrons but **different** numbers of neutrons are called **isotopes**.

- Isotopes have the same chemical properties but slightly different physical properties. For example, there are three isotopes of hydrogen:

Isotope	Symbol	Number of neutrons
normal hydrogen	$_{1}^{1}H$	0
deuterium	$_{1}^{2}H$	1
tritium	$_{1}^{3}H$	2

How are electrons arranged in the atom?

- The electrons are arranged in **shells** around the nucleus. The shells do not all contain the same number of electrons – the shell nearest to the nucleus can only take two electrons whereas the next one further from the nucleus can take eight.

- Oxygen has an atomic number of 8, so has 8 electrons. Of these 2 will be in the first shell and 6 will be in the second shell. This arrangement is written 2, 6. A phosphorus atom with an atomic number of 15 has 15 electrons, arranged 2, 8, 5.

Electron shell	Maximum number of electrons
1	2
2	8
3	8

- The electron arrangements are very important as they determine the way that the atom reacts chemically.

⟦⟧ Atom diagrams

■ The atomic structure of an atom can be shown simply in a diagram.

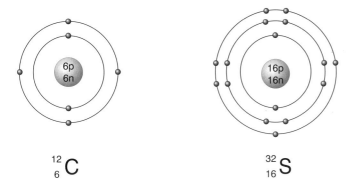

Atom diagrams for carbon and sulphur showing the number of protons, neutrons and the electron arrangements.

CHECK YOURSELF QUESTIONS

Q1 Explain the meanings of:
  a atomic number
  b mass number.

Q2 Copy out and then complete the table.

Atom	Number of protons	Number of neutrons	Number of electrons	Electron arrangement
$^{28}_{14}Si$				
$^{26}_{12}Mg$				
$^{32}_{16}S$				
$^{40}_{18}Ar$				

Q3 The table below shows information about the structure of six particles (A–F).

  a In each of the questions (i) to (v) choose one of the six particles A–F above. Each letter may be used once, more than once or not at all. Choose a particle that:
   i has a mass number of 12
   ii has the highest mass number
   iii has no overall charge
   iv has an overall positive charge
   v is the same element as particle E.
  b Draw an atom diagram for particle F.

Particle	Protons (positive charge)	Neutrons (neutral)	Electrons (negative charge)
A	8	8	10
B	12	12	10
C	6	6	6
D	8	10	10
E	6	8	6
F	11	12	11

Answers are on page 243.

Chemical bonding

☐ How do atoms combine?

- Atoms bond together with other atoms in a chemical reaction to make a **compound**. For example, sodium will react with chlorine to make sodium chloride; hydrogen will react with oxygen to make water.

- This reactivity is due to the electron arrangements in atoms. If atoms have **incomplete electron shells** they will usually react with other atoms. Only atoms with complete electron shells tend to be unreactive. Atoms in group 8 (sometimes referred to as group 0) of the periodic table, the **noble gases**, fall into this category.

- When atoms combine they try to achieve **full outer electron shells**. They do this either by gaining electrons to fill the gaps in the outer shell or by losing electrons from the outer shell to leave an inner complete shell.

- There are two different ways in which atoms can bond together: **ionic** bonding and **covalent** bonding.

☐ What happens in ionic bonding?

- Ionic bonding involves **electron transfer** between metals and non-metals. Both metals and non-metals try to achieve complete outer electron shells.

- **Metals lose electrons** from their outer shells and form **positive** ions. This is an example of **oxidation**.

- **Non-metals gain electrons** into their outer shells and form **negative** ions. This is an example of **reduction**.

- The ions are held together by strong electrical (electrostatic) forces.

- The bonding process can be represented in **dot-and-cross diagrams**. Look at the reaction between sodium and chlorine as an example.

A* EXTRA

When atoms form ions they try to complete their outer electron shell. For metals to do this it is easier to lose electrons than to gain them. For non-metals it is easier to gain electrons than to lose them. The number of electrons that need to be lost or gained is equal to the group number in the periodic table.

Sodium is a metal. It has an atomic number of 11 and so has 11 electrons, arranged 2, 8, 1. Its atom diagram looks like this:

Chlorine is a non-metal. It has an atomic number of 17 and so has 17 electrons, arranged 2, 8, 7. Its atom diagram looks like this:

Sodium has one electron in its outer shell. It can achieve a full outer shell by losing this electron. The sodium atom transfers its outermost electron to the chlorine atom.

Chlorine has seven electrons in its outer shell. It can achieve a full outer shell by gaining an extra electron. The chlorine atom accepts an electron from the sodium.

QUESTION SPOTTER

▸ You may be expected to draw a diagram to show how atoms combine and form ions as part of ionic bonding.
▸ Always show the direction in which the electrons are transferring by using an arrow.
▸ Only draw the electron that is moving once – these diagrams show the electron after it has transferred.

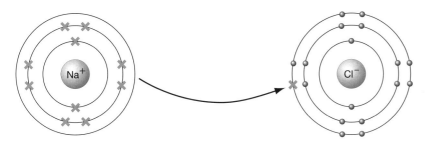

The sodium is no longer an atom; it is now an ion. It does not have equal numbers of protons and electrons, it is no longer neutral. It has one more proton than it has electrons, so it is a positive ion with a charge of 1+. The ion is written as Na^+.

The chlorine is no longer an atom; it is now an ion. It does not have equal numbers of protons and electrons, it is no longer neutral. It has one more electron than protons, so it is a negative ion with a charge of 1–. The ion is written as Cl^-.

A* EXTRA

In ionic bonding the oxygen atom gains two electrons and changes into the oxide ion (O^{2-}). As such the oxygen atom is reduced by the addition of the electrons.

METALS CAN TRANSFER MORE THAN ONE ELECTRON TO A NON-METAL

■ Magnesium combines with oxygen to form **magnesium oxide**. The magnesium (electron arrangement 2, 8, 2) transfers two electrons to the oxygen (electron arrangement 2, 6). Magnesium therefore forms a Mg^{2+} ion and oxygen forms an O^{2-} ion.

Dot and cross diagram for magnesium oxide, MgO

■ Aluminium has an electron arrangement 2, 8, 3. When it combines with fluorine with an electron arrangement 2, 7 three fluorine atoms are needed for each aluminium atom. The formula of **aluminium fluoride** is therefore AlF_3.

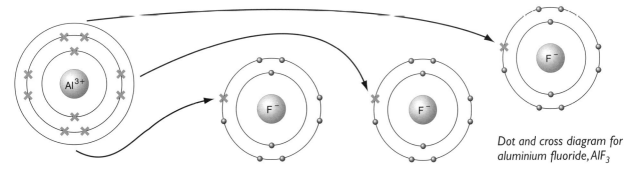

Dot and cross diagram for aluminium fluoride, AlF_3

What ions can an element form?

■ The ion formed by an element can be worked out from the **position of the element in the periodic table**. The elements in group 4 and group 8 (or 0) generally do not form ions.

Group number	1	2	3	4	5	6	7	8 (or 0)
Ion charge	1+	2+	3+	X	3–	2–	1–	X

What is covalent bonding?

■ Covalent bonding involves electron sharing. It occurs between atoms of non-metals. It results in the formation of a **molecule**. The non-metal atoms try to achieve complete outer electron shells.

■ A **single covalent bond** is formed when two atoms each contribute one electron to a shared pair of electrons. For example, hydrogen gas exists as an H_2 molecule. Each hydrogen atom wants to fill its electron shell. They can do this by sharing electrons.

The dot-and-cross diagram and displayed formula of H_2.

represented as

H—H

■ A single covalent bond can be represented by a single line. The formula of the molecule can be written as a **displayed formula**, H–H. The hydrogen and oxygen atoms in water are also held together by single covalent bonds.

Water contains single covalent bonds.

QUESTION SPOTTER

▸ Questions on covalent bonding often ask you to draw a diagram to show how the atoms combine.
▸ Always draw the shared electrons in the region where the electron shells overlap.

■ Some molecules contain **double covalent bonds**. In carbon dioxide, the carbon atom has an electron arrangement of 2, 4 and needs an additional four electrons to complete its outer electron shell. It needs to share its four electrons with four electrons from oxygen atoms (electron arrangement 2, 6). Two oxygen atoms are needed, each sharing two electrons with the carbon atom.

Carbon dioxide contains double bonds.

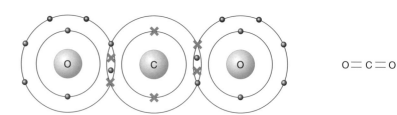

O=C=O

- Compounds containing covalent bonds have very different properties to compounds that contain ionic bonds. These differences are considered in the next section.

How many covalent bonds can an element form?

- The number of covalent bonds a non-metal atom can form is linked to its position in the periodic table. Metals (groups 1, 2, 3) do not form covalent bonds. The noble gases in group 8 are unreactive and usually don't form covalent bonds.

Group in the periodic table	1	2	3	4	5	6	7	8 (or 0)
Covalent bonds formed	X	X	X	4	3	2	1	X

A* EXTRA

- Non-metals can form single, double or triple covalent bonds.
- In a single covalent bond there are 2 shared electrons (1 pair), in a double covalent bond there are 4 shared electrons (2 pairs) and in a triple covalent bond there are 6 shared electrons (3 pairs).

CHECK YOURSELF QUESTIONS

Q1 For each of the following reactions say whether the compound formed is ionic or covalent:
a hydrogen and chlorine
b carbon and hydrogen
c sodium and oxygen
d chlorine and oxygen
e calcium and bromine.

Q2 Write down the ions formed by the following elements:
a potassium
b aluminium
c sulphur
d fluorine.

Q3 Draw dot-and-cross diagrams to show the bonding in the following compounds:
a methane, CH_4
b oxygen, O_2
c nitrogen, N_2
d potassium sulphide
e lithium oxide.

Answers are on page 244.

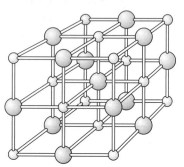

○ chloride ion ○ sodium ion

In solid sodium chloride, the ions are held firmly in place – they are not free to move. Ionic compounds have giant ionic lattice structures like this.

Structures and properties

☐ What structures do ionic compounds form?

■ Ionic compounds form **giant lattice structures**. For example, when sodium chloride is formed by ionic bonding the ions do not exist in pairs. Each sodium ion is surrounded by six chloride ions and each chloride ion is surrounded by six sodium ions.

■ The electrostatic attractions between the ions are very strong. The properties of sodium chloride can be explained using this model of its structure.

Property	Explanation in terms of structure
Hard crystals	Strong forces between the ions
High melting point (801°C)	Strong forces between the ions
Dissolves in water	The water is also able to form strong electrostatic attractions with the ions – the ions are 'plucked' off the lattice structure
Does not conduct electricity when solid	Strong forces between the ions prevent them from moving
Does conduct electricity when molten or dissolved in water	The strong forces between the ions have been broken down and so the ions are able to move

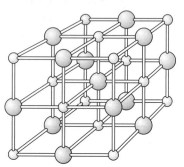

⚡ A* EXTRA

▸ Ionic compounds are electrolytes. They conduct electricity when molten or when dissolved in water (i.e. when the ions are free to move).
▸ Insoluble compounds such as calcium carbonate will only conduct electricity when they are molten.

☐ Covalent compounds

■ Covalent bonds are also strong bonds. They are **intramolecular** bonds – formed *within* each molecule. There are also **intermolecular** bonds – much weaker forces *between* the individual molecules.

■ The properties of covalent compounds can be explained using a simple model involving these two types of bond or forces.

Properties	Explanation in terms of structure	
Hydrogen is a gas with a very low melting point (−259°C)	The intermolecular forces between the molecules are weak	covalent bond
Hydrogen does not conduct electricity	There are no ions or free electrons present. The covalent bond (intramolecular bond) is a strong bond and the electrons cannot be easily removed from it	H—H intermolecular force H—H

■ Some covalently bonded compounds do not exist as simple molecular structures in the way that hydrogen does. Diamond, for example, exists as a **giant structure** with each carbon atom covalently bonded to four others. The bonding is extremely strong – diamond has a melting point of about 3730°C. Another form of carbon is graphite. Graphite has a different giant structure as seen in the diagram. Different forms of the same element are called **allotropes**.

(a)

—— strong bond

(b)

------ weak bond

In diamond (a) each carbon atom forms four strong covalent bonds.
In graphite (b) each carbon atom forms only three strong covalent bonds and one weak intermolecular bond. This explains why graphite is flaky and can be used as a lubricant. The layers of hexagons can slide over each other. The electrical conductivity of graphite can be explained by the fact that each carbon atom has one electron which is not strongly bonded. These electrons can move through the structure.

■ Structures can usually be identified as being giant or molecular from their melting points.

Structure	Atom	Molecule	Ion
Giant	Diamond, graphite, metals High melting points	Sand (silicon oxide molecules) High melting point	All ionic compounds, e.g. sodium chloride High melting points
Simple molecular	Nobel gases, e.g. helium Low melting points	Carbon dioxide, water Low melting points	None

CHECK YOURSELF QUESTIONS

Q1 Explain why an ionic substance such as potassium chloride:
   a has a high melting point
   b behaves as an electrolyte.

Q2 Use the structure of graphite to explain
   a how carbon fibres can add strength to tennis racquets
   b how graphite conducts electricity.

Q3 Explain why methane (CH_4), which has strong covalent bonds between the carbon atom and the hydrogen atoms, has a very low melting point.

Answers are on page 245.

UNIT 9: FUELS AND ENERGY

REVISION SESSION 1

Obtaining fossil fuels

What are fossil fuels?

- Crude oil, natural gas and coal are **fossil fuels**.

- Crude oil was formed millions of years ago from the remains of animals that were pressed together under layers of rock. It is usually found deep underground, trapped between layers of rock that it can't seep through (**impermeable** rock). Natural gas is often trapped in pockets above the crude oil.

- The supply of fossil fuels is limited – they are called 'finite' or **non-renewable** fuels. They are an extremely valuable resource which must be used efficiently.

- Fossil fuels contain many useful chemicals, and we need to separate these chemicals so that they are not wasted. For example, coal is often converted into coke by removing some of the chemicals in the coal. When the coke is burnt as a fuel these chemicals are not wasted.

Separating the fractions

- The chemicals in crude oil are separated into useful **fractions** by a process known as **fractional distillation**.

QUESTION SPOTTER

You could be asked to label the part of the fractionating column where the temperature is the highest and the parts where liquids like petrol and heavy oil are formed.

The fractionating column converts the crude oil into many useful fractions.

	number of carbon atoms in each fraction
gases (butane, propane for gas 'bottles')	1-4
gasoline (petrol)	5-8
naphtha (to make chemicals)	9-12
kerosene (paraffin, fuel)	10-14
gas oil (diesel oil)	14-20
lubricants and waxes	over 20
fuel oil (for ships etc.) bitumen (tar)	

gases bubble up

liquid falls down

preheated crude oil   340 °C

bubble cap

kept hot (over 500° C)

vapour

65 °C
170 °C
250 °C
340 °C
500 °C

- The crude oil is heated in a furnace and passed into the bottom of a **fractionating column**. The vapour mixture given off rises up the column and the different fractions condense out at different parts of the column. The fractions that come off near the top of the column are light-coloured runny liquids. Those removed near the bottom of the column are dark and treacle-like. Thick liquids that are not runny, such as these bottom-most fractions, are described as 'viscous'.

How does fractional distillation work?

- The components present in crude oil separate because they have different boiling points. Why they have different boiling points can be understood using a simple particle model. Crude oil is a mixture of **hydrocarbon** molecules, which contain only carbon and hydrogen. The molecules are chemically bonded in similar ways with strong covalent bonds (see Unit 8), but contain different numbers of carbon atoms.

heptane

octane

You will notice that octane has one more carbon atom and two more hydrogen atoms than heptane. Their formulae differ by CH_2.

- The weak bonds between the molecules have to be broken if the hydrocarbon is to boil. The longer a hydrocarbon molecule is then the stronger the bonds between the molecules. The stronger these bonds, the higher the boiling point as more energy is needed to overcome the larger forces.

> ⚡ **A* EXTRA**
>
> As a general rule, the greater the surface area for contact, the stronger the force between the molecules.

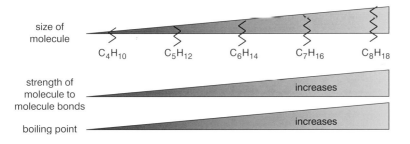

- The smaller molecule hydrocarbons more readily form a vapour – they are more **volatile**. For example, petrol (with molecules containing between 5 and 10 carbon atoms) smells much more than engine oil (with molecules containing between 14 and 20 carbon atoms) because it is more volatile.

■ Another difference between the fractions is how easily they burn and how smoky their flames are.

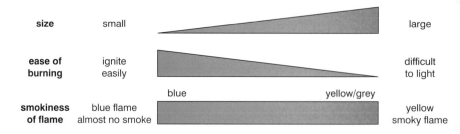

size	small		large
ease of burning	ignite easily		difficult to light
		blue	yellow/grey
smokiness of flame	blue flame almost no smoke		yellow smoky flame

⊡ Cracking the oil fractions

■ The amounts of the different fractions produced by fractional distillation do not match the amounts that are needed or usable. The lower boiling point fractions (e.g. petrol and gas) are in greater demand than the heavier ones (e.g. naphtha and paraffin). The table shows the composition of a sample of crude oil from the Middle East after fractional distillation, and the demand for each fraction.

Fraction (in order of increasing boiling point)	Percentage produced by fractional distillation	Percentage needed (demand)
liquefied petroleum gases (LPG)	3	4
petrol	13	22
naphtha	9	5
paraffin	12	7
diesel	14	24
heavy oils and bitumen	49	38

■ The larger molecules can be broken down into smaller ones by **cracking**. Cracking requires a **high temperature** and a **catalyst**.

The decane molecule ($C_{10}H_{22}$) is converted into the smaller molecules butane (C_4H_{10}) and propene (C_3H_6).

$$C_{10}H_{22} \longrightarrow C_4H_{10} + 2\ C_3H_6$$
decane   butane   propene

■ The butane and propene formed in this example of cracking have different types of structures. These structures will be looked at in more detail in the next section.

CHECK YOURSELF QUESTIONS

Q1 **a** How was crude oil formed?

    b Why is crude oil a non-renewable fuel?

Q2 The diagram shows part of a column used to separate the components present in crude oil.

    a Name the process used to separate crude oil into fractions.

    b What happens to the boiling point of the mixture as it goes up the column?

    c The mixture of vapours arrives at level X. What now happens to the various parts of the mixture?

The table shows some of the properties of the crude oil components:

component	liquid temperature (°C)	how runny?	colour	how it burns
A	up to 70	very	colourless	easily, blue flame
B	70 to 150	fairly	pale yellow	fairly easily, a smoky flame
C	150 to 230	not very	dark yellow	difficult to light, a very smoky flame

    d Another component was collected between 230°C and 300°C. What would it be like?

    e Component A is used as a fuel in a car engine. Suggest why component C would not be suitable as a fuel in a car engine.

Q3 The cracking of decane molecules is shown by the equation $C_{10}H_{22} \rightarrow Y + C_2H_4$

    a Decane is a hydrocarbon. What is a hydrocarbon?

    b What conditions are needed for cracking?

    c Write down the molecular formula for hydrocarbon Y.

Answers are on page 246.

REVISION SESSION 2

How are hydrocarbons used?

⌂ Combustion

- Most of the common fuels used today are hydrocarbons – substances that contain **only** carbon and hydrogen atoms.

- When a hydrocarbon is burnt in a plentiful supply of air it reacts with the oxygen in the air (it is **oxidised**) to form carbon dioxide and water. This reaction is an example of **combustion**.

hydrocarbon	+	oxygen	→	carbon dioxide	+	water

For example, when methane (natural gas) is burnt:

$$CH_4(g) \quad + \quad 2O_2(g) \quad → \quad CO_2(g) \quad + \quad 2H_2O(l)$$

The complete combustion of methane in a plentiful supply of air.

- The air contains only about 20% oxygen by volume. When a hydrocarbon fuel is burnt there is not always enough oxygen for complete combustion. Instead **incomplete combustion** occurs, forming **carbon** or **carbon monoxide**:

methane	+	oxygen	→	carbon monoxide	+	water
$2CH_4(g)$	+	$3O_2(g)$	→	$2CO(g)$	+	$4H_2O(l)$

methane	+	oxygen	→	carbon	+	water
$CH_4(g)$	+	$O_2(g)$	→	$C(s)$	+	$2H_2O(l)$

- Incomplete combustion is **costly** because the full energy content of the fuel is not being released and the formation of carbon or soot reduces the efficiency of the 'burner' being used. It can be **dangerous** as carbon monoxide is extremely poisonous. Carbon monoxide molecules attach to the haemoglobin of the blood, preventing oxygen from doing so. Brain cells deprived of their supply of oxygen will quickly die.

- The tell-tale sign that a fuel is burning incompletely is that the flame is **yellow**. When complete combustion occurs the flame will be **blue**.

⌂ What problems does burning fossil fuels cause?

- **Sulphur** is an impurity in many fuels. When the fuel is burnt the sulphur is oxidised to sulphur dioxide:

sulphur	+	oxygen	→	sulphur dioxide
$S(s)$	+	$O_2(g)$	→	$SO_2(g)$

✭ IDEAS AND EVIDENCE

▸ Burning fossil fuels causes extensive damage to the environment. Particles of soot aggravate health conditions such as asthma and the waste gases cause acid rain and probably contribute to the global warming. However, fossil fuels still form the basis of energy production in this country. This energy is vital to maintain industrial output and the standard of living we have come to expect.

▸ Be prepared to argue the case for and against the continued emphasis on fossil fuels as our major energy source.

UNIT 9 ○ ○ ○ ○ ○ ○ ○ ○ ○ ○ ○ **102** ○ ○ ○ ○ ○ ○ ○ FUELS AND ENERGY

- In the atmosphere, in the presence of oxygen and water, **sulphuric acid** is formed:

sulphur dioxide	+	oxygen	+	water	$\rightarrow$	sulphuric acid
$2SO_2(g)$	+	$O_2(g)$	+	$2H_2O(l)$	$\rightarrow$	$2H_2SO_4(aq)$

This falls as **acid rain**.

- Buildings, particularly those made of limestone and marble, are damaged by acid rain. Metal constructions are also attacked by the sulphuric acid. Acid rain can also damage trees and kill fish.

- Power stations are now being fitted with 'Flue Gas Desulphurisation Plants' (FGD) to reduce the release of sulphur dioxide into the atmosphere.

- Acid rain is also caused by solutions of the oxides of **nitrogen**, which are produced in the exhaust fumes of cars and aeroplanes. Catalytic converters are fitted to car exhaust systems to convert the oxides of nitrogen into harmless nitrogen gas.

- **Carbon dioxide** in the atmosphere traps energy from the Sun as heat instead of reflecting it straight back into space – this is the **greenhouse effect**. If there is too much carbon dioxide in the Earth's atmosphere the overall temperature of the planet will increase (**global warming**), causing the polar ice caps to melt and the sea level to rise. The level of carbon dioxide in the atmosphere is rising because we are increasing our use of fossil fuels and cutting down vast areas of forest. The effect of these changes can be seen by understanding the **carbon cycle** (see also Unit 5).

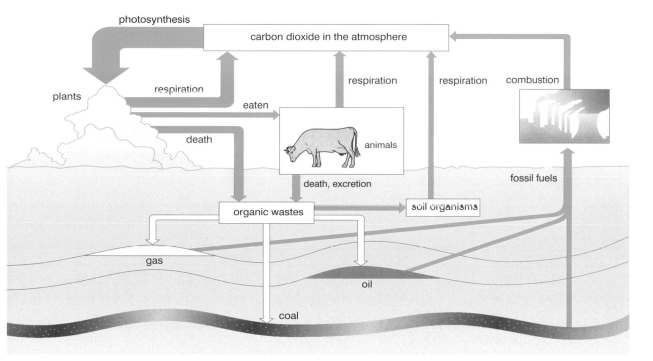

The importance of plants in the carbon cycle is that they remove carbon dioxide from the atmosphere by photosynthesis. Carbon dioxide is also removed from the atmosphere as it dissolves in the oceans.

- Many people feel that the best way to minimise the greenhouse effect is to reduce emissions of carbon dioxide but others feel that the problem may be caused by other **greenhouse gases**. Some scientists are not even sure that there is such a thing as global warming, and say that the recent rises in average temperature are just one of many climatic changes that have occurred on Earth over the last 1000 years. See Unit 5 for more on this.

Alkanes and alkenes

- There are two common families of hydrocarbons, the **alkanes** and the **alkenes**. Members of a family have similar chemical properties, and physical properties that change gradually from one member to the next.

		Molecular formula	Displayed formula	Boiling point (°C)	State at room temperature and pressure
Alkanes	methane	CH_4		−162	gas
	ethane	C_2H_6		−89	gas
	propane	C_3H_8		−42	gas
	butane	C_4H_{10}		0	gas
	pentane	C_5H_{12}		36	liquid
Alkene	ethene	C_2H_4		−104	gas
	propene	C_3H_6		−48	gas
	butene	C_4H_8		−6	gas
	pentene	C_5H_{10}		30	liquid

- Many alkanes are obtained from **crude oil** by **fractional distillation**. The first members of the family are used extensively as fuels. Apart from burning, however, they are remarkably unreactive. Alkanes are made up of atoms joined by single covalent bonds, so they are known as **saturated** hydrocarbons.

- The alkenes are often formed in the cracking process. They contain a carbon–carbon double bond. Hydrocarbons with at least one double bond are known as **unsaturated** hydrocarbons. Alkenes burn well and are reactive in other ways as well. Their reactivity is due to the carbon–carbon double bond.

- Alkenes can be distinguished from alkanes by adding **bromine water** to the hydrocarbon. Alkanes do not react with bromine water, but an alkene will decolourise it. The type of reaction is known as an **addition** reaction:

many small molecules

catalyst and heat

one large molecule

Ethene molecules link together to produce a long polymer chain of poly(ethene).

Polymers

- Alkenes can be used to make **polymers**, very large molecules made up of many identical smaller molecules called **monomers**. Alkenes are able to react with themselves. They join together into long chains like adding beads to a necklace. When the monomers add together like this the material produced is called an **addition polymer**. Poly(ethene) or polythene is made this way.

- By changing the atoms or groups of atoms attached to the carbon–carbon double bond a whole range of different polymers can be made:

name of monomer	displayed formula of monomer	name of polymer	displayed formula of polymer	uses of polymer
ethene		poly(ethene)		buckets, bowls, plastic bags
chloroethene (vinyl chloride)		poly(chloroethene) (polyvinylchloride)		plastic sheets, artificial leather
phenylethene (styrene)		poly(phenylethene) (polystyrene)		yoghurt cartons, packaging
tetrafluoroethene		poly(tetrafluroethene) or PTFE		non-stick coating in frying pans

QUESTION SPOTTER

Questions will either give you the displayed formula of the monomer and ask you to write the displayed formula of a polymer or ask you to write the displayed formula of the monomer by working back from the formula of the polymer.

■ **Plastics** are very difficult to dispose of. Most of them are not **biodegradable** – they cannot be decomposed by bacteria in the soil. Currently most waste plastic material is buried in landfill sites or is burnt, but burning plastics produces toxic fumes and landfill sites are filling up.

■ Some types of plastic can be melted down and used again. These are **thermoplastics**. Other types of plastic decompose when they are heated. These are **thermosetting** plastics. Recycling is difficult because the different types of plastic must be separated.

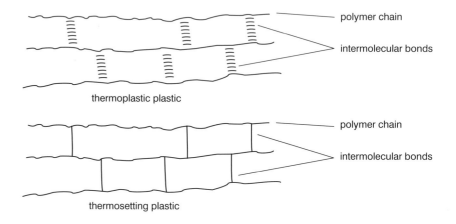

thermoplastic plastic

thermosetting plastic

In thermoplastics the intermolecular bonds are weak and break on heating. The plastic can be melted and re-moulded. In thermosetting plastics the intermolecular bonds are strong inter-linking covalent bonds. The whole structure breaks down when these bonds are broken by heating.

IDEAS AND EVIDENCE

▸ Thermosetting plastics have many uses as they are much more rigid than most thermoplastic plastics. However, they cannot be recycled as the whole structure breaks down at its melting point. The only way they can be disposed of is by burning or in landfill sites.
▸ How do you balance the convenience of such plastics against the longer-term environmental issues?

CHECK YOURSELF QUESTIONS

Q1 a Petrol is a hydrocarbon. Write a word equation for the reaction when petrol burns in a plentiful supply of air.
b When petrol is burnt in a car engine carbon monoxide may be formed. What condition causes the formation of carbon monoxide?
c Explain what effect carbon monoxide has on the body.

Q2 a Draw displayed formulae for
(i) hexane;
(ii) hexene.
b Describe a test that could be used to distinguish between hexane and hexene.

Q3 a Draw the displayed formula for propene.
b Write an equation using displayed formulae to show how propene can be polymerised.
c What is the name of the polymer formed in **b**?
d Explain why propane cannot form polymers as propene does.

Answers are on page 246.

Energy transfers

☐ Measuring energy transfers

- In most reactions energy is transferred to the surroundings and the temperature goes up. These reactions are **exothermic**. In a minority of cases energy is absorbed from the surroundings as a reaction takes place and the temperature goes down. These reactions are **endothermic**.

temperature goes up
EXOTHERMIC

temperature goes down
ENDOTHERMIC

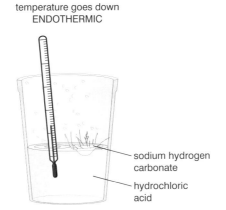

magnesium ribbon

hydrochloric acid

sodium hydrogen carbonate

hydrochloric acid

Energy transfers in a wide range of chemical reactions can be measured using a polystyrene cup as a calorimeter. If a lid is put on the cup, very little energy is transferred to the air and quite accurate results can be obtained.

- All reactions involving the combustion of fuels are exothermic. The energy transferred when a fuel burns can be measured using a **calorimetric technique**, as shown in the figure on the right.

- The rise in temperature of the water is a measure of the energy transferred to the water. This technique will not give a very accurate answer because much of the energy will be transferred to the surrounding air. Nevertheless, the technique can be used to compare the energy the same amounts of different fuels release.

- It is often worth calculating the exact amount of energy transferred using the equation:

energy transferred to the water	=	mass of water	×	specific heat capacity of water	×	rise in temperature of water

The specific heat capacity of water is 4.2 J/g/°C (or 4200 J/kg/°C). As the density of water is 1 g/cm^3, the mass of water in grams is the same as the volume of water in cm^3.

400g of water

metal can

draught excluder

paraffin burner

Measuring the energy produced on burning a liquid fuel.

WORKED EXAMPLE

2.0 g of paraffin were burned in a spirit burner under a metal can containing 400cm^3 of water. The temperature of the water rose from 20°C to 70°C. Calculate the energy produced by the paraffin.

Equation:	Energy	=	mass of water × 4.2 × temperature rise
Substitute values:	E	=	400 × 4.2 × 50
Calculate:	E	=	84000 J per 2 g of paraffin
		=	42000 J per g of paraffin

QUESTION SPOTTER

In a question asking you to calculate the energy change in a reaction you might not be given the equation E = *mst*. So you will need to remember it.

■ When a fuel is burnt the reaction can be considered to take place in two stages. In the first stage the **covalent bonds** between the atoms in the fuel molecules and the oxygen molecules are **broken**. In the second stage the atoms combine and **new covalent bonds are formed**. For example, in the combustion of propane:

propane	+	oxygen	→	carbon dioxide	+	water
$C_3H_8(g)$	+	$5O_2(g)$	→	$3CO_2(g)$	+	$4H_2O(l)$

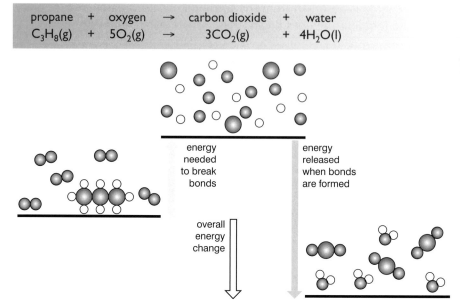

energy needed to break bonds

energy released when bonds are formed

overall energy change

The two stages of the chemical reaction between propane and oxygen. Existing bonds are broken and new bonds are formed.

Stage 1: Energy is needed (absorbed from the surroundings) to break the bonds. This process is endothermic.

Stage 2: Energy is released (transferred to the surroundings) as the bonds form. This process is exothermic.

■ The overall reaction is exothermic because more energy is released when bonds are formed than is needed initially to break the bonds. A simplified **energy level diagram** showing the exothermic nature of the reaction is shown on the left.

■ The larger the alkane molecule the more energy is released on combustion. This is because, although more bonds have to be broken in the first stage of the reaction, more bonds are formed in the second stage.

■ The increase in energy from one alkane to the next is almost constant, due to the extra CH_2 unit in the molecule. In the table the energy released on combustion has been worked out per mole of alkane. In this way the comparison can be made when the same number of molecules of each alkane is burnt. (More information on moles is given in Unit 13.)

Alkane		Energy of combustion (kJ/ mole)
methane	CH_4	882
ethane	C_2H_6	1542
propane	C_3H_8	2202
butane	C_4H_{10}	2877
pentane	C_5H_{12}	3487
hexane	C_6H_{14}	4141

CHECK YOURSELF QUESTIONS

Q1 A 0.2 g strip of magnesium ribbon is added to 40 cm^3 of hydrochloric acid in a polystyrene beaker. The temperature rises by 32°C. (The specific heat capacity of the hydrochloric acid can be assumed to be the same as that of water, i.e. 4.2 J/g/°C.) Calculate **a** the energy released in the reaction and **b** the energy released per gram of magnesium.

Q2 Calcium oxide reacts with water as shown in the equation:

$$CaO(s) + H_2O(l) \rightarrow Ca(OH)_2(s)$$

An energy level diagram for this reaction is shown below.

a What does the energy level diagram tell us about the type of energy change that takes place in this reaction?

b What does the energy level diagram indicate about the amounts of energy required to break bonds and form new bonds in this reaction?

Q3 Chlorine (Cl_2) and hydrogen (H_2) react together to make hydrogen chloride (HCl). The equation can be written as:

$$H–H \; + \; Cl–Cl \; \rightarrow \; H–Cl \; + \; H–Cl$$

When this reaction occurs energy is transferred to the surroundings. Explain this in terms of the energy transfer processes taking place when bonds are broken and when bonds are made.

Answers are on page 247.

UNIT 10: ROCKS AND METALS

Geological change

⬚ Layers of the Earth

■ Evidence obtained by monitoring the shock waves produced by earthquakes suggests that the Earth is made up of three layers: a thin rocky **crust**, the **mantle** and the **core.**

The layered structure of the Earth.

continental crust (30–70 km thick)

ocean crust (5–10 km thick)

liquid outer core: here it is hot enough for nickle and iron to melt

mantle

crust

solid inner core: high pressure makes the liquid metals solid again

■ Due to large amounts of energy released by the decay of radioactive material in the core, the outer core and the mantle are in a liquid state.

■ So the outer crust is really 'floating' on the liquid material of the mantle, which is called **magma.**

■ Energy from the hot core is transferred out through the magma by the process of convection. This results in the formation of huge **convection currents** in the magma.

⬚ Plate tectonics

■ Until the beginning of the 20th century scientists thought that the Earth's crust had remained unchanged for millions of years. Then in 1912 the theory of **plate tectonics** was proposed.

■ The crust is made up of large **tectonic plates** with boundaries between the different plates. Millions of years ago the continents were joined together. Some plates carry continents (**continental plates**), others carry oceans (**oceanic plates**). The convection currents in the mantle cause these plates to move by a few centimetres each year.

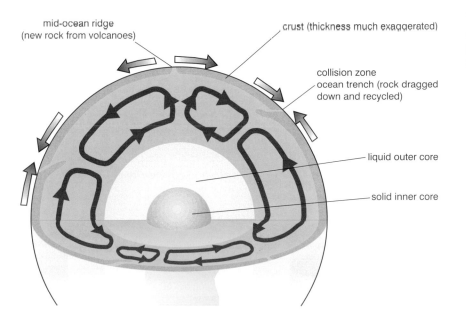

mid-ocean ridge (new rock from volcanoes)

crust (thickness much exaggerated)

collision zone
ocean trench (rock dragged down and recycled)

liquid outer core

solid inner core

The huge convection currents in the mantle cause the plates to move across the surface of the Earth.

■ When the tectonic plates grind together, **earthquakes** occur. When they move apart, a weakness or gap forms in the crust and magma forces its way up through this gap, forming a **volcano** – or, if the gap is in the ocean, a **mid-ocean ridge**. If continental plates collide **mountain ranges** can be formed – the Himalayas are thought to have been formed in this way. If the collision is between an oceanic plate and a continental plate, the denser oceanic plate is pushed down into the mantle, forming an **ocean trench**. This process is known as **subduction**.

 A* EXTRA

Subduction is the process where rock at the plate edges is forced into the mantle and melts. The denser plate is forced into the mantle and the less dense plate 'floats' on top of it.

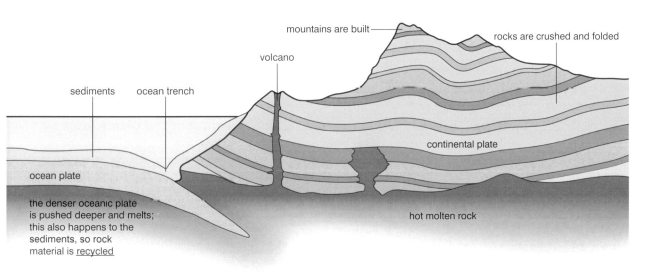

mountains are built

rocks are crushed and folded

volcano

sediments   ocean trench

continental plate

ocean plate

the denser oceanic plate is pushed deeper and melts; this also happens to the sediments, so rock material is <u>recycled</u>

hot molten rock

■ By identifying areas of volcanic action, the occurrence of ocean trenches, and areas prone to earthquakes, scientists have been able to identify the separate plates and their boundaries.

What happens when plates collide. This shows the process of subduction – 'drawing under'. This is happening along the west coast of America.

☐ The rock cycle

- Rocks are constantly being broken down and new rocks are constantly forming in the **rock cycle**.

- Molten rocks in the magma cool and form **igneous rocks**.

- **Weathering** and **erosion** produce small sediments of rock, which are transported (**transportation**) by water into streams and rivers. Here they are ground into even smaller particles, which are compressed by the particles above them, eventually forming **sedimentary rock**. This process can take millions of years.

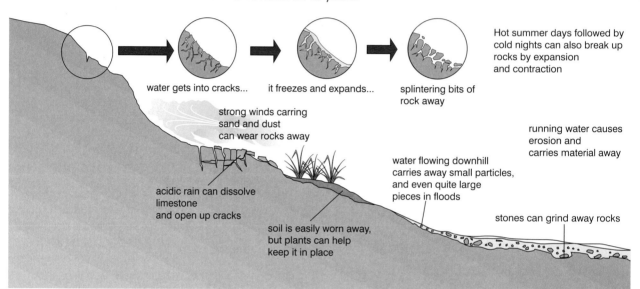

water gets into cracks...

it freezes and expands...

splintering bits of rock away

Hot summer days followed by cold nights can also break up rocks by expansion and contraction

strong winds carring sand and dust can wear rocks away

running water causes erosion and carries material away

acidic rain can dissolve limestone and open up cracks

water flowing downhill carries away small particles, and even quite large pieces in floods

soil is easily worn away, but plants can help keep it in place

stones can grind away rocks

Weathering, erosion and transportation – all important processes in the formation of sedimentary rocks.

- When sedimentary rocks are subjected to high temperature and pressure **metamorphic rocks** are formed. If the sedimentary or metamorphic rocks are forced into the magma in the process of subduction, igneous rocks are formed and the rock cycle is completed.

Type of rock	Method of formation	Appearance	Examples
Igneous	Cooling of hot, liquid rock (lava from a volcano or underground magma).	Hard, containing crystals of different minerals. Crystal size depends on how quickly the molten rock crystallised. Large crystals are produced on slow cooling; small crystals are formed when the cooling is quick.	Granite, basalt
Sedimentary	Layers of mud, sand or the shells and bones of living creatures are compressed under high pressure.	The rocks exist in layers with newer layers forming on top of older layers. Fossils are commonly found.	Limestone, sandstone.
Metamorphic	Formed from igneous and sedimentary rocks under conditions of high temperature and pressure.	Grains and crystals are often distorted and fossils are rarely present.	Marble (made from limestone), slate.

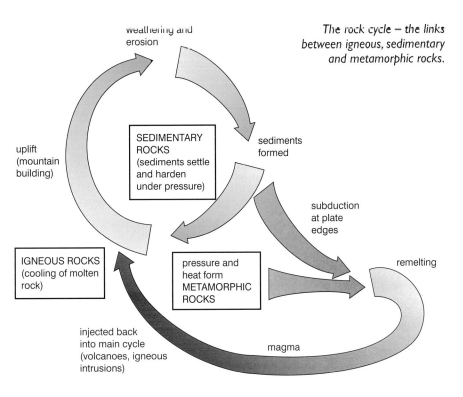

weathering and
erosion

*The rock cycle – the links
between igneous, sedimentary
and metamorphic rocks.*

SEDIMENTARY
ROCKS
(sediments settle
and harden
under pressure)

sediments
formed

uplift
(mountain
building)

subduction
at plate
edges

IGNEOUS ROCKS
(cooling of molten
rock)

pressure and
heat form
METAMORPHIC
ROCKS

remelting

injected back
into main cycle
(volcanoes, igneous
intrusions)

magma

QUESTION SPOTTER

▸ Questions are likely to focus on the formation of the different types of rock and may require extended answers.
▸ When writing about the formation of sedimentary rocks you should mention the separate processes of weathering, erosion, transportation and sedimentation.

■ Evidence obtained from the structure of rocks (the **rock record**) has provided information on the age of the Earth and about the changes that have taken place over billions of years. When sedimentary rocks are formed the lower layers are older than the upper layers. The thickness of the layers and the **fossils** they contain have provided a lot of information about the evolution of plants and animals.

CHECK YOURSELF QUESTIONS

Q1 In the diagram A, B and C represent plates of the Earth's crust moving in the direction of the arrows.

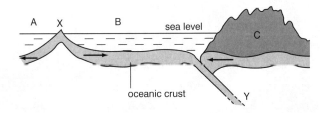

a Write down one natural occurrence that could happen at the boundary between plates.
b Explain how igneous rock is formed at the plate boundary X.
c Metamorphic rock forms at Y. What two conditions are needed for the formation of metamorphic rock?

Q2 The crust of the Earth is divided into several tectonic plates.
a What causes the tectonic plates to move?
b Describe what happens to tectonic plates when they collide.

Q3 Sedimentary rock can be made from igneous rock. Three processes are involved. These are weathering, erosion and transportation. Explain how these three processes lead to the formation of sedimentary rock.

Answers are on page 247.

Extraction of metals

⬜ How are metals extracted?

- Metals are found in the form of ores containing minerals mixed with waste rock. In almost all cases the mineral is a compound of the metal, not the pure metal. One exception is gold, which can be found in a pure state.

- Extracting a metal from its ore usually involves two steps:

  1 the mineral is physically separated from unwanted rock

  2 the mineral is chemically broken down to obtain the metal.

⬜ Reactivity of metals

- The chemical method chosen to break down a mineral depends on the reactivity of the metal. The **more reactive** a metal is the **harder** it is to break down its compounds. The more reactive metals are obtained from their minerals by a process known as **electrolysis**.

- The less reactive metals can be obtained by heating their oxides with carbon. This method will only work for metals below carbon in the reactivity series. It involves the **reduction** of a metal oxide to the metal.

☀ QUESTION SPOTTER

The most frequently asked questions test understanding of the relationship between the method chosen for extracting a metal from its ore and the reactivity of that metal.

Metal	Extraction method
potassium sodium calcium magnesium aluminium	The most reactive metals are obtained using electrolysis.
(carbon)	
zinc iron tin lead copper	These metals are below carbon in the reactivity series and so can be obtained by heating their oxides with carbon.
silver gold	The least reactive metals are found as pure elements.

✦ IDEAS AND EVIDENCE

▶ The mining of metal ores and the extraction of metals from them cause damage to the environment and yet modern society depends on metal objects at work, in the home and in leisure pursuits.

▶ Do you think there will come a point in the future when the advantages of using metals are outweighed by the disadvantages?

⬜ Using carbon to extract copper

- Copper is extracted by heating the mineral **malachite** (copper(II) carbonate) with carbon. The reaction takes place in two stages:

Stage 1 – The malachite decomposes:

copper(II) carbonate → copper(II) oxide + carbon dioxide

$$CuCO_3(s) \rightarrow CuO(s) + CO_2(g)$$

Stage 2 – The copper(II) oxide is reduced by the carbon:

copper(II) oxide + carbon → copper + carbon dioxide

$$2CuO(s) + C(s) \rightarrow 2Cu(s) + CO_2(g)$$

- The copper produced by this process is purified by electrolysis (see page 117).

⌊⌋ The blast furnace

- Iron is produced on a very large scale by reduction using carbon. The reaction is undertaken in a huge furnace called a **blast furnace**.

- Three important raw materials are put in the top of the furnace: **iron ore** (iron(III) oxide) – the source of iron – **coke** (the source of carbon needed for the reduction) and **limestone**, needed to remove the impurities as a 'slag'.

A blast furnace is used to reduce iron(III) oxide to iron.

1 Iron ore, limestone and coke are fed into the top of the blast furnace

2 Hot air is blasted up the furnace from the bottom

3 Oxygen from the air reacts with coke to form carbon dioxide:
$$C(s) + O_2(g) \longrightarrow CO_2(g)$$

4 Carbon dioxide reacts with more coke to form carbon monoxide:
$$CO_2(g) + C(s) \longrightarrow 2CO(g)$$

5 Carbon monoxide is a reducing agent. Iron (III) oxide is reduced to iron:
reduction = loss of oxygen
$$Fe_2O_3(s) + 3CO(g) \longrightarrow 2Fe(l) + 3CO_2(g)$$

6 Dense molten iron runs to the bottom of the furnace and is run off. There are many impurities in iron ore. The limestone helps to remove these as shown in 7 and 8.

7 Limestone is broken down by heat to calcium oxide:
$$CaCO_3(s) \longrightarrow CaO(s) + CO_2(g)$$

8 Calcium oxide reacts with impurities like sand (silicon dioxide) to form a liquid called 'slag':
$$CaO(s) + SiO_2(s) \longrightarrow CaSiO_3(l)$$
impurity   slag
The liquid slag falls to the bottom of the furnace and is tapped off.

- The overall reaction is:

iron oxide	+	carbon	→	iron	+	carbon dioxide
$2Fe_2O_3(s)$	+	$3C$	→	$4Fe$	+	$3CO_2$

- The reduction happens in three stages.

Stage 1 – The coke (carbon) reacts with oxygen 'blasted' into the furnace:

carbon	+	oxygen	→	carbon dioxide
$C(s)$	+	$O_2(g)$	→	$CO_2(g)$

Stage 2 – The carbon dioxide is reduced by unreacted coke to form carbon monoxide:

carbon dioxide	+	carbon	→	carbon monoxide
$CO_2(g)$	+	$C(s)$	→	$2CO(g)$

Stage 3 – The iron(III) oxide is reduced by the carbon monoxide to iron:

iron(III) oxide	+	carbon monoxide	→	iron	+	carbon dioxide
$Fe_2O_3(s)$	+	$3CO(g)$	→	$2Fe(s)$	+	$3CO_2(g)$

⚡ A* EXTRA

In a blast furnace the iron oxide is reduced to iron by carbon monoxide, formed when the carbon reacts with the air blasted into the furnace. In this reaction the carbon monoxide is oxidised to carbon dioxide.

Extraction of other metals

- Lead and zinc are also extracted in large quantities by heating their oxides with carbon.

- Metals that are above carbon in the reactivity series cannot be obtained by heating their oxides with carbon. They are reduced by **electrolysis**. Electrolysis is the breakdown of a chemical compound by an electric current.

Conditions for electrolysis

- The substance being electrolysed (the **electrolyte**) must contain ions and these ions must be free to move. In other words the substance must either be molten or dissolved in water.

- A d.c. voltage must be used. The **electrode** connected to the **positive** terminal of the power supply is known as the **anode**. The electrode connected to the **negative** terminal of the power supply is known as the **cathode**. The electrical circuit can be drawn as follows:

QUESTION SPOTTER

▸ Common questions ask you to define terms such as electrode, electrolyte and electrolysis.
▸ You could also be asked to label a diagram to show these, together with the anode and cathode.

A typical electrical circuit used in electrolysis.

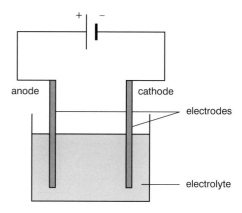

How does the electrolyte change?

- The negative ions are attracted to the anode and release electrons. (Loss of electrons is oxidation.) For example:

chloride ions	→	chlorine molecules	+	electrons
$2Cl^-(aq)$	→	$Cl_2(g)$	+	$2e^-$

- The positive ions are attracted to the cathode and gain electrons. (Gaining electrons is reduction.) For example:

copper ions	+	electrons	→	copper atoms
$Cu^{2+}(aq)$	+	$2e^-$	→	$Cu(s)$

- The electrons move through the external circuit from the anode to the cathode.

Extracting aluminium

- Aluminium is extracted from the ore **bauxite** (aluminium oxide) by electrolysis. The aluminium oxide is insoluble so it is **melted** to allow the ions to move when an electric current is passed through it. The anodes are made from carbon and the cathode is the carbon-lined steel case.

The extraction of aluminium is expensive. A mineral called cryolite is added to the aluminum oxide to lower the melting point and save energy costs.

carbon anodes

pure aluminium oxide is added continually

carbon lining of the cell is the cathode

the electrolyte is molten cryolite and aluminium oxide

molten aluminium tapped off

molten aluminium

- At the cathode **aluminium** is formed:

aluminium ions	+	electrons	→	aluminium
$Al^{3+}(l)$	+	$3e^-$	→	$Al(l)$

- At the anode **oxygen** is formed:

oxide ions	→	oxygen molecules	+	electrons
$2O^{2-}(l)$	→	$O_2(g)$	+	$4e^-$

- The oxygen reacts with the carbon anodes to form carbon dioxide. The rods constantly need to be replaced because of this.

Using electrolysis to purify copper

- Copper is extracted from its ore by reduction with carbon but the copper produced is not pure enough for some of its uses, such as making electrical wiring. It can be purified using electrolysis.

- The impure copper is made the anode in a cell with copper(II) sulphate as an electrolyte. The cathode is made from a thin piece of pure copper.

- At the anode the copper atoms dissolve, forming copper ions:

copper atoms	→	copper ions	+	electrons
$Cu(s)$	→	$Cu^{2+}(aq)$	+	$2e^-$

- At the cathode the copper ions are deposited to form copper atoms:

copper ions	+	electrons	→	copper atoms
$Cu^{2+}(aq)$	+	$2e^-$	→	$Cu(s)$

Copper is purified by electrolysis.

To positive of electricity supply

To negative of electricity supply

+ −

Copper sulphate in

Copper sulphate out

Copper sulphate solution (electrolyte)

impure copper slab

pure copper

impurities (waste)

Check Yourself Questions

Q1 Iron is made from iron ore (iron oxide) in a blast furnace by heating with carbon.
  a Write a word equation for the overall reaction.
  b Is the iron oxide oxidised or reduced in this reaction? Explain your answer.
  c Why is limestone also added to the blast furnace?

Q2 Explain the following terms:
  a electrolysis
  b electrolyte
  c electrode
  d anode
  e cathode.

Q3 Aluminium is extracted from aluminium oxide (Al_2O_3) by electrolysis. Aluminium oxide contains Al^{3+} and O^{2-} ions. The aluminium oxide is heated until it is in a molten state.
  a Why is the electrolysis carried out on molten rather than solid aluminium oxide?
  b Which electrode does the aluminium form at?
  c Explain how aluminium atoms are formed from aluminium ions. Write an ionic equation for this change.
  d The carbon electrodes need to be replaced regularly. Explain why.

Answers are on page 248.

UNIT 11: CHEMICAL REACTIONS

REVISION SESSION 1

▰ Chemical change ▰

⊡ What happens in chemical reactions?

- A chemical change, or **chemical reaction**, is quite different from the physical changes that occur, for example, when sugar dissolves in water.

FEATURES OF A CHEMICAL REACTION

- One or more **new substances** are produced.

- In many cases an **observable change** is apparent, for example the colour changes or a gas is produced.

- An **apparent change in mass** occurs. This change is often quite small and difficult to detect unless accurate balances are used. (Mass is conserved in a chemical reaction – the apparent change in mass usually occurs because one of the reactants or products is a gas.)

- An **energy change** is almost always involved. In most cases energy is released and the surroundings become warmer. In some cases energy is absorbed from the surroundings and so the surroundings become colder. Note: Some physical changes, such as evaporation, also produce energy changes.

⊡ Collision theory

- For a chemical reaction to occur, the reacting particles (atoms, molecules or ions) must **collide**. The energy involved in the collision must be enough to break the chemical bonds in the reacting particles – or the particles will just bounce off one another.

- A collision that has enough energy to result in a chemical reaction is an **effective collision**

QUESTION SPOTTER

Questions on the collision theory are very common. You will often be asked why not every collision leads to a reaction.

unsuccessful

successful

Particles must collide with sufficient energy to make an effective collision.

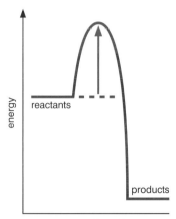

energy

reactants

products

course of reaction

If the activation energy of a reaction is low, more of the collisions will be effective and the reaction will proceed quickly. If the activation energy is high a smaller proportion of collisions will be effective and the reaction will be slow.

■ Some chemical reactions occur extremely quickly (for example, the explosive reaction between petrol and oxygen in a car engine) and some more slowly (for example, iron rusts over days or weeks). This is because they have different **activation energies**. Activation energy is the minimum amount of energy required in a collision for a reaction to occur. As a general rule, the bigger the activation energy the slower the reaction will be at a particular temperature.

⊡ Speed, rate and time

■ A quick reaction takes place in a short time. It has a high **rate of reaction**. As the time taken for a reaction to be completed increases, the rate of the reaction decreases. In other words:

$$\text{rate} \; \alpha \; \frac{1}{\text{time}}$$

Speed	Rate	Time
quick or fast	high	short
slow	low	long

⊡ Monitoring the rate of a reaction

■ When marble (calcium carbonate) reacts with hydrochloric acid the following reaction starts straight away:

calcium carbonate	+	hydrochloric acid	→	calcium chloride	+	carbon dioxide	+	water
$CaCO_3(s)$	+	$2HCl(aq)$	→	$CaCl_2(aq)$	+	$CO_2(g)$	+	$H_2O(l)$

■ The reaction can be monitored as it proceeds either by measuring the **volume of gas** being formed or by measuring the **change in mass** of the reaction flask.

The volume of gas can be measured every 10 seconds.

gas syringe

dilute hydrochloric acid

marble chips

stop clock

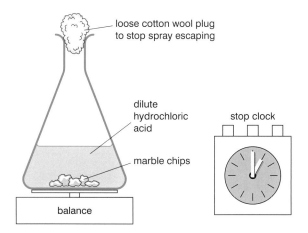

loose cotton wool plug
to stop spray escaping

dilute
hydrochloric
acid

stop clock

marble chips

balance

The change in mass can be measured every 10 seconds. The carbon dioxide produced in the reaction escapes into the air. The cotton wool plug is there to stop acid spray from escaping.

■ Graphs of the results from both experiments have almost identical shapes.

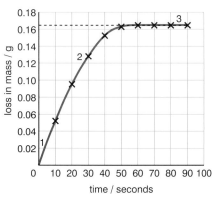

The rate of the reaction decreases as the reaction proceeds.

■ The **rate of the reaction** at any point can be calculated from the **gradient** of the curve. The shapes of the graphs can be divided into three regions:

1 The curve is the steepest (has the greatest gradient) and the reaction has its highest rate at this point. The maximum number of reacting particles are present and the number of effective collisions per second is at its greatest.

2 The curve is not as steep (has a lower gradient) at this point and the rate of the reaction is lower. Fewer reacting particles are present and so the number of effective collisions per second will be less.

3 The curve is horizontal (gradient is zero) and the reaction is complete. At least one of the reactants has been completely used up and so no further collisions can occur between the two reactants.

QUESTION
SPOTTER

You will often be given a graph showing the change in rate during a reaction. You will be asked questions about *how* the rate changes and *why* it changes during the reaction.

CHECK YOURSELF QUESTIONS

Q1 For a chemical reaction to occur the reacting particles must collide. Why don't all collisions between the particles of the reactants lead to a chemical reaction?

Q2 The diagrams below show the activation energies of two different reactions A and B. Which reaction is likely to have the greater rate of reaction at a particular temperature?

Q3 Look at the table of results obtained when dilute hydrochloric acid is added to marble chips.

Time/seconds	0	10	20	30	40	50	60	70	80	90
Volume of gas/cm^3	0	20	36	49	58	65	69	70	70	70

a What is the name of the gas produced in this reaction?
b Use the results to calculate the volume of gas produced:
  i in the first 10 seconds
  ii between 10 and 20 seconds
  iii between 20 and 30 seconds
  iv between 80 and 90 seconds.
c Explain how your answers to part (b) show that the rate of reaction decreases as the reaction proceeds.
d Use collision theory to explain why the rate of reaction decreases as the reaction proceeds.
e In this experiment the rate of the reaction was followed by measuring the volume of gas produced every 10 seconds. What alternative measurement could have been used?

Answers are on page 249.

Controlling the rate of reaction

What can change the rate of a reaction?

- There are six key factors that can change the rate of a reaction:
  - **concentration** (of a solution)
  - **temperature**
  - **surface area** (of a solid)
  - **pressure** (of a gas)
  - **light**
  - a **catalyst**.

- A simple **collision theory** can be used to explain how these factors affect the rate of a reaction. Two important parts of the theory are:

  1 The reacting particles must collide with each other.

  2 There must be sufficient energy in the collision to overcome the activation energy.

Concentration

- **Increasing the concentration** of a reactant will **increase the rate** of a reaction. If a piece of magnesium ribbon is added to a solution of hydrochloric acid the following reaction occurs:

  magnesium + hydrochloric acid → magnesium chloride + hydrogen
  $Mg(s)$ + $2HCl(aq)$ → $MgCl_2(aq)$ + $H_2(g)$

- As the magnesium and acid come into contact, the acid **effervesces** – hydrogen is given off. The graph below shows the volume of gas collected every 10 seconds when two different concentrations of hydrochloric acid are used.

> ### QUESTION SPOTTER
>
> ▸ You are often asked to explain the differences in shapes of the graphs in experiments like these.
> ▸ You may also be asked to add further lines to a graph to represent what you would expect when conditions changed. (e.g. if the temperature was increased).

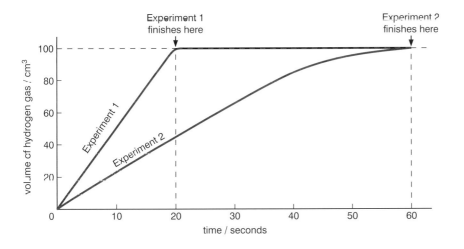

The same length of magnesium was used in each experiment. In experiment 1 the concentration of the acid was 2.0 M, in experiment 2 it was 0.5 M.

- In experiment 1 the curve is steeper (has a greater gradient) than in experiment 2. In experiment 1 the reaction is complete after 20 seconds whereas in experiment 2 it takes 60 seconds. The rate of the reaction is higher with 2.0 M hydrochloric acid than with 0.5 M hydrochloric acid. In the 2.0 M hydrochloric acid solution the hydrogen ions are more likely to collide with the surface of the magnesium ribbon than in the 0.5 M hydrochloric acid.

dilute solution

0.5M
hydrochloric
acid

magnesium
ribbon

concentrated solution

2.0M
hydrochloric
acid

magnesium
ribbon

⌗ Temperature

■ **Increasing the temperature** will **increase the rate** of reaction. Warming a chemical transfers kinetic energy to the chemical's particles. More kinetic energy means that the particles move faster. As they are moving faster there will be more collisions each second. The increased energy of the collisions also means that the proportion of collisions that are effective will increase.

■ Increasing the temperature of a reaction such as that between calcium carbonate and hydrochloric acid will not increase the final amount of carbon dioxide produced. The **same amount** of gas will be produced in a **shorter time**.

20° C

30° C

The rates of the two reactions are different but the final loss in mass is the same.

Surface area

- **Increasing the surface area** of a solid reactant will **increase the rate** of a reaction. The reaction can only take place if the reacting particles collide. This means that the reaction takes place at the surface of the solid. The particles within the solid cannot react until those on the surface have reacted and moved away.

- Powdered calcium carbonate has a much larger surface area than the same mass of marble chips. A lump of coal will burn slowly in the air whereas coal dust can react explosively.

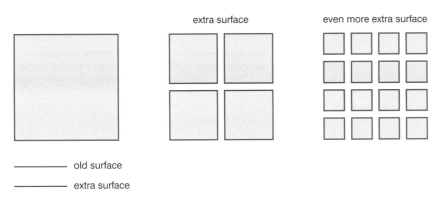

extra surface   even more extra surface

————— old surface

————— extra surface

On a large lump of marble hydrochloric acid can only react with the outside surfaces. Breaking the lump into smaller pieces creates extra surfaces for the reaction.

Pressure

- **Increasing the pressure** on the reaction between gases will **increase the rate** of the reaction. Increasing the pressure reduces the volume of the gas, moving the particles closer together. If the particles are closer together there will be more collisions and therefore more effective collisions.

low pressure   high pressure

The same number of particles are closer together in a smaller volume. There will be more effective collisions each second.

Light

- **Increasing the intensity of light** will **increase the rate** of some reactions. This fact is important in photography. The photographic film is coated with chemicals that react when in contact with the light.

- Some laboratory chemicals, for example silver nitrate and hydrogen peroxide, are stored in brown glass bottles to reduce the effect of the light.

Catalysts

- A **catalyst** is a substance that alters the rate of a chemical reaction without being used up itself. The mass of the catalyst remains unchanged throughout the reaction.

- Hydrogen peroxide decomposes slowly at room temperature into water and oxygen. This reaction is catalysed by manganese(IV) oxide.

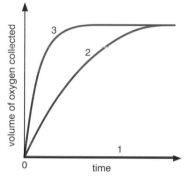

The manganese(IV) oxide has a dramatic effect on the rate of decomposition of hydrogen peroxide. The catalyst doesn't produce any extra oxygen but gives the same amount at a higher rate.
1 = no catalyst
2 = one spatula measure
3 = two spatula measures

- Most catalysts work by providing an alternative 'route' for the reaction that has a lower activation energy 'barrier'. This increases the number of effective collisions each second.

- Some catalysts slow down reactions. These are called negative catalysts or **inhibitors**. Inhibitors are added to petrol to prevent 'pre-ignition' of the petrol vapour in the engine.

The catalyst provides a lower energy route from reactants to products.

CHECK YOURSELF QUESTIONS

Q1 Why does increasing the temperature increase the rate of a reaction?

Q2 The graph shows the results obtained in three different experiments. In each experiment marble chips were added to 50 cm^3 of 1 M hydrochloric acid (an excess) at room temperature. The same mass of marble was used each time but different sized chips were used in each experiment.

a i In which experiment was the reaction the fastest?
ii Give a reason for your answer.
b i Which experiment used the largest marble chips?
ii Give a reason for your answer.
c i How long did it take for the reaction in experiment 2 to finish?
ii Why did the reaction finish?
d Why was the same mass of carbon dioxide lost in each experiment?

e Experiment 3 was repeated at 50°C rather than room temperature. How would the results be different from those shown for experiment 3?

Q3 a What is a catalyst?
b How does the catalyst affect the rate of a reaction?

Answers are on page 250.

REVISION SESSION 3 — Making use of enzymes

⊡ What are enzymes?

- An **enzyme** is a biological catalyst. Enzymes are protein molecules that control many of the chemical reactions that occur in living cells.

- Enzymes are used in a wide range of manufacturing processes – some of the more important ones are shown in the table.

Process	Enzyme involved	Description
Brewing	Enzymes present in yeast	A mixture of sugar solution and yeast will produce ethanol (alcohol) and carbon dioxide. This process is called fermentation and is the basis of the beer and wine making industries.
Baking	Enzymes present in yeast	This also depends on the fermentation process. The carbon dioxide produced helps the bread dough rise. The ethanol evaporates during the baking process.
Washing using biological washing powders	Proteases	These enzymes break down proteins found in stains (e.g. blood, egg) on clothing.
Making cheese	Lipases	These enzymes speed up the ripening of cheese.

- Increasing the temperature of a reaction will usually increase its rate. This is not the case in reactions where an enzyme is involved. The protein structure of an enzyme is affected by temperature. Above a certain temperature the protein becomes **denatured** and it will cease to function as a catalyst.

- Enzymes are also sensitive to **pH**. Inside cells, most enzymes work best in neutral conditions, around pH 7. However, the enzymes in the stomach work best at about pH 2.

⚡ A* EXTRA

- ▸ Enzymes are protein molecules with an active site where the reaction occurs. The active site has a certain shape and will only accommodate the shape of a particular molecule (sometimes referred to as the 'lock and key' model).
- ▸ This active site can be caused to lose its shape by changes in pH or temperature. If this happens it will no longer 'hold' the reacting molecule.

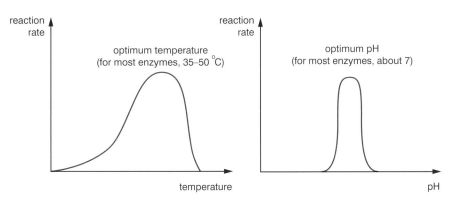

The effect of temperature and pH on the rate of a reaction involving enzymes.

How enzymes work

■ How enzymes work can best be understood by using a simple model. The enzyme provides a surface for the reaction to take place on. The surface of the enzyme molecule contains a cavity known as an **active site**. Reactant molecules become 'trapped' in the active site and so collide more frequently, resulting in more effective collisions and a greater rate of reaction.

■ This model also explains why enzymes cease to function above a certain temperature. The protein molecule is a long folded chain. As the temperature is increased the folded chain jostles and reforms and so the shape of the active site changes. Above a certain temperature the active site has changed so much that it is no longer able to 'trap' reactant molecules. Such an enzyme is said to be **denatured**.

IDEAS AND EVIDENCE

▸ Industry uses micro-organisms or pure enzymes as catalysts to bring about changes at normal temperatures and pressures. Their *advantages* are that they avoid the need for expensive equipment and also save on the use of energy for processes. The fact that they are also bio-degradable prevents environmental problems in their disposal.

▸ There are some *disadvantages* of using pure enzymes. They are expensive to produce and are wasteful because they cannot be recovered at the end of the process.

CHECK YOURSELF QUESTIONS

Q1 What is an enzyme?

Q2 In fermentation, glucose ($C_6H_{12}O_6$) is broken down to ethanol (C_2H_5OH) and carbon dioxide (CO_2).
  a What is used as a source of enzymes for this reaction?
  b Which two major industries make use of this reaction?
  c The optimum temperature for this reaction is about 40°C. Why isn't a higher temperature used?
  d Write a word equation for the reaction.
  e Write a balanced symbol equation for the reaction.

Q3 a What is an active site?
  b Use the active site model to explain why enzymes usually only act as catalysts for one reaction.

Answers are on page 250.

■ Reversible reactions ■

⬚ Types of reversible reaction

■ Carbon burns in oxygen to form carbon dioxide:

carbon	+	oxygen	→	carbon dioxide
$C(s)$	+	$O_2(g)$	→	$CO_2(g)$

Carbon dioxide cannot be changed back into carbon and oxygen. The reaction cannot be reversed.

■ When blue copper(II) sulphate crystals are heated a white powder is formed (anhydrous copper(II) sulphate) and water is lost as steam. If water is added to this white powder, blue copper(II) sulphate is re-formed. The reaction is **reversible**:

copper(II) sulphate crystals	⇌	anhydrous copper(II) sulphate	+	water
$CuSO_4.5H_2O(s)$	⇌	$CuSO_4(s)$	+	$5H_2O(l)$

When copper(II) sulphate crystals are heated they turn from blue to white.

The reaction can then be reversed by adding water.

■ A reversible reaction can go from left to right or from right to left – notice the double-headed '⇌' arrow used when writing these equations.

■ Another reversible reaction is the reaction between ethene and water to make ethanol. This is one of the reactions used industrially to make ethanol:

ethene	+	water	⇌	ethanol
$C_2H_4(g)$	+	$H_2O(g)$	⇌	$C_2H_5OH(g)$

If ethene and water are heated in the presence of a catalyst in a sealed container ethanol is produced.

■ As the ethene and water are used up, the rate of the forward reaction decreases. As the amount of ethanol increases the rate of the back reaction (the decomposition of ethanol) increases. Eventually the rate of formation of ethanol will be exactly equal to the rate of decomposition of ethanol. The amounts of ethene, water and ethanol will be constant. The reaction is said to be in **equilibrium**.

⚡ A* EXTRA

A chemical equilibrium is an example of a dynamic equilibrium (a moving equilibrium). Reactants are constantly forming products and products are constantly reforming the reactants. Equilibrium is reached when the rates of the forward and backward reactions are the same.

⬚ Changing the position of equilibrium

■ Reversible reactions can be a nuisance to an industrial chemist. You want to make a particular product but as soon as it forms it starts to change back into the reactants! Fortunately scientists have found ways of increasing the amount of product that can be obtained (the **yield**) in a reversible reaction by moving the position of balance to favour the products rather than the reactants.

■ The position of equilibrium or yield can be changed in the following ways:
  • changing **concentrations**
  • changing **pressure**
  • changing **temperature**.

⬚ The Haber process

■ Ammonia is used to make nitrogen-containing fertilisers.

■ It is manufactured in the **Haber process** from nitrogen and hydrogen. The conditions include an iron catalyst, a temperature of 450°C and 200 times atmospheric pressure.

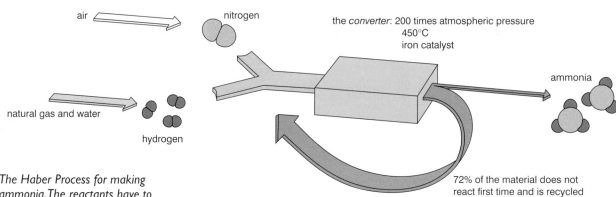

The Haber Process for making ammonia. The reactants have to be recycled to increase the amount of ammonia produced.

nitrogen	+	hydrogen	⇌	ammonia
$N_2(g)$	+	$3H_2(g)$	⇌	$2NH_3(g)$

■ The temperature of 450°C is a compromise between rate and equilibrium requirements. If it were lower more ammonia would be formed, but the reaction would be much slower. The catalyst is used to increase the rate of the reaction – it does not change the yield.

✦ IDEAS AND EVIDENCE

▸ Ammonia is used extensively in the production of artificial fertilisers which can dramatically improve the yield of crops. As a result more food is available to feed the world's population. There are drawbacks, including the effect these fertilisers can have on rivers and streams.
▸ A significant proportion of the people in this country now prefer organic food which has been produced without the use of artificial fertilisers.
▸ You should be able to give both sides of the argument for using or not using artificial fertilisers.

⊏⊐ The contact process

■ Sulphuric acid is a very important starting material in the chemical industry. It is used in the manufacture of many other chemicals, from fertilisers to plastics.

■ It is manufactured in a process known as the **contact process** – sulphur dioxide is oxidised to sulphur trioxide, then water is added to make sulphuric acid.

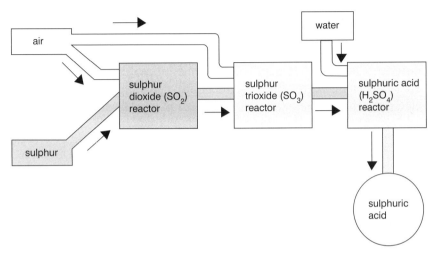

The conversion of sulphur dioxide to sulphur trioxide takes place at 450°C in the presence of a vanadium(V) oxide catalyst.

sulphur dioxide	+	oxygen	⇌	sulphur trioxide
$2SO_2(g)$	+	$O_2(g)$	⇌	$2SO_3(g)$

■ The temperature of 450°C is a compromise between rate and equilibrium requirements. A catalyst is used to increase the rate of the reaction. High pressure is not used as this would be costly and, as 98% conversion can be achieved at normal atmospheric pressure, it is unnecessary.

⚡ A* EXTRA

▸ Low temperature often gives a good conversion of reactant into product but a very slow rate of reaction.
▸ The temperature chosen in an industrial process is often a compromise between one that favours the forward reaction (rather than the backward reaction) and one that gives a suitable rate of reaction.

? CHECK YOURSELF QUESTIONS

Q1 When a chemical reaction is in equilibrium what does this mean?

Q2 What effect does a catalyst have on:
a the rate of reaction
b the yield of a reaction?

Q3 In the Haber process for making ammonia the forward reaction is favoured by a low temperature. Why is a temperature as high as 450°C used?

Answers are on page 251.

UNIT 12: THE PERIODIC TABLE

Organising the elements

⬚ How are elements classified?

- Elements are the building blocks from which all materials are made. Over 100 elements have been identified so far and each element has its own properties and reactions. The elements are arranged in the **periodic table**, which puts elements with similar reactions and properties close together.

- The periodic table arranges the elements in order of **increasing atomic number**. The atomic number is the number of protons in the atom. As atoms are neutral, the atomic number also gives the number of electrons. The elements are then arranged in **periods** and **groups**.

groups	1	2											3	4	5	6	7	8(0)
periods																		
1							H hydrogen 1											He helium 2
2	Li lithium 3	Be beryllium 4				transition metals							B boron 5	C carbon 6	N nitrogen 7	O oxygen 8	F fluorine 9	Ne neon 10
3	Na sodium 11	Mg magnesium 12											Al aluminium 13	Si silicon 14	P phosphorus 15	S sulphur 16	Cl chlorine 17	Ar argon 18
4	K potassium 19	Ca calcium 20	Sc scandium 21	Ti titanium 22	V vanadium 23	Cr chromium 24	Mn manganese 25	Fe iron 26	Co cobalt 27	Ni nickel 28	Cu copper 29	Zn zinc 30	Ga gallium 31	Ge germanium 32	As arsenic 33	Se selenium 34	Br bromine 35	Kr krypton 36
5	Rb rubidium 37	Sr strontium 38	Y yttrium 39	Zr zirconium 40	Nb niobium 41	Mo molybdenum 42	Tc technetium 43	Ru ruthenium 44	Rh rhodium 45	Pd palladium 46	Ag silver 47	Cd cadmium 48	In indium 49	Sn tin 50	Sb antimony 51	Te tellurium 52	I iodine 53	Xe xenon 54
6	Cs caesium 55	Ba barium 56	La lanthanum 57	Hf hafnium 72	Ta tantalum 73	W tungsten 74	Re rhenium 75	Os osmium 76	Ir iridium 77	Pt platinum 78	Au gold 79	Hg mercury 80	Tl thallium 81	Pb lead 82	Bi bismuth 83	Po polonium 84	At astatine 85	Rn radon 86

metal	non metal	transition metal	metalloid

Part of the modern periodic table showing periods and groups.

⬚ Periods

- Rows of elements arranged in increasing atomic number from left to right. They are numbered from 1 to 7.

- The first period contains only two elements, hydrogen and helium.

- The elements in the middle block of the periodic table in periods 4, 5 and 6 are called the **transition metals**.

⬚ Groups

- Columns of elements with the atomic number increasing down the column. They are numbered from 1 to 8 (group 8 is often referred to as group 0).

- Elements in a group have similar properties – they are a 'chemical family'.

- Some groups have family names – the **alkali metals** (group 1), the **halogens** (group 7) and the **noble gases** (group 8/0).

- The fact that elements in the same group have similar reactions can be explained in terms of the electron structures of their atoms (see Unit 8). If elements have the same number of electrons in their outer shells they will have similar chemical properties. The relationship between the group number and the number of electrons in the outer electron shell of the atom is shown in the table.

Group number	1	2	3	4	5	6	7	0 (8)
Electrons in the outer electron shell	1	2	3	4	5	6	7	2 or 8 (full)

Metals and non-metals

- Most elements can be classified as either **metals** or **non-metals**. In the periodic table the metals are arranged on the left-hand side and in the middle, the non-metals are on the right-hand side.

- **Metalloid** elements are close to the boundary between metals and non-metals, and have some properties of metals and some of non-metals. Examples are silicon and germanium.

- Metals and non-metals have quite different physical and chemical properties.

Good conductors of electricity

High melting point

Good conductors of heat

Typical properties of metals

Shiny

Malleable can be hammered into shape

Ductile can be drawn into a wire

Sonorous rings when struck

Exceptions:
- the alkali metals have low melting points and are not sonorous
- mercury has a low melting point

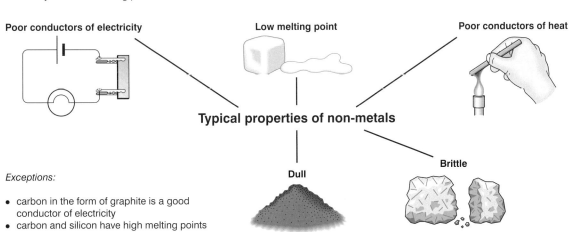

Poor conductors of electricity

Low melting point

Poor conductors of heat

Typical properties of non-metals

Dull

Brittle

Exceptions:
- carbon in the form of graphite is a good conductor of electricity
- carbon and silicon have high melting points

- The **oxides** of elements can often be made by heating the element in air or oxygen. For example, a metal such as magnesium burns in oxygen to form magnesium oxide:

$$magnesium \ + \ oxygen \ \rightarrow \ magnesium \ oxide$$
$$2Mg(s) \ + \ O_2(g) \ \rightarrow \ 2MgO(s)$$

- The magnesium oxide forms as a white ash. If distilled water is added to the ash and the mixture is tested with universal indicator the pH will be greater than 7 – the oxide has formed an **alkaline** solution.

- If sulphur is burned in oxygen, sulphur dioxide gas is formed:

$$sulphur \ + \ oxygen \ \rightarrow \ sulphur \ dioxide$$
$$S(s) \ + \ O_2(g) \ \rightarrow \ SO_2(g)$$

- If this is dissolved in water and then tested with universal indicator solution the pH will be less than 7 – the oxide has formed an **acidic** solution.

- The oxides of most elements can be classified as **basic oxides** or **acidic oxides**. Some elements form **neutral oxides**, for example water is a neutral oxide. Basic oxides or bases that dissolve in water are called **alkalis**.

- Bases and alkalis react with acids to form salts in reactions known as **neutralisation** reactions. A typical neutralisation reaction occurs when sodium hydroxide (an alkali) reacts with hydrochloric acid. The salt formed is sodium chloride, common salt:

$$alkali \ + \ acid \ \rightarrow \ salt \ + \ water$$
$$sodium \ hydroxide \ + \ hydrochloric \ acid \ \rightarrow \ sodium \ chloride \ + \ water$$
$$NaOH(aq) \ + \ HCl(aq) \ \rightarrow \ NaCl(aq) \ + \ H_2O(l)$$

⚡ A* EXTRA

▸ Salts are formed when the hydrogen of an acid is replaced by a metal.
▸ Hydrochloric acid forms salts called chlorides, sulphuric acid forms salts called sulphates and nitric acid forms salts called nitrates.

Oxide	Type of oxide	pH of solution	Other reactions of the oxide
Metal oxide	basic	more than 7 (alkaline)	reacts with an acid to form a salt + water
Non-metal oxide	acidic	less than 7 (acidic)	reacts with a base to form a salt + water

CHECK YOURSELF QUESTIONS

Q1 Look at the diagram representing the periodic table. The letters stand for elements.

	a																
													b				
			c														d
e																f	

a Which element is in group 4?
b Which element is in the second period?
c Which element is a noble gas?
d Which element is a transition metal?
e Which element is a metalloid?
f Which elements are non-metals?
g Which element is most likely to be a gas?

Q2 Why do elements in the same group react in similar ways?

Q3 Look at the table of experimental results at the end of the question.
a Which of the oxides is/are acidic? Explain how you decided.
b Which of the oxides is/are basic? Explain how you decided.
c Copper(II) oxide reacts with sulphuric acid (H_2SO_4).
  i What is the name given to this type of reaction?
  ii Write a word equation for the reaction.
  iii Write a symbol equation for the reaction.
  iv Which oxide A to D is most likely to be copper(II) oxide?

Oxide of element	pH of solution	Does it react with an acid?	Does it react with an alkali?
A	7	✓	✗
B	3	✗	✓
C	7	✗	✗
D	10	✓	✗

Answers are on page 251.

The metals

Most elements are metals. Some metals are highly reactive whilst others are almost completely unreactive. These types of metals are found in different parts of the periodic table.

Group 1 – the alkali metals

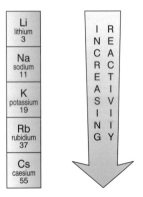

| Li |
| lithium |
| 3 |
| Na |
| sodium |
| 11 |
| K |
| potassium |
| 19 |
| Rb |
| rubidium |
| 37 |
| Cs |
| caesium |
| 55 |

INCREASING REACTIVITY

Group 1 elements become more reactive as you go further down the group.

- These very reactive metals all have only **one electron** in their outer electron shell. This electron is readily given away when the metal reacts with non-metals. The more electrons a metal atom has to lose in a reaction, the more energy is needed to start the reaction. This is why the group 2 elements are less reactive – they have to lose two electrons when they react (see Chapter 8).

- **Reactivity increases down the group** because, as the atom gets bigger, the outer electron is further away from the nucleus and so is removed more easily.

Properties of group 1 metals

- **Soft to cut**.

- **Shiny when cut**, but quickly tarnish in the air.

- **Very low melting points** compared with most metals.

- **Very low densities** compared with most metals (lithium, sodium and potassium will float on water).

- **React very easily** with air, water and other elements such as chlorine. The alkali metals are so reactive that they are stored in oil to prevent reaction with air and water.

QUESTION SPOTTER

▸ A typical question will ask you to describe what you would observe when an alkali metal is added to water.
▸ You could also be asked to write the equation for the reaction.

Reaction	Observations	Equations
Air or oxygen	The metals burn easily with coloured flames: ••lithium – red ••sodium – orange ••potassium – lilac A white solid oxide is formed.	lithium + oxygen $\rightarrow$ lithium oxide $4Li(s) + O_2(g) \rightarrow 2Li_2O(s)$ sodium + oxygen $\rightarrow$ sodium oxide $4Na(s) + O_2(g) \rightarrow 2Na_2O(s)$ potassium + oxygen $\rightarrow$ potassium oxide $4K(s) + O_2(g) \rightarrow 2K_2O(s)$

Reaction	Observations	Equations
Water	The metals react vigorously. They float on the surface; moving around rapidly; the heat of the reaction melts the metal so it forms a sphere; effervescence occurs and a gas is given off; the metal rapidly dissolves. With the more reactive metals (e.g. potassium) the hydrogen gas produced burns. The resulting solution is alkaline.	lithium + water → lithium hydroxide + hydrogen $2Li(s) + 2H_2O(l) → 2LiOH(aq) + H_2(g)$ sodium + water → sodium hydroxide + hydrogen $2Na(s) + 2H_2O(l) → 2NaOH(aq) + H_2(g)$ potassium + water → potassium hydroxide + hydrogen $2K(s) + 2H_2O(l) → 2KOH(aq) + H_2(g)$
Chlorine	The metals react easily burning in the chlorine to form a white solid.	lithium + chlorine → lithium chloride $2Li(s) + Cl_2(g) → 2LiCl(s)$ sodium + chlorine → sodium chloride $2Na(s) + Cl_2(g) → 2NaCl(s)$ potassium + chlorine → potassium chloride $2K(s) + Cl_2(g) → 2KCl(s)$

Uses for group 1 metals

■ The compounds of the alkali metals are widely used:

- lithium carbonate – in light sensitive lenses for glasses
- lithium hydroxide – removes carbon dioxide in air conditioning systems
- sodium chloride – table salt
- sodium carbonate – a water softener
- sodium hydroxide – used in paper manufacture
- mono-sodium glutamate – a flavour enhancer
- sodium sulphite – a preservative
- potassium nitrate – a fertiliser also used to make explosives.

The transition metals

■ The transition metals are listed in the centre of the periodic table.

■ All the transition metals have **more than one electron in their outer electron shell**, which is why they are much less reactive than the alkali metals and so are more 'everyday' metals. They have much higher melting points and densities. Iron, cobalt and nickel are the only magnetic elements. They react much more slowly with water and with oxygen. Some, like iron, will react with dilute acids – others, like copper, show no reaction.

■ They are widely used as construction metals (particularly iron), and they are frequently used as **catalysts** in the chemical industry.

Property	Group I metal	Transition metal
Melting point	low	high
Density	low	high
Colours of compounds	white	coloured
Reactions with water/air	vigorous	slow or no reaction
Reactions with acid	violent (dangerous)	slow or no reaction

■ The **compounds** of the transition metals are usually **coloured**. Copper
compounds are usually blue or green; iron compounds tend to be either
green or brown. If sodium hydroxide solution is added to the solution of
a transition metal compound, a precipitate of the metal hydroxide will
be formed. The colour of the precipitate will help to identify the metal.
For example:

copper sulphate	+	sodium hydroxide	→	copper(II) hydroxide	+	sodium sulphate
$CuSO_4(aq)$	+	$2NaOH(aq)$	→	$Cu(OH)_2(s)$	+	$Na_2SO_4(aq)$

■ This can be written as an ionic equation (see Unit 7):

$$Cu^{2+}(aq) + 2OH^-(aq) \rightarrow Cu(OH)_2(s)$$

A* EXTRA

In this equation the sulphate
ions and sodium ions are
spectator ions – they play no
part in the reaction. This ionic
equation would be given by any
soluble compound containing
Cu^{2+} ions.

Colour of metal hydroxide	Likely metal present
blue	copper
green	nickel
green turning to brown	iron
greenish/blue	chromium

■ Transition metal compounds and other metal compounds produce
characteristic colours in **flame tests**.

Metal ion	Flame colour
lithium	red
sodium	orange
potassium	lilac
copper	turquoise
calcium	brick red
strontium	crimson
barium	green

*The colour of the flame can be
used to identify the metal ions
present.*

CHECK YOURSELF QUESTIONS

Q1 This question is about the group 1 elements.

    a Which is the most reactive of the elements?

    b Why are the elements stored in oil?

    c Which element will be the easiest to cut?

    d Why do the elements tarnish quickly when they are cut?

    e Why is the group known as the alkali metals?

    f Why does sodium float when added to water?

    g Write word equations and symbol equations for the following reactions:

        i rubidium and oxygen

        ii caesium and water

        iii potassium and chlorine.

Q2 This question is about the transition metals.

    a Give two differences in the physical properties of the transition metals compared with the alkali metals.

    b Transition metals are used as catalysts. What is a catalyst?

    c Suggest why the alkali metals are more reactive than the transition metals.

Q3 Look at the table of observations below.

Compound tested	Colour of compound	Colour produced in a flame test	Effect of adding sodium hydroxide solution to a solution of the compound
A	white	orange	no change
B	green	turquoise	blue precipitate formed
C	white	brick red	white precipitate formed

    a Identify the metal present in each of the three compounds.

    b Explain why C could not contain a metal from group 1 of the periodic table.

    c Write an ionic equation for the reaction of a solution of B with sodium hydroxide solution.

Answers are on page 252.

The non-metals

There are only about 20 non-metal elements. There is a wide range of reactivity between different groups of non-metals. The most reactive non-metals are found in group 7, the least reactive are found in the next group, group 0.

| F
fluorine
9 |
| Cl
chlorine
17 |
| Br
bromine
35 |
| I
iodine
53 |
| At
astatine
85 |

INCREASING REACTIVITY

The elements become more reactive as you go further up the group.

⬚ Group 7 – The halogens

■ The term 'halogen' means 'salt-maker' and the halogens react with most metals to make salts.

■ The halogen elements have **seven electrons in their outermost electron shell**, which means they only need to gain one electron to obtain a full outer electron shell and so are **very reactive**. The halogens react with metals, gaining an electron and forming a singly charged negative ion (see ionic bonding in Unit 8).

■ The reactivity of the elements **decreases down the group** because as the atom gets bigger the extra electron will be further from the attractive force of the nucleus. This means it is harder for this electron to be gained.

⬚ Differences between the group 7 elements

■ **Appearance**: fluorine is a pale yellow gas; chlorine is a yellow/green gas; bromine is a brown liquid; iodine is a black solid.

⬚ Similarities between the group 7 elements

■ All have **7 electrons** in their outermost electron shell.

■ All exist as **diatomic** molecules (molecules containing two atoms – e.g. F_2, Cl_2, Br_2, I_2).

■ All react with water and react quickly with metals to form **salts**.

■ All undergo **displacement** reactions.

> ### ⚡ A* EXTRA
>
> A more reactive halogen will displace a less reactive halogen from a solution of one of its salts – for example, chlorine will displace bromine from sodium bromide solution. The ionic equation is: $Cl_2(aq) + 2Br^-(aq) \rightarrow 2Cl^-(aq) + Br_2(aq)$

Reaction	Observations	Equations
Water chlorine gas water	The halogens dissolve in water and also react with it forming solutions that behave as bleaches. Chlorine solution is pale yellow. Bromine solution is brown. Iodine solution is brown.	chlorine + water → hydrochloric acid + hypochlorous acid (bleach) $Cl_2(g) + H_2O(l) \rightarrow HCl(aq) + HClO(aq)$
Metals chlorine iron wool	The halogens will form salts with all metals. For example, gold leaf will catch fire in chlorine without heating. With a metal such as iron, brown fumes of iron(III) chloride form.	iron + chlorine → iron (III) chloride $2Fe(s) + 3Cl_2(g) \rightarrow 2FeCl_3(s)$ Fluor*ine* forms salts called fluor*ides* Chlor*ine* forms salts called chlor*ides* Brom*ine* forms salts called brom*ides* Iod*ine* forms salts called iod*ides*

Reaction	Observations	Equations

Displacement
 	
chlorine gas →
 	
potassium iodide solution
iodine being formed
	A more reactive halogen will displace a less reactive halogen from a solution of a salt.
	Chlorine displaces bromine from sodium bromide solution. The colourless solution (sodium bromide) will turn brown as the chlorine is added due to the formation of bromine.
	Chlorine displaces iodine from sodium iodide solution. The colourless solution (sodium iodide) will turn brown as the chlorine is added due to the formation of iodine.
		chlorine + sodium bromide →
		        sodium chloride + bromine
		$Cl_2(g) + 2NaBr(aq) \rightarrow 2NaCl(aq) + Br_2(aq)$
		
		chlorine + sodium iodide →
		        sodium chloride + iodine
		$Cl_2(g) + 2NaI(aq) \rightarrow 2NaCl(aq) + I_2(aq)$

Uses of halogens

- The halogens and their compounds have a wide range of uses:
  - fluorides – in toothpaste help to prevent tooth decay
  - fluorine compounds – make plastics like Teflon (the non-stick surface on pans)
  - chloro-fluorocarbons – propellants in aerosols (now being phased out due to their effect on the ozone layer)
  - chlorine – a bleach
  - chlorine compounds – kill bacteria in drinking water and are used in antiseptics
  - hydrochloric acid – widely used in industry
  - bromine compounds – make pesticides
  - silver bromide – the light sensitive film coating in photography
  - iodine solution – an antiseptic.

Group 0 – The noble gases

- This is a group of **very unreactive** non-metals. They used to be called the inert gases as it was thought that they didn't react with anything! Scientists have more recently managed to produce fluorine compounds of some of the noble gases. As far as the school laboratory is concerned, however, they are completely unreactive.

- This can be explained in terms of their electronic structures. The atoms all have **complete outer electron shells**. They don't need to lose electrons (as metals do), or gain electrons (as most non-metals do).

IDEAS AND EVIDENCE

- The use of chloro-fluorocarbons (CFCs) has been drastically reduced in the last ten years and yet there remains a 'hole' in the ozone layer.
- You should be able to analyse an article on the ozone layer and identify the reasons why there is still a problem.

Name	Symbol
Helium	He
Neon	Ne
Argon	Ar
Krypton	Kr
Xenon	Xe
Radon	Rn

Similarities of the noble gases

■ Full outer electron shells.

■ Very unreactive.

■ Gases.

■ Exist as single atoms – they are **monatomic** (He, Ne, Ar, Kr, Xe, Rn).

How are the noble gases used?

■ Helium   in balloons.

■ Neon – in 'red lights'.

■ Argon – in light bulbs.

■ Krypton – in some lasers.

CHECK YOURSELF QUESTIONS

Q1 This question is about the group 7 elements.

a Which is the most reactive of the elements?

b Which of the elements exists as a liquid at room temperature and pressure?

c Which of the elements exists as a solid at room temperature and pressure?

d Why are halogens such reactive elements?

e Write word and symbol equations for the following reactions:

  i sodium and chlorine

  ii magnesium and bromine

  iii hydrogen and fluorine.

Q2 The table below records the results of some reactions.

	sodium chloride	sodium bromide	sodium iodide
chlorine	✗		✓
bromine		✗	✓
iodine			✗

a ✓ indicates a reaction occurred, a ✗ indicates no reaction occurred.)

a What are the colours of the following solutions:

  i aqueous chlorine (chlorine water)

  ii aqueous bromine

  iii aqueous iodine

  iv aqueous sodium bromide?

b What would be observed in the reaction between aqueous chlorine and sodium bromide solution?

c Complete the table of results. Use a ✓ or ✗ as appropriate.

d Write a word equation and symbol equation for the reaction between bromine and sodium iodide.

Q3 Explain why the noble gases are so unreactive.

Answers are on page 253.

UNIT 13: CHEMICAL CALCULATIONS

Atomic masses and the mole

Working out the mass of atoms

- Atoms are far too light to be weighed. Instead scientists have developed a **relative atomic mass** scale. Initially the hydrogen atom, the lightest atom, was chosen as the unit that all other atoms were weighed in terms of.

- On this scale, a carbon atom weighs the same as 12 hydrogen atoms, so carbon's relative atomic mass was given as 12.

- Using this relative mass scale you can see, for example, that:
  - 1 atom of magnesium has 24 × the mass of 1 atom of hydrogen
  - 1 atom of magnesium has 2 × the mass of 1 atom of carbon
  - 1 atom of copper has 2 × the mass of 1 atom of sulphur.

	Hydrogen	Carbon	Oxygen	Magnesium	Sulphur	Calcium	Copper
Symbol	H	C	O	Mg	S	Ca	Cu
Relative atomic mass	1	12	16	24	32	40	64

- Recently, the reference point has been changed to carbon and the relative atomic mass is defined as:

  the mass of an atom on a scale where the mass of a carbon atom is 12 units.

- This change does not really affect the work that is done at GCSE. The relative atomic masses are not changed.

Moles of atoms

- The **mole** is a very large number, approximately 6×10^{23}. That is 600 000 000 000 000 000 000 000.

- 6×10^{23} atoms of hydrogen have a mass of 1 g.

- 6×10^{23} atoms of carbon have a mass of 12 g.

- 6×10^{23} atoms of magnesium have a mass of 24 g.

- So the relative atomic mass (RAM) of an element expressed in grams contains one mole of atoms. This means that the number of atoms of an element can be worked out by weighing.

these all contain 1 mole of atoms:

 12 g Carbon

 24 g Magnesium

 32 g Sulphur

 56 g Iron

 64 g Copper

- Calculations can be done using the simple equation:

$$\text{moles of atoms} = \frac{\text{mass}}{\text{RAM}}$$

Put your finger over the quantity you are trying to work out. The triangle will then tell you whether to multiply or divide the other quantities.

QUESTION SPOTTER

Calculation questions are very common. You will be asked to convert moles into mass in grams and vice versa. You will need to remember the equation moles of atoms = mass/RAM.

WORKED EXAMPLES

1 How many moles of atoms are there in 72 g of magnesium? (RAM of magnesium = 24)

Write down the formula:	$\text{moles} = \dfrac{\text{mass}}{\text{RAM}}$
Rearrange if necessary:	(None needed)
Substitute the numbers:	$\text{moles} = \dfrac{72}{24}$
Write the answer and units:	moles = 3 moles

2 What is the mass of 0.1 moles of carbon atoms? (RAM of carbon = 12)

Write down the formula:	$\text{moles} = \dfrac{\text{mass}}{\text{RAM}}$
Rearrange if necessary:	mass = moles × RAM
Substitute the numbers:	mass = 0.1 × 12
Write the answer and units:	mass = 1.2 g

How do we work out chemical formulae?

- A chemical formula shows the number of atoms of each element that combine together. For example:

H_2O A water molecule contains 2 hydrogen atoms and 1 oxygen atom.

Alternatively:

H_2O 1 mole of water molecules is made from 2 moles of hydrogen atoms and 1 mole of oxygen atoms.

- The formula of a compound can be calculated if the number of moles of the combining elements are known.

1 What is the simplest formula of a hydrocarbon that contains 60 g of carbon combined with 20 g of hydrogen? (RAMs: H = 1, C = 12)

	C	H
Write down the mass of each element:	60	20
Work out the number of moles of each element:	$\frac{60}{12} = 5$	$\frac{20}{1} = 20$
Find the simplest ratio (divide by the smaller number):	$\frac{5}{5} = 1$	$\frac{20}{5} = 4$
Write the formula showing the ratio of atoms:	CH_4	

2 What is the simplest formula of calcium carbonate if it contains 40% calcium, 12% carbon and 48% oxygen? (C = 12, O = 16, Ca = 40)

	Ca	C	O
Write down the mass of each element:	40	12	48
Work out the number of moles of each element:	$\frac{40}{40} = 1$	$\frac{12}{12} = 1$	$\frac{48}{16} = 3$
Find the simplest ratio:	(Already in the simplest ratio)		
Write the formula showing the ratio of atoms:	$CaCO_3$		

⬚ Moles of molecules

■ You can also refer to a mole of molecules. A mole of water molecules will be 6×10^{23} water molecules. The **relative molecular mass** of a molecule can be worked out by simply adding up the relative atomic masses of the atoms in the molecule. For example:

Water, H_2O (H = 1, O = 16)

The relative molecular mass (RMM) = 1 + 1 + 16 = 18.

Carbon dioxide, CO_2 (C = 12, O = 16)

The RMM = 12 + 16 + 16 = 44.

(Note: The '2' only applies to the oxygen atom.)

■ A similar approach can be used for any formula, including ionic formulae. As ionic compounds do not exist as molecules the **relative formula mass** (RFM) can be worked out.

WORKED EXAMPLES

Sodium chloride, NaCl (Na = 23, Cl = 35.5)

The relative formula mass (RFM) = 23 + 35.5 = 58.5

Potassium nitrate, KNO_3 (K = 39, N = 14, O = 16)

RFM = 39 + 14 + 16 + 16 + 16 = 101

(Note: The '3' only applies to the oxygen atoms.)

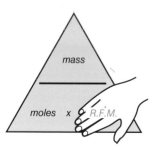

Put your finger over the quantity you are trying to work out.

Calcium hydroxide, $Ca(OH)_2$ ($Ca = 40, O = 16, H = 1$)

RFM = 40 + (16 + 1)2 = 40 + 34 = 74

(Note: The '2' applies to everything in the bracket.)

Magnesium nitrate, $Mg(NO_3)_2$ ($Mg = 24, N = 14, O = 16$)

RFM = 24 + (14 + 16 + 16 + 16)2 = 24 + (62)2 = 24 + 124 = 148

■ An equation can be written that can be used with atoms, molecules and ionic compounds.

$$\text{number of moles} = \frac{\text{mass}}{\text{RFM}}$$

CHECK YOURSELF QUESTIONS

Q1 Calculate the number of moles in the following:
 a 56 g of silicon (Si = 28)
 b 3.1 g of phosphorus (P = 31)
 c 11 g of carbon dioxide, CO_2 (C = 12, O = 16)
 d 50 g of calcium carbonate, $CaCO_3$ (Ca = 40, C = 12, O = 16)

Q2 Calculate the mass of the following:
 a 2 moles of magnesium atoms (Mg = 24)
 b 2 moles of hydrogen molecules, H_2 (H = 1)
 c 0.1 moles of sulphuric acid, H_2SO_4 (H = 1, O = 16, S = 32)

Q3 Titanium chloride contains 25% titanium and 75% chlorine by mass.
 Work out the simplest formula of titanium chloride. (Ti = 48, Cl = 35.5)

Answers are on page 254.

Equations and reacting masses

▢ Linking reactants and products

- Chemical equations allow quantities of **reactants** and **products** to be linked together. They tell you how much of the products you can expect to make from a fixed amount of reactants.

- In a balanced equation the numbers in front of each symbol or formula indicate the number of moles represented. The number of moles can then be converted into a mass in grams.

- For example, when magnesium (RAM 24) reacts with oxygen (RAM 16):

Write down the balanced equation:	$2Mg(s)$	+	$O_2(g)$	→	$2MgO(s)$
Write down the number of moles:	2	+	1	→	2
Convert moles to masses:	48 g	+	32 g	→	80 g

So when 48 g of magnesium reacts with 32 g of oxygen, 80 g of magnesium oxide is produced. From this you should be able to work out the mass of magnesium oxide produced from any mass of magnesium. All you need to do is work out a **scaling factor**.

WORKED EXAMPLES

1 What mass of magnesium oxide can be made from 6 g of magnesium? (O = 16, Mg = 24.)

Equation:	$2Mg(s)$	+	$O_2(g)$	→	$2MgO(s)$
Moles:	2		1		2
Masses:	48 g		32 g		80 g

Instead of 48 g of magnesium, the question asks about 6 g. We can scale down all the quantities by dividing them by 8. Therefore $\frac{48}{8}$ g = 6 g of magnesium would make $\frac{80}{8}$ g = 10 g of magnesium oxide.

Note: In this example, there was no need to work out the mass of oxygen needed. It was assumed that there would be as much as was necessary to convert all the magnesium to magnesium oxide.

2 What mass of ammonia can be made from 56 g of nitrogen? (H = 1, N = 14)

Equation:	$N_2(g)$	+	$3H_2(g)$	→	$2NH_3(g)$
Moles:	1		3		2
Masses:	28 g		6 g		34 g

In this case we need to multiply the mass of nitrogen by 2 to get the amount asked about in the question. Use the same scaling factor on the other quantities. So 28 g × 2 = 56 g of nitrogen makes 34 g × 2 = 68 g of ammonia.

Note: In this example there was no need to work out the mass of hydrogen required.

QUESTION SPOTTER

▸ You should be able to use equations and relative atomic masses to work out calculations like those shown here.

▸ Sometimes the question will refer to tonnes rather than grams. The method is just the same.

Each of these contains 1 mole
(6×10^{23}) of molecules.

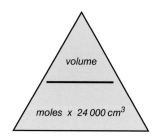

The triangle can be used as
before to work out whether to
multiply or divide the quantities.

⬜ Moles of gases

- In reactions involving gases it is often more convenient to measure the **volume** of a gas rather than its mass.

- One mole of any gas occupies the same volume under the same conditions of temperature and pressure. The conditions chosen are usually room temperature (20°C) and normal atmospheric pressure.

  1 mole of any gas occupies 24 000 cm³ (24 litres) at room temperature and pressure.

- The following equation can be used to convert moles and volumes:

$$\text{moles} = \frac{\text{volume in cm}^3}{24000}$$

WORKED EXAMPLE

What volume of hydrogen is formed at room temperature and pressure when 4 g of magnesium is added to excess dilute hydrochloric acid? (H = 1, Mg = 24)

Equation:	Mg(s)	+	2HCl(aq)	→	MgCl₂(aq)	+	H₂(g)
Moles:	1		2		1		1
Masses/volumes:	24 g						24 000 cm³

Now work out the scaling factor needed and use the same scaling factor on the other quantities. Here we divide 24 g by 6 to get 4 g of magnesium. This produces $\frac{24\,000}{6}$ cm³ = 4000 cm³ of hydrogen gas.

Note: The hydrochloric acid is in excess. This means that there is enough to react with all the magnesium.

⬜ Moles of solutions

- A solution is made when a **solute** dissolves in a **solvent**. The concentration of a solution depends on how much solute is dissolved in how much solvent. The concentrations of a solution are defined in terms of moles per litre (1000 cm³) and are referred to as the **molarity** of the solution.

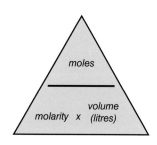

This triangle will help you to
calculate concentrations of
solutions.

  1 mole of solute dissolved to make 1000 cm³ of solution produces a 1 molar (1 M) solution

  2 moles dissolved to make a 1000 cm³ solution produces a 2 M solution

  0.5 moles dissolved to make a 1000 cm³ solution produces a 0.5 M solution

  1 mole dissolved to make a 500 cm³ solution produces a 2 M solution

  1 mole dissolved to make a 250 cm³ solution produces a 4 M solution.

- If the same amount of solute is dissolved to make a smaller amount of solution the solution will be more concentrated.

WORKED EXAMPLE

How much sodium chloride can be made from reacting 100 cm³ of 1 M hydrochloric acid with excess sodium hydroxide solution?
(Na = 23, Cl = 35.5)

Equation:	HCl(aq)	+	NaOH(aq)	→	NaCl(aq)	+	$H_2O(l)$
Moles:	1		1		1		1
Masses/volumes:	(1000 cm³ 1 M)				58.5 g		

Now work out the scaling factor and use the same scaling factor on the other quantities. In this case we divide by 10 to get 100 cm³ of reactant, which means we get $\frac{58.5}{10}$ g = 5.85 g of product.

Note: 100 cm³ of 1 M solution is equal to 0.1 mole.

CHECK YOURSELF QUESTIONS

Q1 What mass of sodium hydroxide can be made by reacting 2.3 g of sodium with water? (H = 1, O = 16, Na = 23)

$$2Na(s) + 2H_2O(l) \rightarrow 2NaOH(aq) + H_2(g)$$

Q2 Iron(III) oxide is reduced to iron by carbon monoxide.
(C = 12, O = 16, Fe = 56)

$$Fe_2O_3(s) + 3CO(g) \rightarrow 2Fe(s) + 3CO_2(g)$$

a Calculate the mass of iron that could be obtained by the reduction of 800 tonnes of iron(III) oxide.

b What volume of carbon dioxide would be obtained by the reduction of 320 g of iron(III) oxide?

Q3 What mass of barium sulphate can be produced from 50 cm³ of 0.2 M barium chloride solution and excess sodium sulphate solution?
(O = 16, S = 32, Ba = 137)

$$BaCl_2(aq) + Na_2SO_4(aq) \rightarrow$$
$$BaSO_4(s) + 2NaCl(aq)$$

Answers are on page 254.

UNIT 14: ELECTRICITY

Electric circuits

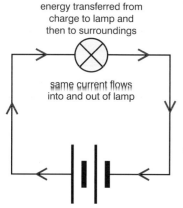

energy transferred from charge to lamp and then to surroundings

same current flows into and out of lamp

battery transfers energy to charge and pushes charge around circuit

In this simple circuit the arrows show the direction of the current.

What does electricity do?

- You cannot see electricity but you can see the effects it has. It is very good at **transferring energy**, and can:
  - make things **hot** – as in the heating element of an electric fire
  - make things **magnetic** – as in an electromagnet
  - produce **light** – as in a light bulb
  - **break down** certain compounds and solutions – as in electrolysis.

A simple model of an electrical circuit

- The battery in an electrical circuit can be thought of as pushing electrical charge round the circuit to make a current. It also transfers energy to the electrical charge. The **voltage** of the battery is a measure of how much 'push' it can provide and how much energy it can transfer to the charge.

- Scientists now know that electric current is really a **flow of electrons** around the circuit from negative to positive. Unfortunately, early scientists guessed the direction of flow incorrectly. Consequently all diagrams were drawn showing the current flowing from positive to negative. This way of showing the current has not been changed and so the **conventional current** that everyone uses gives the direction that positive charges would flow.

free electron   positive ion

positive ion and nearby electron

The electrons move down the wire

CONVENTIONAL CURRENT

It is as if the positive ions move up the wire

ELECTRON FLOW

Conventional current is drawn in the opposite direction to electron flow.

- There are two different ways of connecting two lamps to the same battery. Two very different kinds of circuit can be made. These circuits are called **series** and **parallel** circuits.

	Series	Parallel
Circuit diagram		
Appearance of the lamps	Both lamps have the same brightness, both lamps are dim.	Both lamps have the same brightness, both lamps are bright.
Battery	The battery is having a hard time pushing the same charge first through one bulb, then another. This means less charge flows each second, so there is a low current and energy is slowly transferred from the battery.	The battery pushes the charge along two alternative paths. This means more charge can flow around the circuit each second, so energy is quickly transferred from the battery.
Switches	The lamps cannot be switched on and off independently.	The lamps can be switched on and off independently by putting switches in the parallel branches.
Advantages/ disadvantages	A very simple circuit to make. The battery will last longer. If one lamp 'blows' then the circuit is broken so the other one goes out too.	The battery won't last as long. If one lamp 'blows' the other one will keep working.
Examples	Christmas tree lights are often connected in series.	Electric lights in the home are connected in parallel.

Charge, current and potential difference

- Electric charge is measured in **coulombs** (C). Electric current is measured in **amperes** (A).

- The electric current is the amount of charge flowing every second – the number of coulombs per second:

$$I = \frac{Q}{t}$$

I = current in amperes (A)

Q = charge in coulombs (C)

t = time in seconds (s)

- The charge flowing round a circuit has some **potential energy**. As charge flows around a circuit it transfers energy to the various components in the circuit. For example, when the charge flows through a lamp it transfers some of its energy to the lamp.

- The amount of energy that a unit of charge (a coulomb) transfers between one point and another (the number of joules per coulomb) is called the **potential difference** (p.d.). Potential difference is measured in **volts** and so it is often referred to as **voltage**:

$$V = \frac{E}{Q}$$

V = potential difference in volts

E = energy transferred in joules

Q = charge in coulombs

⚡ A* EXTRA

▸ In a conductor the charge carriers are electrons and flow round the circuit from negative to positive.
▸ In an electrolyte (e.g. sulphuric acid in a car battery) the charge carriers are ions. The negative ions (anions) move to the anode and the positive ions (cations) move to the cathode.

💡 QUESTION SPOTTER

You will be expected to remember the equation that links current, charge and time and carry out calculations which use it. Don't forget that charge is measured in coulombs and current in amps.

A* EXTRA

The potential difference is measured between two points in a circuit. It is like an electrical pressure difference and measures the energy transferred per unit of charge flowing

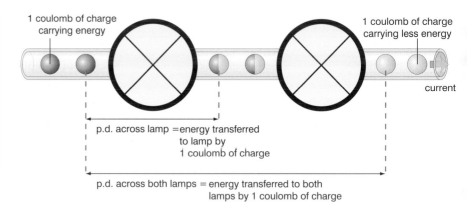

1 coulomb of charge carrying energy

1 coulomb of charge carrying less energy

current

p.d. across lamp =energy transferred to lamp by 1 coulomb of charge

p.d. across both lamps = energy transferred to both lamps by 1 coulomb of charge

Potential difference (p.d.) is the difference in energy of a coulomb of charge between two parts of a circuit.

⌷ Measuring electricity

■ Potential difference is measured using a **voltmeter**. If you want to measure the p.d. across a component then the voltmeter must be connected **in parallel** to that component. Testing with a voltmeter does not interfere with the circuit at all.

■ A voltmeter can be used to show how the potential difference varies in different parts of a circuit. In a series circuit you get different values of the voltage depending on where you attach the voltmeter. You can assume that energy is only transferred when the current passes through

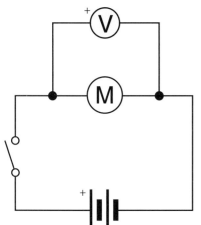

The voltmeter can be added after the circuit has been made.

p.d. = 6 V
 6 joules transferred from each coulomb

power = 2 coulombs per second, of 6 joules each
 12 joules per second

p.d. = 3 V
 = 3 J/C

power = 2 C/s × 3 J/C
 = 6 J/s

V_1

V_2

6 V lamp

3 V lamp

current = 2 A
(2 coulombs every second)

A

9 V battery

V

p.d. = 9 V = 9 joules transferred to each coulomb

power = 2 coulombs per second, of 9 joules each
 = 18 joules per second

The potential difference across the battery equals the sum of the potential differences across each lamp. That is $V = V_1 + V_2$.

electrical components such as lamps and motors – the energy transfer as the current flows through copper connecting wire is very small. It is only possible therefore to measure a p.d. or voltage across a component.

■ The current flowing in a circuit can be measured using an **ammeter**. If you want to measure the current flowing through a particular component, such as a lamp or motor, the ammeter must be connected **in series** with the component. In a series circuit the current is the same no matter where the ammeter is put. This is not the case with a parallel circuit.

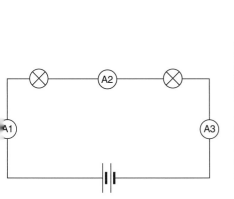

In this series circuit the current will be the same throughout the circuit so the readings $A_1 = A_2 = A_3$.

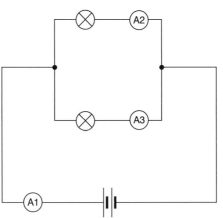

The current flow splits between the two branches of the parallel circuit so the readings $A_1 = A_2 + A_3$.

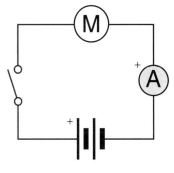

The circuit has to be broken to include the ammeter.

⟲ Direct and alternating currents

■ A battery produces a steady current. The electrons are constantly flowing from the negative terminal of the battery round the circuit and back to the positive terminal. This produces a **direct current** (d.c.).

■ The mains electricity used in the home is quite different. The electrons in the circuit move backwards and forwards. This kind of current is called **alternating current** (a.c.). Mains electricity moves forwards and backwards 50 times each second, that is, with a frequency of 50 hertz (Hz).

■ The advantage of using an a.c. source of electricity rather than a d.c. source is that it can be transmitted from power stations to the home at very high voltages, which reduces the amount of energy that is lost in the overhead cables (see Unit 15).

CHECK YOURSELF QUESTIONS

Q1 Look at the following circuit diagrams. They show a number of ammeters and in some cases the readings on these ammeters. All the lamps are identical.

circuit X

circuit Y

a For circuit X, what readings would you expect on ammeters A_1 and A_2?

b For circuit Y, what readings would you expect on ammeters A_3 and A_4?

Q2 Look at the circuit diagram. It shows how three voltmeters have been added to the circuit. What reading would you expect on V_1?

Q3 a A charge of 10 coulombs flows through a motor in 30 seconds. What is the current flowing through the motor?

b A heater uses a current of 10 A. How much charge flows through the lamp in:

i 1 second, **ii** 1 hour?

Answers are on page 255.

REVISION SESSION 2 — What affects resistance?

☐ Ohm's Law

■ The relationship between voltage, current and resistance in electrical circuits is given by **Ohm's law**:

$V = I R$

V is the voltage in volts (V)

I is the current in amps (A)

R is the resistance in ohms (Ω)

■ It is important to be able to rearrange this equation when performing calculations. Use the triangle on the right to help you.

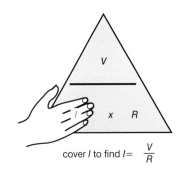

cover I to find $I = \frac{V}{R}$

WORKED EXAMPLES

1 Calculate the resistance of a heater element if the current is 10 A when it is connected to a 230 V supply.

Write down the formula in terms of R: $R = \frac{V}{I}$

Substitute the values for V and I: $R = \frac{230}{10}$

Work out the answer and write down the unit: $R = 23\ \Omega$

2 A 6 V supply is applied to 1000 Ω resistor. What current will flow?

Write down the formula in terms of I: $I = \frac{V}{R}$

Substitute the values for V and R: $I = \frac{6}{1000}$

Work out the answer and write down the unit: $I = 0.006\ A$

> ## 🔆 QUESTION SPOTTER
>
> Calculations involving Ohm's Law are very common. You will need to remember the equation and be able to change the subject. Marks will usually be given for the correct units.

☐ Effect of material on resistance

■ Substances that allow an electric current to flow through them are called **conductors**. Those which do not are called **insulators**.

■ Metals are conductors. In a metal structure the metal atoms exist as ions surrounded by an electron cloud. If a potential difference is applied to the metal the electrons in this cloud are able to move and a current flows.

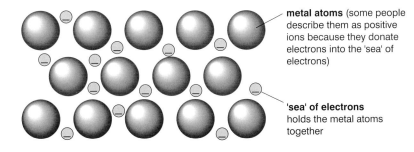

metal atoms (some people describe them as positive ions because they donate electrons into the 'sea' of electrons)

'sea' of electrons holds the metal atoms together

In a metal structure metal ions are surrounded by a cloud or 'sea' of electrons.

- When the electrons are moving through the metal structure they bump into the metal ions and this causes **resistance** to the electron flow or current. In different conductors the ease of flow of the electrons is different and so the conductors have different resistances. For instance, copper is a better conductor than iron.

Effects of length and cross-sectional area

- For a particular conductor the resistance is **proportional to length**. The longer the conductor, the further the electrons have to travel, the more likely they are to collide with the metal ions and so the greater the resistance.

Two wires in series are like one long wire, because the electrons have to travel twice as far.

QUESTION SPOTTER

Questions often ask you to state and explain how the resistance of a conductor is affected by its length or its thickness. Using the simple models shown here should help.

- Resistance is **inversely proportional to cross-sectional area.** The greater the cross-sectional area of the conductor, the more electrons there are available to carry the charge along the conductor's length and so the lower the resistance.

Two wires in parallel are like one thick wire, so the electrons have more routes to travel along the same distance.

IDEAS AND EVIDENCE

Using the idea of electrons to explain how a material behaves is a good example of scientists using a mental model.

- The amount of current flowing through a circuit can be controlled by changing the resistance of the circuit using a **variable resistor** or **rheostat**. Adjusting the rheostat changes the length of the wire the current has to flow through.

re-wrapped variable resistor — terminals — slider — long wire with high resistance

variable resistor made from carbon ring — metal slider — carbon ring — terminals — control (turn to move slider)

symbol for a variable resistor (rheostat)

Variable resistors are commonly used in electrical equipment, for example in the speed controls of model racing cars or in volume controls on radios and hi-fi systems.

Effect of temperature on resistance

■ If the resistance of a conductor remains constant a graph of voltage against current will give a **straight line**. The gradient of the line will be the resistance of the conductor.

■ The resistance of most conductors becomes higher if the temperature of the conductor increases. As the temperature rises the metal ions vibrate more and provide greater resistance to the flow of the electrons. For example, the resistance of a filament lamp becomes greater as the voltage is increased and the lamp gets hotter.

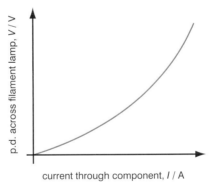

In an 'ohmic' resistor, such as carbon, Ohm's law applies and the voltage is directly proportional to the current – a straight line is obtained. In a filament lamp, Ohm's law is not obeyed because the heating of the lamp changes its resistance.

■ In some substances, increasing the temperature actually **lowers** the resistance. This is the case with **semiconductors** such as silicon. Silicon has few free electrons and so behaves more like an insulator than a conductor. But if silicon is heated, more electrons are removed from the outer electron shells of the atoms producing an increased electron cloud. The released electrons can move throughout the structure, creating an electric current. This effect is large enough to outweigh the increase in resistance that might be expected from the increased movement of the silicon ions in the structure as the temperature increases.

QUESTION SPOTTER

You will often be shown graphs of potential difference against current and asked to explain how the current varies with the p.d.

■ Semiconducting silicon is used to make **thermistors**, which are used as temperature sensors, and **light-dependent resistors** (LDRs), which are used as light sensors.

A light-dependent resistor, (top left) conducts better when light shines on it. A thermistor (top right) conducts better when it is hot. A diode (bottom left) only conducts in one direction. An ordinary (ohmic) resistor is shown bottom right.

■ In LDRs it is light energy that removes electrons from the silicon atoms, increasing the electron cloud.

■ Silicon **diodes** also use resistance as a means of controlling current flow in a circuit. In one direction the resistance is very high, effectively preventing current flow, in the other direction the resistance is relatively low and current can flow. Diodes are used to **protect** sensitive electronic equipment that would be damaged if a current flowed in the wrong direction.

LDR

thermistor

diode

resistor

CHECK YOURSELF QUESTIONS

Q1
a Draw a circuit diagram to show how you could measure the resistance of a piece of nichrome wire. Explain how you would calculate the resistance of the wire.
b How would the resistance of the wire change if: i its length was doubled, ii its cross-sectional area was doubled?

Q2 Use Ohm's law to calculate the following:
a The voltage required to produce a current of 2 A in a 12 Ω resistor.
b The voltage required to produce a current of 0.1 A in a 200 Ω resistor.
c The current produced when a voltage of 12 V is applied to a 100 Ω resistor.
d The current produced when a voltage of 230 V is applied to a 10 Ω resistor.
e The resistance of a wire which under a potential difference of 6 V allows a current of 0.1 A to flow.
f The resistance of a heater which under a potential difference of 230 V allows a current of 10 A to flow.

Q3 A graph of current against voltage is plotted for a piece of wire. The graph is shown below.

a Describe how the resistance of the wire changes as the voltage is increased.
b Suggest an explanation for this change.

Answers are on page 255.

Power in electrical circuits

⌂ Calculating power ratings

■ All electrical equipment has a **power rating**, which indicates how many joules of energy are supplied each second. The unit of power used is the **watt** (W). Light bulbs often have power ratings of 60 W or 100 W. Electric kettles have ratings of about 2 kilowatts (2 kW = 2000 W). A 2 kW kettle supplies 2000 J of energy each second.

■ The power of a piece of electrical equipment depends on the voltage and the current:

	P = power in watts (W)
$P = V\,I$	V = voltage in volts (V)
	I = current in amps (A)

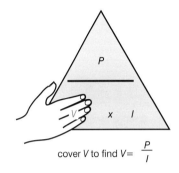

cover V to find $V = \dfrac{P}{I}$

WORKED EXAMPLES

1 What is the power of an electric toaster if a current of 7 A is obtained from a 230V supply?

Write down the formula in terms of P:	$P = V\,I$
Substitute the values:	$P = 230 \times 7$
Work out the answer and write down the unit:	$P = 1610\,W$

2 An electric oven has a power rating of 2 kW. What current will flow when the oven is used with a 230 V supply?

Write down the formula in terms of I:	$I = \dfrac{P}{V}$
Substitute the values:	$I = \dfrac{2000}{230}$
Work out the answer and write down the unit:	$I = 8.7\,A$

QUESTION SPOTTER

Questions on the equation $P = V\,I$ are very common. You will need to be able to change the subject of the equation and give the units for P, V and I.

⌂ How do suppliers charge for electricity?

■ Electricity meters in the home and in industry measure the amount of energy used in **kilowatt–hours** (kWh). 1 kilowatt-hour (1 kWh) is the amount of energy transferred by a 1 kW device in 1 hour.

1 kWh = 3600000 J.

WORKED EXAMPLE

Calculate the energy transferred by a 3 kW electrical immersion heater which is used for 30 minutes.

Write down the formula:	Energy = power (kW) × time (h)
Substitute the values:	Energy = 3 × 0.5
Work out the answer and write down the unit:	Energy = 1.5 kWh

An off-peak white meter has two displays. The lower display shows the number of kWh units used at the standard rate. The upper display shows the units used at off-peak rate.

Balancing supply and demand

- Because they can't close the power stations at night when demand is lower, the electricity companies sell electricity at two different rates.

- **Standard rate** applies to electricity used during the day.

- **Off-peak rate** electricity is used at night, and costs less than half standard rate electricity. Users need a special meter for this type of electricity. Off-peak electricity is usually available from midnight until 7 a.m. – hence it is sometimes called '**Economy 7**' electricity.

WORKED EXAMPLE

A 3 kW night storage heater is switched on full power for 7 hours one night. The rate on the Economy 7 tariff is 4p per unit. Calculate the cost of using the heater.

Write down the formula:	Units = power (kW) × time (h)
Substitute the values:	Units = 3 × 7 = 21
Include cost of each unit:	Cost = units × 4p = 21 × 4 = 84p

Using electricity safely

- Electrical appliances can be damaged if the current flowing through them is too high. The electric current usually has to pass through the **fuse** in the plug before it reaches the appliance. If there is a sudden surge in the current the wire in the fuse will heat up and melt – it 'blows'. This breaks the circuit and stops any further current flowing.

- The fuse must have a value above the normal current that the appliance needs but should be as small as possible. The most common fuses are rated at 3 A, 5 A and 13 A. Any electrical appliance with a heating element in it should be fitted with a 13 A fuse.

The fuse fits between the live brown wire and the pin. The brown live wire and the blue neutral wire carry the current. The green and yellow striped earth wire is needed to make metal appliances safer.

1 What fuse should be fitted in the plug of a 2.2 kW electric kettle used with a supply voltage of 230 V?

Calculate the normal current: $I = \frac{P}{V} = \frac{2000}{230} = 9.6$ A.

Choose the fuse with the smallest rating bigger than the normal current: the fuse must be 13 A.

2 What fuse should be fitted to the plug of a reading lamp which has a 60 W lamp and a supply of 230 V?

Calculate the normal current: $I = \frac{P}{V} = \frac{60}{230} = 0.26$ A.

Choose the fuse with the smallest rating bigger than the normal current: the fuse must be 3 A.

Other safety measures

- **Circuit breakers** spring open ('trip') a switch if there is an increase in current in the circuit. They can be reset easily once the fault in the circuit has been corrected.

- Metal-cased appliances must have an **earth wire** as well as a fuse. If the live wire worked loose and came into contact with the metal casing, the casing would become live and the user could be electrocuted. The earth wire provides a very low resistance route to the 0 V earth – usually water pipes buried deep underground. This low resistance means that a large current passes from the live wire to earth, causing the fuse to melt and break the circuit.

- Appliances that are made with plastic casing do not need an earth wire. The plastic is an insulator and so can never become live. Appliances like this are said to be **double insulated**.

The earth wire and fuse work together to make sure that the metal outer casing of this appliance can never become live and electrocute someone.

CHECK YOURSELF QUESTIONS

Q1 A hairdryer works on mains electricity of 230V and takes a current of 4 A. Calculate the power of the hairdryer.

Q2 a An iron has a power rating of 1000 W. Calculate the cost of using the iron for 3 hours if electricity costs 8p per kilowatt-hour.
  b The power of a television set is 200 W. Calculate how much it costs to watch the television for 5 hours. A unit (kWh) of electricity costs 8p.

Q3 A 3 kW immersion heater transfers energy to water for 10 minutes. How much energy does the heater transfer in 10 minutes?

Answers are on page 256.

Static electricity

⟲ What is static electricity?

■ Electric charge doesn't flow in an insulator. However, when two insulators are rubbed together electrons from the atoms on the surface of one insulator are transferred to the surface of the other. This leaves an excess of electrons – a negative charge – on one insulator and a shortage of electrons – a positive charge – on the other insulator. The charge is fixed in place – it is **static electricity**.

Charging up a plastic ruler.

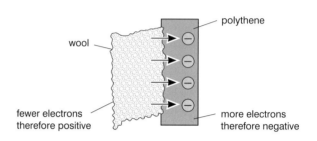

polythene

wool

fewer electrons therefore positive

more electrons therefore negative

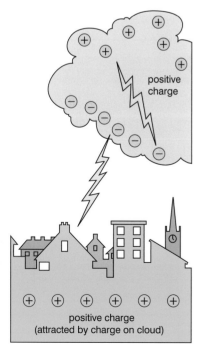

electrons repelled away from surface

ceiling

negative balloon

The balloon induces a charge on the ceiling's surface.

■ Static charges interact in a simple way: **like charges repel – unlike charges attract**. For example, when a balloon is rubbed against clothing it will 'stick' to a wall or ceiling. This is because of **electrostatic induction**. The balloon 'sticks' because of the attraction between the negative charges on the balloon and the induced positive charges on the ceiling.

⟲ What problems can static electricity cause?

■ Air currents in thunderclouds, rub past water molecules and charge them up. The bottom of the cloud is left with a negative charge, which induces a positive charge in buildings and trees on the ground and creates a strong electric field in the air between the cloud and the ground. A short burst of electric current can occur in the air – **lightning**.

■ The sudden discharge of electricity caused by friction between two insulators can cause **shocks in everyday situations** – for example:
  • combing your hair
  • pulling clothes over your head
  • walking on synthetic carpets
  • getting out of a car.

■ Sparks can also cause **explosions** and so great care has to be taken when emptying fuel tankers at service stations and airports or in grain silos or flour factories.

positive charge

positive charge (attracted by charge on cloud)

Thunderclouds have a high concentration of negative charge at the bottom. They have very high voltages. They ionise the air so that it conducts electricity. Lightning is caused by a burst of electric current through the air.

☀ QUESTION SPOTTER

A common question will ask you to explain how a flash of lightning occurs. It is easier to explain if you include a diagram showing the build up of charges.

⬚ Uses of static electricity

■ The properties of static electricity are put to good effect in **ink-jet printers** and **photocopiers**.

charged wire

drum

1 high voltage wire charges drum

2 drum is charged evenly

light reflected off original

lens

3 light removes charge from parts that are not to be printed

In a photocopier, charged particles attract the toner. Light is used to remove charge from parts that are not to be printed.

4 charged parts attract toner particles

5 toner rolled onto paper

6 toner melted on to paper by heating

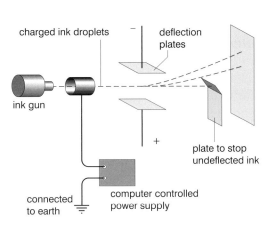

charged ink droplets

deflection plates

ink gun

plate to stop undeflected ink

connected to earth

computer controlled power supply

In inkjet printers, uncharged ink droplets do not reach the paper. This is how the spaces between words are made.

✦ IDEAS AND EVIDENCE

You need to be aware of evidence supporting the idea of two 'opposite' types of charge: positive and negative. Remind yourself of the experiments involving attraction and repulsion.

CHECK YOURSELF QUESTIONS

Q1 A plastic rod is rubbed with a cloth.
   a How does the plastic become positively charged?
   b The charged plastic rod attracts small pieces of paper. Explain why this attraction occurs.

Q2 a A car stops and one of the passengers gets out. When she touches a metal post she feels an electric shock. Explain why she feels this shock.
   b Write down two other situations where people might get this type of shock.

Q3 Give two examples of where static electricity can be dangerous.

Answers are on page 256.

Electromagnetism

Magnetic fields are created around any wire that carries a current.

▢ What is electromagnetism?

■ An electric current flowing through a wire creates a magnetic field in the region of the wire. Magnetism created in this way is known as electromagnetism. The magnetic field is stronger if the wire is made into a coil. It is even stronger if the coil is wrapped around a piece of magnetic material such as iron.

■ The strength of the electromagnet can be increased by:
  • increasing the number of coils in the wire
  • increasing the current flowing through the wire
  • placing a soft iron core inside the coils.

▢ How do relay switches work?

■ **Electromagnets** produce magnetic fields that can be turned on and off at will. A **relay** is an electromagnetic switch. It has the advantage of using a small current from a low-voltage circuit to switch on a higher current in a higher-voltage circuit.

■ A relay switch operates the **starter motor** of a car. Thin low-current wires are used in the circuit that contains the ignition switch operated by the driver. Much thicker wires are used in the circuit containing the battery and the high-current starter motor. Turning the ignition key causes a current to flow through the relay coil. This creates a magnetic field which attracts the armature to the core. The armature pivots and connects the starter motor to the car battery.

A relay circuit used to switch on a starter motor.

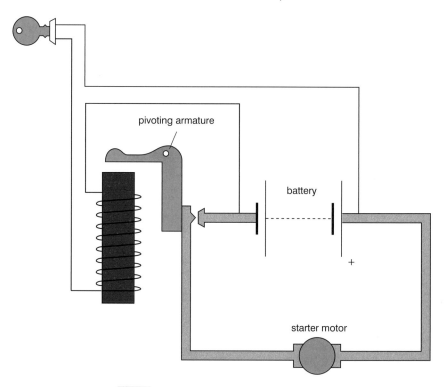

pivoting armature

battery

+

starter motor

⌗ D.C. Motors

■ An **electric motor** transfers electrical energy to kinetic energy. It is made from a coil of wire positioned between the poles of two permanent magnets. When a current flows through the coil of wire, it creates a magnetic field, which interacts with the magnetic field produced by the two permanent magnets. The two fields exert a force that pushes the wire at right angles to the permanent magnetic field.

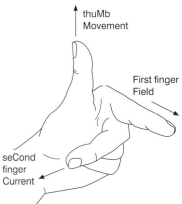

Fleming's left-hand rule predicts the direction of the force on a current carrying wire.

■ A motor coil as set up in the diagram will be forced round as indicated by the arrows (1 and 2 below). The split–ring commutator ensures that the motor continues to spin. Without the commutator, the coil would rotate 90° and then stop. This would not make a very useful motor! The commutator reverses the direction of the current at just the right point (3) so that the forces on the coil flip around and continue the rotating motion (4).

CHECK YOURSELF QUESTIONS

Q1 In a recycling plant an electromagnet separates scrap metal from household rubbish.

a Can this method be used to separate aluminium drinks cans from other household rubbish? Explain your answer.
b How can the operator drop the scrap metal into the skip?

Q2 The diagram shows a simple electromagnet made by a student.

Suggest two ways in which the electromagnet can be made to pick up more nails.

Q3 The diagram shows an electric bell.

Explain how the bell works when the switch is closed.

Answers are on page 257.

■ Electromagnetic induction ■

⬚ Generating electricity

- Michael Faraday was the first person to generate electricity from a magnetic field using **electromagnetic induction**. The large generators in power stations generate the electricity we need using this process.

- Current is created in a wire when:
  - the wire is moved through a magnetic field ('cutting' the field lines)
  - the magnetic field is moved past the wire (again 'cutting' the field lines)
  - the magnetic field around the wire changes strength.

- Current created in this way is said to be **induced**.

- The faster these changes, the larger the current.

⬚ Dynamos and generators

- A **dynamo** is a simple current generator. A dynamo looks very like an electric motor. Turning the permanent magnet near to the coil induces a current in the wires. The split-ring commutator ensures that the current generated flows in only one direction.

In a bicycle dynamo the magnet rotates and the coil is fixed.

- Power station generators don't have a commutator, so they produce **alternating current**. Power stations use electromagnets rather than permanent magnets.

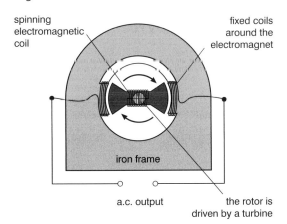

The generator rotates at 50 times per second, producing a.c. at 50 hertz.

◻ Transformers

- A **transformer** consists of two coils of insulated wire wound on a piece of iron. If an alternating voltage is applied to the first (primary) coil the alternating current produces a changing magnetic field in the core. This changing magnetic field induces an alternating current in the second (the secondary) coil.

- If there are more turns on the secondary coil than on the primary coil, then the voltage in the secondary coil will be greater than the voltage in the primary coil. The exact relationship between turns and voltage is:

$$\frac{\text{primary coil voltage (Vp)}}{\text{secondary coil voltage (Vs)}} = \frac{\text{number of primary turns (Np)}}{\text{number of secondary turns (Ns)}}$$

- When the secondary coil has more turns than the primary coil, the voltage increases in the same proportion. This is a **step-up transformer**.

- A transformer with fewer turns on the secondary coil than on the primary coil is a **step-down transformer**, which produces a smaller voltage in the secondary coil.

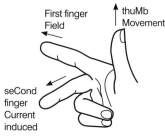

First finger — Field
thuMb — Movement
seCond finger — Current induced

Fleming's right-hand rule predicts the direction of the current induced in a moving wire.

12V
primary
1000 turns
6V
secondary
500 turns

transformer   circuit symbol

step-down transformer
ratio of number of turns is 2:1
voltage ratio is 2:1

12V
primary
1000 turns
48V
secondary
4000 turns

step-up transformer
ratio of number of turns is 1:4
voltage ratio is 1:4

Transformers are widely used to change voltages. They are frequently used in the home to step down the mains voltage of 230V to 6V or 12V.

WORKED EXAMPLE

Calculate the output voltage from a transformer when the input voltage is 230 V and the number of turns on the primary coil is 2000 and the number of turns on the secondary coil is 100.

Write down the formula:	$\dfrac{Vp}{Vs} = \dfrac{Np}{Ns}$
Substitute the values known:	$\dfrac{230}{Vs} = \dfrac{2000}{100} = 20$
Rewrite this so that Vs is the subject:	$Vs = \dfrac{230}{20}$
Work out the answer and write down the unit:	$Vs = 11.5\,V$

⬚ Transmitting electricity

■ Most power stations **burn fuel** to heat water into high–pressure steam, which is then used to drive a **turbine**. The turbine turns an a.c. generator, which produces the electricity.

The most common fuels used in power stations are still coal, oil and gas.

■ The **National Grid** links all the power stations to all parts of the country. To minimise the power loss in transmitting electricity around the grid the current has to be kept as low as possible. The higher the current the more the transmission wires will be heated by the current and the more energy is wasted as heat.

■ This is where transformers come in useful. This is also the reason that mains electricity is generated as alternating current. When a transformer steps up a voltage it also steps down the current and vice versa. Power stations generate electricity with a voltage of 25 000 V. Before this is transmitted on the grid it is converted by a step-up transformer to 400 000 V. This is then reduced by a series of step-down transformers to 230 V before it is supplied to homes.

Mains electricity is a.c. so that it can be easily stepped up and down. High-voltage/low-current transmission lines waste less energy than low-voltage/high-current lines.

CHECK YOURSELF QUESTIONS

Q1 Two students are using the equipment shown in the diagram.

The students cannot decide whether it is an electric motor or a generator. Explain how you would know which it is.

Q2 The diagram shows a transformer.

a What material is used for the transformer core?

b What happens in the core when the primary coil is switched on?

c What happens in the secondary coil when the primary coil is switched on?

d If the primary coil has 12 turns and the secondary coil has 7 turns, what will the primary voltage be if the secondary voltage is 14 V?

Q3 Explain why electricity is transmitted on the National Grid at very high voltages.

Answers are on page 257.

UNIT 16: FORCES AND MOTION

REVISION SESSION 1 ◼ The effects of forces ◼

⛶ How do forces act on objects?

◼ It is very unusual for a single force to be acting on an object. Usually there will be two or more. The size and direction of these forces determine whether the object will move and the direction it will move in.

◼ Forces are measured in **newtons**. They take many forms and have many effects including pushing, pulling, bending, stretching, squeezing and tearing. Forces can:
- **change the speed** of an object
- **change the direction** of movement of an object
- **change the shape** of an object.

⛶ What is friction?

◼ **Friction** is a very common force. It is the force that tries to stop movement between touching surfaces by opposing the force that causes the movement.

◼ In many situations friction can be a disadvantage, e.g. friction in the bearings of a bicycle wheel. In other situations friction can be an advantage, e.g. between brake pads and a bicycle wheel.

⛶ The effects of weight

◼ **Weight** is another common force. It is also measured in **newtons**. The weight of an object depends on its **mass** and **gravity**. Any mass near the Earth has weight due to the Earth's gravitational pull.

◼ On the Moon, your mass will be the same as on Earth, but your weight will be less. This is because the gravity on the Moon is about one-sixth of that on the Earth, and so the force of attraction of an object to the Moon is about one-sixth of that on the Earth.

Who cares how much you weigh? It's your mass that people really care about.

Earth

mass = 90 kg

weight = 900 N

Moon

mass = 90 kg

weight = 150 N

FORCES AND MOTION ○ ○ ○ ○ ○ ○ 171 ○ ○ ○ ○ ○ ○ ○ ○ ○ ○ ○ ○ ○ UNIT 16

Balanced forces

- Usually there are at least two forces acting on an object. If these two forces are **balanced** then the object will either be stationary or moving at a constant speed.

- A spacecraft in deep space will have no forces acting on it – no air resistance (no air!), no force of gravity – and because there is no need to produce a forward force from its rockets it will travel at a constant speed.

Unbalanced forces

- For an object's speed or direction of movement to change the forces acting on it must be **unbalanced**.

Acceleration. The force provided by the engine is greater than the force provided by air resistance and so the car increases its speed.

Deceleration. The engine is now providing no forward force. The 'drag' force provided by the parachute will slow the car down.

- As a gymnast first steps on to a trampoline, his weight is much greater than the opposing supporting force of the trampoline, so he moves downwards, stretching the trampoline. As the trampoline stretches, its supporting force increases until the supporting force is equal to the gymnast's weight. When the two forces are balanced the trampoline stops stretching. If an elephant stood on the trampoline it would break because it could never produce a supporting force equal to the elephant's weight.

A trampoline stretches until it supports the weight on it.

gymnast moves down pulled by his own weight

gymnast stops moving when trampoline's supporting force equals his weight

- As a skydiver jumps from a plane, the force of gravity will be much greater than the opposing force caused by air resistance. The skydiver's speed will increase rapidly – and the force caused by the air resistance increases as the skydiver's speed increases. Eventually it will exactly match the force of gravity, the forces will be balanced and the speed of the skydiver will remain constant. This speed is known as the **terminal speed**.

■ If the skydiver spreads out so that more of his or her surface is in contact with the air, the resistive force will be greater and the terminal speed will be lower than if he or she adopted a more compact shape. A parachute has a very large surface, and produces a very large resistive force, so the terminal speed of a parachutist is quite low. This means that he or she can land relatively safely.

CHECK YOURSELF QUESTIONS

Q1 Look at the diagrams A, B and C. In each case describe the effect the forces would have on the object.

A — Stationary wooden block
20N ← → 20N

B
2000N ← → 6000N

C — ice skater (moving)
400N ← → 400N

Q2 Skiers can travel at very high speeds. A friction force acts on the skis.

a Use the diagram to show the direction of the friction force acting on the skier.
b Explain why it is important for the friction forces to be as small as possible.
c Describe one way the skier could reduce the friction force.

Q3 The diagram shows the stages in the descent of a skydiver.

1 — 600N
2 — 600N / 600N
3 — 1000N / 600N
4 — 600N / 600N
5 — 600N / 600N

a Describe and explain the motion of the skydiver in each case.
b In stage 5 explain why the parachutist doesn't sink into the ground.

Answers are on page 258.

Velocity and acceleration

Both cars have the same speed. Car A has a velocity of +10m/s, car B has a velocity of −10m/s.

⊡ Are speed and velocity the same?

■ The **speed** of an object can be calculated using the following formula:

$$speed = \frac{distance}{time}$$

$$v = \frac{s}{t}$$

v = speed in m/s
s = distance in m
t = time in s

■ **Velocity** is almost the same as speed. It has a **size** (called speed) and a **direction**.

WORKED EXAMPLES

1 Calculate the average speed of a motor car that travels 500 m in 20 seconds.

Write down the formula:	$v = \frac{s}{t}$
Substitute the values for s and t:	$v = \frac{500}{20}$
Work out the answer and write down the units:	$v = 25$ m/s

2 A horse canters at an average speed of 5 m/s for 2 minutes. Calculate the distance it travels.

Write down the formula in terms of s:	$s = v \times t$
Substitute the values for v and t:	$s = 5 \times 2 \times 60$
Work out the answer and write down the units:	$s = 600$ m

Cover speed to find that
$$speed = \frac{distance}{time}$$

☀ QUESTION SPOTTER

Calculation questions involving $v = \frac{s}{t}$ are very common. You will need to remember the equation and be able to change the subject of the equation to match the question. (For example, write $s = v \times t$.) Don't forget to include the correct units.

⊡ What is acceleration?

■ How much an object's **speed or velocity changes** in a certain time is its **acceleration**. Acceleration can be calculated using the following formula:

$$acceleration = \frac{change\ in\ speed}{time\ taken}$$

$$a = \frac{(v - u)}{t}$$

a = acceleration

v = final speed in m/s

u = starting speed in m/s

t = time in s

■ The units of acceleration m/s/s (metres per second per second) are sometimes written as m/s² (metres per second squared).

WORKED EXAMPLE

Calculate the acceleration of a car that travels from 0 m/s to 28 m/s in 10 seconds.

Write down the formula:	$a = \dfrac{(v - u)}{t}$
Substitute the values for v, u and t:	$a = \dfrac{(28 - 0)}{10}$
Work out the answer and write down the units:	$a = 2.8$ m/s/s

Using graphs to study motion

- Journeys can be summarised using **graphs**. The simplest type is a **distance–time graph** where the distance travelled is plotted against the time of the journey.

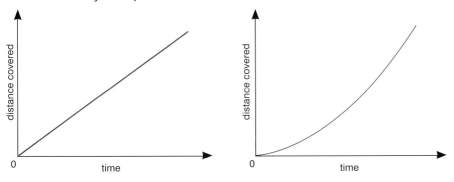

Steady speed is shown by a straight line. Steady acceleration is shown by a smooth curve.

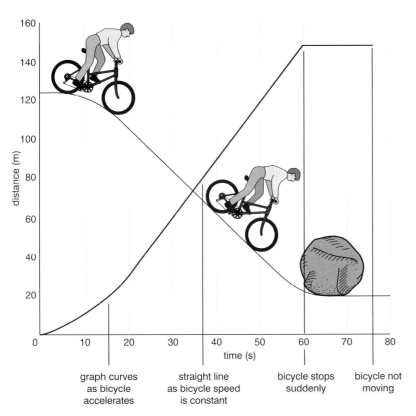

graph curves as bicycle accelerates

straight line as bicycle speed is constant

bicycle stops suddenly

bicycle not moving

A distance–time graph for a bicycle travelling down a hill. The graph slopes when the bicycle is moving. The slope gets steeper when the bicycle goes faster. The slope is straight (has a constant gradient) when the bicycle's speed is constant. The line is horizontal when the bicycle is at rest.

■ A **speed–time graph** provides information on speed, acceleration and distance travelled.

Steady speed is shown by a horizontal line. Steady acceleration is shown by a line sloping up.

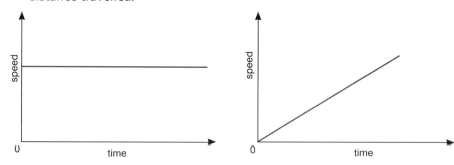

■ The graph shows a car travelling between two sets of traffic lights. It can be divided into three regions.

A speed–time graph for a car travelling between two sets of traffic lights.

■ In region A, the car is **accelerating at a constant rate** (the line has a constant positive gradient). The distance travelled by the car can be calculated:

average velocity $= \dfrac{(16 + 0)}{2} = 8$ m/s

time $= 40$ s

so distance $= v \times t = 8 \times 40 = 320$ m

This can also be calculated from the area under the line
($\frac{1}{2}$ base $\times$ height $= \frac{1}{2} \times 40 \times 16 = 320$ m).

■ In region B, the car is travelling at a **constant speed** (the line has a gradient of zero). The distance travelled by the car can be calculated:

velocity $= 16$ m/s

time $= 30$ s

so, distance $= v \times t = 16 \times 30 = 480$ m

This can also be calculated from the area under the line
(base $\times$ height $= 30 \times 16 = 480$ m).

- In region C, the car is **decelerating at a constant rate** (the line has a constant negative gradient). The distance travelled by the car can be calculated:

$$\text{average velocity} = \frac{(16 + 0)}{2} = 8 \text{ m/s}$$

time = 30 s

so, distance = $v \times t$ = 8 × 30 = 240 m

This can also be calculated from the area under the line

($\frac{1}{2}$ base × height = $\frac{1}{2}$ × 30 × 16 = 240 m).

▢ Thinking, braking and stopping distances

- When a car driver has to brake it takes time for him or her to react. During this time the car will be travelling at its normal speed. The distance it travels in this time is called the **thinking distance**.

- The driver then puts on the brakes. The distance the car travels while it is braking is called the **braking distance**. The overall stopping distance is made up from the thinking distance and the braking distance.

- The thinking distance can vary from person to person and from situation to situation – the braking distance can vary from car to car.

Factors affecting thinking distance	Factors affecting braking distance
speed	speed
tiredness	condition of tyres (amount of tread)
alcohol	condition of brakes
medication, drugs	road conditions (dry, wet, icy, gravel, etc.)
level of concentration and distraction	mass of the car

Shortest stopping distances for a car on a good, dry road.

20 mph — 6 m, 6 m = 12 m
30 mph — 9 m, 14 m = 23 m
40 mph — 12 m, 24 m = 36 m
50 mph — 15 m, 38 m = 53 m
60 mph — 18 m, 55 m = 73 m
70 mph — 21 m, 75 m = 96 m

thinking distance ⟶ braking distance ⟶

▢ How are mass, force and acceleration related?

■ The acceleration of an object depends on its **mass** and the **force** that is applied to it. The relationship between these factors is given by the formula:

force = mass × acceleration	F = force in newtons
$F = m\,a$	m = mass in kg
	a = acceleration in m/s/s

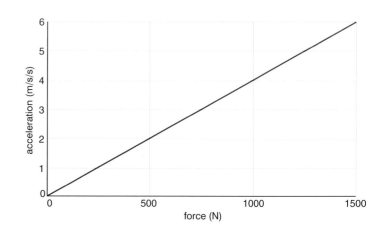

Acceleration is directly proportional to force. Acceleration is inversely proportional to mass.

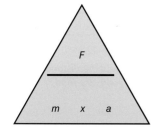

WORKED EXAMPLES

1 What force would be required to give a mass of 5 kg an acceleration of 10 m/s/s?

Write down the formula:	$F = m\,a$
Substitute the values for m and a:	$F = 5 \times 10$
Work out the answer and write down the units:	$F = 50$ N

2 A car has a resultant driving force of 6000 N and a mass of 1200 kg. Calculate the car's initial acceleration.

Write down the formula in terms of a:	$a = \dfrac{F}{m}$
Substitute the values for F and m:	$a = \dfrac{6000}{1200}$
Work out the answer and write down the units:	$a = 5$m/s/s

⚡ A* EXTRA

The equation $F = m\,a$ shows that the acceleration of an object is directly proportional to the force acting (if its mass is constant) and is inversely proportional to its mass (if the force is constant).

UNIT 16 ● ● ● ● ● ● ● ● ● ● ●   178   ● ● ● ● ● ●   FORCES AND MOTION

CHECK YOURSELF QUESTIONS

Q1 The graph shows a distance–time graph for a journey.

a What does the graph tell us about the speed of the car between 20 and 60 seconds?

b How far did the car travel between 20 and 60 seconds?

c Calculate the speed of the car between 20 and 60 seconds.

d What happened to the car between 80 and 100 seconds?

Q2 Look at the velocity–time graph for a toy tractor.

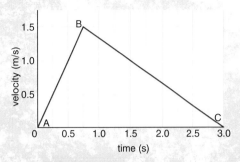

a Calculate the acceleration of the tractor from A to B.

b Calculate the total distance travelled by the tractor from A to C.

Q3 The manufacturer of a car gave the following information:
Mass of car 1000 kg. The car will accelerate from 0 to 30 m/s in 12 seconds.

a Calculate the average acceleration of the car during the 12 seconds.

b Calculate the force needed to produce this acceleration.

Answers are on page 258.

UNIT 17: ENERGY

REVISION SESSION 1

Where does our energy come fron

◻ Sources of energy

- Most of the energy we use is obtained from **fossil fuels** – coal, oil and natural gas.

- Once supplies of these fuels have been used up they cannot be replaced – they are **non-renewable**.

- At current levels of use, oil and gas supplies will last for about another 40 years, and coal supplies for about a further 300 years. The development of **renewable** sources of energy is therefore becoming increasingly important.

◻ Renewable energy sources

- **Solar power** is energy from the Sun. The Sun's energy is trapped by solar panels and transferred into electrical energy or, as with domestic solar panels, is used to heat water. The cost of installing solar panels is high, and the weather limits the time when the panels are effective.

- The **wind** is used to turn windmill-like turbines which generate electricity directly from the rotating motion of their blades. Modern wind turbines are very efficient but several thousand would be required to equal the generating capacity of a modern fossil-fuel power station.

- The motion of **waves** can be used to move large floats and generate electricity. A very large number of floats are needed to produce a significant amount of electricity.

- Dams on tidal estuaries trap the water at high tide. When the water is allowed to flow back at low tide, **tidal power** can be generated. This obviously limits the use of the estuary.

A 'pumped storage' hydroelectric power station.

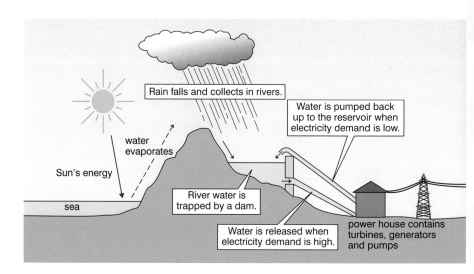

Rain falls and collects in rivers.

Water is pumped back up to the reservoir when electricity demand is low.

water evaporates

Sun's energy

sea

River water is trapped by a dam.

Water is released when electricity demand is high.

power house contains turbines, generators and pumps

- Dams can be used to store **water** which is allowed to fall in a controlled way that generates electricity. This is particularly useful in mountainous regions for generating **hydroelectric power**. When demand for electricity is low, electricity can be used to pump water back up into the high dam for use in times of high demand.

- **Plants** use energy from the Sun in photosynthesis. Plant material can then be used as a **biomass fuel** – either directly by burning it or indirectly. A good example of indirect use is to ferment sugar cane to make ethanol, which is then used as an alternative to petrol. Waste plant material can be used in 'biodigesters' to produce methane gas. The methane is then used as a fuel.

- **Geothermal power** is obtained using the heat of the Earth. In certain parts of the world, water forms hot springs which can be used directly for heating. Water can also be pumped deep into the ground to be heated.

IDEAS AND EVIDENCE

For a particular energy source, you should be able to give reasons *for* and *against* its use. For example, in favour of wind power, you might say that it is renewable and cheap to run, whilst you could say that wind farms cause visual pollution and are expensive to set up. Remember that there are reasons in favour of fossil fuels, particularly that they store large amounts of energy, as well as disadvantages such as the release of greenhouse gases when they are burned.

? CHECK YOURSELF QUESTIONS

Q1
 a What is meant by a non-renewable energy source?
 b Name three non-renewable energy sources.
 c Which non-renewable energy source is likely to last the longest?

Q2 Look at the graph, which shows the amount of energy from different sources used in the UK in 1955, 1965, 1975 and 1985.

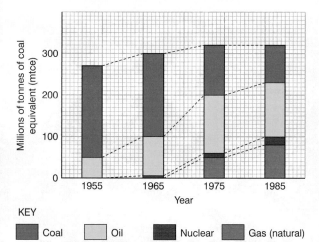

KEY

■ Coal ☐ Oil ■ Nuclear ■ Gas (natural)

 a Describe the trend in the total energy used in this period.
 b Describe the main changes in the sources of this energy.

Q3 A site has been chosen for a wind farm (a series of windmill-like turbines).
 a Give two important factors in choosing the site.
 b Give one advantage and one disadvantage of using wind farms to generate electricity.

Answers are on page 259.

Transferring energy

Conduction in a solid. Particles in a hot part of a solid (top) vibrate further and faster than particles in a cold part (bottom). The vibrations are passed on through the bonds from particle to particle.

Conduction plays an important part in cooking food.

⟲ How is energy transferred?

■ Energy flows from high temperatures to low temperatures – this is called **thermal transfer**. Thermal energy can be transferred in four main ways:
  • **conduction**
  • **convection**
  • **radiation**
  • **evaporation**.

⟲ Conduction

■ Materials that allow thermal energy to transfer through them quickly are called **conductors**. Those that do not are called **insulators**.

■ If one end of a conductor is heated the atoms that make up its structure start to vibrate more vigorously. As the atoms in a solid are linked together by chemical bonds the increased vibration can be passed on to other atoms. The energy of movement (kinetic energy) passes through the whole material.

■ **Metals** are particularly good conductors because they contain freely moving electrons which transfer energy very rapidly. **Air** is a good insulator. As air is a gas there are no bonds between the particles and so energy can only be transferred by the particles colliding with each other. Conduction cannot occur when there are no particles present, so a vacuum is a perfect insulator.

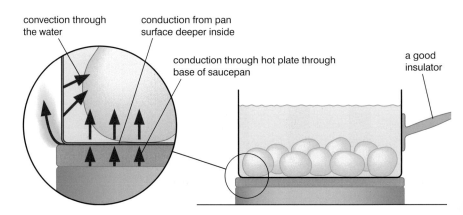

convection through the water

conduction from pan surface deeper inside

conduction through hot plate through base of saucepan

a good insulator

QUESTION SPOTTER

Examination questions often ask for explanations of processes that combine conduction and convection – for example, in explaining the energy transfer in cooking potatoes (see diagram).

⟲ Convection

■ Convection occurs in **liquids** and **gases** because these materials flow (they are 'fluids'). The particles in a fluid move all the time. When a fluid is heated, energy is transferred to the particles, causing them to move faster and further apart. This makes the heated fluid less dense than the unheated fluid. The less dense warm fluid will rise above the more dense colder fluid, causing the fluid to circulate. This **convection current** is how the thermal energy is transferred.

- If a fluid's movement is restricted, then energy cannot be transferred. That is why many insulators, such as ceiling tiles, contain trapped air pockets. Wall cavities in houses are filled with fibre to prevent air from circulating and transferring thermal energy by convection.

⟦⟧ Radiation

- Radiation, unlike conduction and convection, **does not need particles** at all. Radiation can travel through a vacuum.

- All objects take in and give out infrared radiation all the time. Hot objects radiate more infrared than cold objects. The amount of radiation given out or absorbed by an object depends on its temperature and on its surface.

Type of surface	As an emitter of radiation	As an absorber of radiation	Examples
Dull black	Good	Good	Cooling fans on the back of a refrigerator are dull black to radiate away more energy.
Bright shiny	Poor	Poor	Marathon runners wrap themselves in shiny blankets to prevent thermal transfer by radiation. Fuel storage tanks are sprayed with shiny silver paint to reflect radiation from the Sun.

⟦⟧ Evaporation

- When particles break away from the surface of a liquid and form a vapour, the process is known as evaporation.

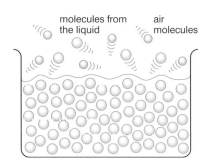

The more energetic molecules of the liquid escape from the surface. This reduces the average energy of the molecules remaining in the liquid and so the liquid cools down.

- Evaporation causes cooling. The evaporation of sweat helps to keep a body cool in hot weather. The cooling obtained in a refrigerator is also due to evaporation.

Convection currents caused by a room heater.

A vacuum flask has a hollow glass lining. The absence of air in the lining prevents thermal transfer by conduction and convection. The insides of the lining are silvered to reduce thermal transfer by radiation. The flask will therefore keep hot drinks hot, or cold drinks cold, for hours.

⚡ **A* EXTRA**

Convection currents in gases and liquids are caused by changes in density.
- When a liquid is heated the particles move more quickly and move further apart, making that part of the liquid less dense than cooler parts.
- The less dense part then rises and the cooler or denser liquid takes its place.

How can we keep our energy costs low?

■ Heating a house can account for over 60% of a family's total energy bill. Reducing thermal energy transfer from the house to the outside can greatly reduce the amount of energy that is being used and save a lot of money.

There are a number of ways of reducing wasteful energy transfer.

curtains reduce radiation

loft insulation

porch to reduce warm air loss

double-glazed windows insulate

draught excluder on door

wall cavity filled with insulation

carpet underlay acts as insulation

Source of energy wastage	% of energy wasted	Insulation technique
Walls	35	*Cavity wall insulation.* Modern houses have cavity walls, that is, two single walls separated by an air cavity. The air reduces energy transfer by conduction but not by convection as the air is free to move within the cavity. Fibre insulation is inserted into the cavity to prevent the air from moving and so reduces convection.
Roof	25	*Loft insulation.* Fibre insulation is placed on top of the ceiling and between the wooden joists. Air is trapped between the fibres, reducing energy transfer by conduction and convection.
Floors	15	*Carpets.* Carpets and underlay prevent energy loss by conduction and convection. In some modern houses foam blocks are placed under the floors.
Draughts	15	*Draught excluders.* Cold air can get into the home through gaps between windows and doors and their frames. Draught excluder tape can be used to block these gaps.
Windows	10	*Double glazing.* Energy is transferred through glass by conduction and radiation. Double glazing has two panes of glass with a layer of air between the panes. It reduces energy transfer by conduction but not by radiation. Radiation can be reduced by drawing the curtains.

Means of insulation	Approximate pay-back time (years)
Cavity wall	5
Loft	2
Carpets	10
Draught excluders	1
Double glazing	20

■ One thing to consider when insulating a house is the balance of the cost of the insulation against the potential saving in energy costs. The **pay-back time** is the time it takes for the savings to repay the costs of installation. The different methods of insulation have very different pay-back times.

■ The pay-back time is not the only thing to think about when considering different means of insulation. For instance, glazing reduces noise and condensation inside the home, and carpets provide increased comfort.

⊡ Efficiency of energy transfers

■ Energy transfers can be summarised using simple **energy transfer diagrams** or **Sankey diagrams**. The thickness of each arrow is drawn to scale to show the amount of energy.

■ Energy is always conserved – the total amount of energy after the transfer must be the same as the total amount of energy before the transfer. Unfortunately, in nearly all energy transfers some of the energy will end up as 'useless' heat.

■ In a power station only some of the energy originally produced from the fuel is transferred to useful electrical output. Energy **efficiency** can be calculated from the following formula:

$$\text{efficiency} = \frac{\text{useful energy output} \times 100\%}{\text{energy input}}$$

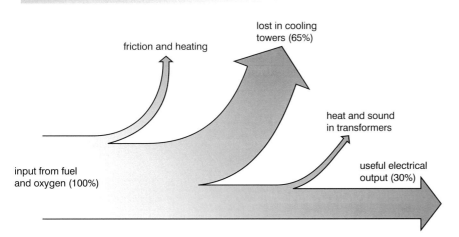

lost in cooling towers (65%)

friction and heating

heat and sound in transformers

input from fuel and oxygen (100%)

useful electrical output (30%)

■ Many power stations are now trying to make use of the large amounts of energy 'lost' in the cooling towers.

In a power station as much as 70% of the energy transfers do not produce useful energy. The power station is only 30% efficient.

QUESTION SPOTTER

You may be asked to label or complete a Sankey diagram like the one shown. Remember that the thickness of each section is directly related to its percentage contribution.

? CHECK YOURSELF QUESTIONS

Q1 Why are several thin layers of clothing more likely to reduce thermal transfer than one thick layer of clothing?

Q2 Hot water in an open container transfers energy by evaporation. Explain how the loss of molecules from the surface of the liquid causes the liquid to cool.

Q3 The diagram shows a cross-section of a steel radiator positioned in a room next to a wall.

still air

hot water circulated from boiler through pipes

wall

steel radiator

Describe how energy from the hot water reaches the wall behind the radiator.

Answers are on page 260.

Work, power and energy

In this position the gymnast is not doing any work against his body weight – he is not moving (he will be doing work pumping blood around his body though!).

⌗ Work

■ **Work** is done when the application of a force results in movement. Work can only be done if the object or system has energy. When work is done energy is transferred.

■ Work done can be calculated using the following formula:

> work done = force × distance moved
>
> $W = F s$
>
> W = work done in joules (J)
>
> F = force in newtons (N)
>
> s = distance moved in the direction of the force in metres (m)

WORKED EXAMPLES

1 A cyclist pedals along a flat road. She exerts a force of 60 N and travels 150 m. Calculate the work done by the cyclist.

Write down the formula:	$W = F s$
Substitute the values for F and s:	$W = 60 \times 150$
Work out the answer and write down the unit:	$W = 9000$ J

2 A person does 3000 J of work in pushing a supermarket trolley 50 m across a level car park. What force was the person exerting on the trolley?

Write down the formula with F as the subject:	$F = \dfrac{W}{s}$
Substitute the values for W and s:	$F = \dfrac{3000}{50}$
Work out the answer and write down the unit:	$F = 60$ N

The gymnast is doing work. He is moving upwards against the force of gravity. Energy is being transferred as he does the work.

⌗ Power

■ **Power** is defined as the rate of doing work or the rate of transferring energy. The more powerful a machine is the quicker it does a fixed amount of work or transfers a fixed amount of energy.

■ Power can be calculated using the formula:

> power = $\dfrac{\text{work done}}{\text{time taken}}$ = $\dfrac{\text{energy transfer}}{\text{time taken}}$
>
> $P = \dfrac{W}{t}$
>
> P = power in joules per second or watts (W)
>
> W = work done in joules (J)
>
> t = time taken in seconds (s)

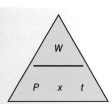

WORKED EXAMPLES

1 A crane does 20 000 J of work in 40 seconds. Calculate its power over this time.

Write down the formula:	$P = \dfrac{W}{t}$
Substitute the values for W and t:	$P = \dfrac{20000}{40}$
Work out the answer and write down the unit:	$P = 500\ W$

2 A student with a weight of 600 N runs up the flight of stairs shown in the diagram (right) in 4 seconds. Calculate the student's power.

The student is lifting his body against the force of gravity, which acts in a vertical direction. The distance measured must be in the direction of the force (that is, the vertical height).

Write down the formula for work done:	$W = F\,s$
Substitute the values for F and s:	$W = 600 \times 5 = 3000\ J$
Write down the formula for power:	$P = \dfrac{W}{t}$
Substitute the values for W and t:	$P = 3000/4 = 750\ W$

Potential energy

■ Stored, or hidden, energy is called **potential energy** (P.E.). If a spring is stretched the spring will have potential energy. If a load is raised above the ground it will have **gravitational potential energy**. If the spring is released or the load moves back to the ground the stored potential energy is transferred to movement energy, which is called **kinetic energy** (K.E.).

■ Gravitational potential energy can be calculated using the following formula:

gravitational potential energy = mass × gravitational field strength × height

P.E. = $m\,g\,h$

P.E. = gravitational potential energy in joules (J)

m = mass in kilograms (kg)

g = gravitational field strength of 10 N/kg

h = height in metres (m)

A* EXTRA

An object gains gravitational potential energy as it gains height. Work has to be done to increase the height of the object above the ground. Therefore:

> gain in gravitational potential energy of an object = work done on that object against gravity.

WORKED EXAMPLE

A skier has a mass of 70 kg and travels up a ski lift a vertical height of 300 m. Calculate the change in the skier's gravitational potential energy.

Write down the formula:	P.E. = $m\,g\,h$
Substitute values for m, g and h:	P.E. = $70 \times 10 \times 300$
Work out the answer and write down the unit:	P.E. = 210 000 J or 210 kJ

The kinetic energy given to the stone when it is thrown is transferred to potential energy as it gains height and slows down. At the top of its flight practically all the kinetic energy will have been converted into gravitational potential energy. A small amount of energy will have been lost due to friction between the stone and the air.

⚡ A* EXTRA

As a skier skis down a mountain the loss in potential energy should equal the gain in kinetic energy (assuming no other energy transfers take place, as a result of friction, for example). Calculations can then be performed using:

Loss in P.E. = Gain in K.E.
$$(mgh = \tfrac{1}{2}mv^2)$$

⊡ Kinetic energy

■ The kinetic energy of an object depends on its mass and its velocity. The kinetic energy can be calculated using the following formula:

kinetic energy = $\tfrac{1}{2}$ × mass × velocity²

K.E. = $\tfrac{1}{2}mv^2$

K.E. = kinetic energy in joules (J)

m = mass in kilograms (kg)

v = velocity in m/s

WORKED EXAMPLE

An ice skater has a mass of 50 kg and travels at a velocity of 5 m/s. Calculate the ice-skater's kinetic energy.

Write down the formula:	K.E. = $\tfrac{1}{2}mv^2$
Substitute the values for m and v:	K.E. = $\tfrac{1}{2}$ × 50 × 5 × 5
Work out the answer and write down the unit:	K.E. = 625 J

❓ CHECK YOURSELF QUESTIONS

Q1 50 000 J of work are done as a crane lifts a load of 400 kg. How far did the crane lift the load? (Gravitation field strength, g, is 10 N/kg.)

Q2 A student is carrying out a personal fitness test.

She steps on and off the 'step' 200 times. She transfers 30 J of energy each time she steps up.
a Calculate the energy transferred during the test.
b She takes 3 minutes to do the test. Calculate her average power.

Q3 A child of mass 35 kg climbed a 30 m high snow-covered hill.
a Calculate the change in the child's potential gravitational energy.
b The child then climbed onto a lightweight sledge and slid down the hill. Calculate the child's maximum speed at the bottom of the hill. (Ignore the mass of the sledge.)
c Explain why the actual speed at the bottom of the hill is likely to be less than the value calculated in part (b).

Answers are on page 260.

UNIT 18: WAVES

The properties of waves

There are two types of waves

- **Longitudinal waves.** This type of wave can be shown by pushing and pulling a spring. The spring stretches in places and squashes in others. The stretching produces regions of **rarefaction**, whilst the squashing produces regions of **compression**. Sound is an example of a longitudinal wave.

- **Transverse waves.** In a transverse wave the vibrations are at right angles to the direction of motion. Light, radio and other electromagnetic waves are transverse waves. Water waves are often used to demonstrate the properties of waves because the **wavefront** of a water wave is easy to see. A wavefront is the moving line that joins all the points on the crest of a wave.

QUESTION SPOTTER

You will often be asked to label a transverse wave showing features such as crest, trough, amplitude and wavelength.

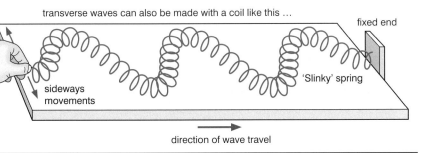

transverse waves can also be made with a coil like this …

fixed end

sideways movements

'Slinky' spring

direction of wave travel

Transverse and longitudinal waves are made by vibrations

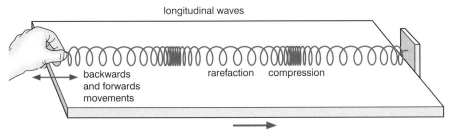

longitudinal waves

backwards and forwards movements

rarefaction   compression

What features do all waves have?

- The speed a wave travels at depends on the substance or **medium** it is passing through.

- Waves have a **repeating shape** or pattern.

- Waves **carry energy** without moving material along.

- Waves have a wavelength, frequency and amplitude.
  - **Wavelength** – the length of the repeating pattern.
  - **Frequency** – the number of repeated patterns that go past any point each second.
  - **Amplitude** – the maximum displacement of the medium's vibration. In transverse waves, this is half the crest-to-trough height.

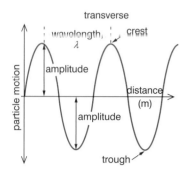

transverse

wavelength, λ

crest

amplitude

particle motion

distance (m)

amplitude

trough

longitudinal

wavelength (λ)

■ **The speed of a wave in a given medium is constant.** If you change the wavelength the frequency *must* change as well. Speed, frequency and wavelength of a wave are related by the equation:

wave speed = frequency × wavelength

$v = f \times \lambda$

v = wave speed, usually measured in metres/second (m/s)

f = frequency, measured in cycles per second or hertz (Hz)

λ = wavelength, usually measured in metres (m)

WORKED EXAMPLES

1 A loudspeaker makes sound waves with a frequency of 300 Hz. The waves have a wavelength of 1.13 m. Calculate the speed of the sound waves.

Write down the formula:	$v = f \times \lambda$
Substitute the values for f and λ:	$v = 300 \times 1.13$
Work out the answer and write down the unit:	$v = 339$ m/s

2 A radio station broadcasts on a wavelength of 250 m. The speed of the radio waves is 3×10^8 m/s. Calculate the frequency.

Write down the formula with f as the subject: $f = \dfrac{v}{\lambda}$

Substitute the values for v and λ: $f = \dfrac{3 \times 10^8}{250}$

Work out the answer and write down the unit: $f = 12000000$ Hz
or 12000 kHz

⌑ Reflection, refraction and diffraction

■ When a wave hits a barrier the wave will be **reflected**. If it hits the barrier at an angle then the angle of reflection will be equal to the angle of incidence. Echoes are a common consequence of the reflection of sound waves.

wave direction

wavefront

angle of incidence

Waves hit a barrier. The angle between a wavefront and the barrier is the angle of incidence.

new direction

old direction

The waves bounce off.

wave direction

angle of reflection

The angle of reflection is the same as the angle of incidence.

- When a wave moves from one medium into another, it will either speed up or slow down. When a wave **slows down**, the wavefronts crowd together – the **wavelength gets smaller**. When a wave **speeds up**, the wavefronts spread out – the **wavelength gets larger**.

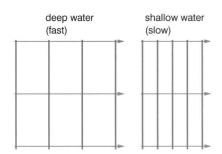

When waves slow down, their wavelength gets shorter.

- If a wave enters a new medium at an angle then the wavefronts also change direction. This is known as **refraction**. Refraction happens whenever there is a change in wave speed. Water waves are slower in shallower water than in deep water, so water waves will refract when the depth changes.

QUESTION SPOTTER

Calculations involving the wave equation are very common. You will need to be able to remember the equation and change its subject if required.

If waves cross into a new medium at an angle, their wavelength and direction changes.

- Wavefronts change shape when they pass the edge of an obstacle or go through a gap. This process is known as **diffraction**. Diffraction is strong when the width of the gap is similar in size to the wavelength of the waves.

- Diffraction is a problem in communications when radio and television signals are transmitted through the air in a narrow beam. Diffraction of the wavefront means that not all the energy transmitted with the wavefront reaches the receiving dishes. On the other hand, diffraction allows long-wave radio waves to spread out and diffract around buildings and hills.

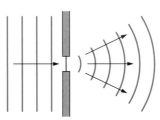

Diffraction is most noticeable when the size of the gap equals the wavelength of the waves.

⌨ Seismic waves

■ Earthquakes make waves that travel right through the Earth. These waves are called **seismic waves**. There are longitudinal waves called **P-waves** (primary) and transverse waves called **S-waves** (secondary).

■ The waves travel through rock and are partially reflected at the boundaries between different types of rock. Instruments called **seismometers** detect the waves. Monitoring these seismic waves after earthquakes has provided geologists with evidence that the Earth is made up of layers and that part of the core is liquid.

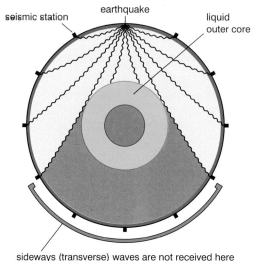

S-waves can travel through solid rock but not through liquid. P-waves can travel through solid and liquid rock. Only the P-waves from an earthquake, not the S-waves, are received at seismic stations on the opposite side of the world.

sideways (transverse) waves are not received here

CHECK YOURSELF QUESTIONS

Q1 The diagram shows a trace of a sound wave obtained on a cathode ray oscilloscope.

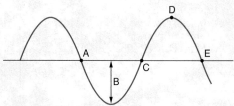

a Which letter shows the crest of the wave?

b The wavelength is the distance between which two letters?

c Which letter shows the amplitude?

d The frequency of the wave is 512 Hz. How many waves are produced each second?

Q2 Radio waves of frequency 900 MHz are used to send information to and from a portable phone. The speed of the waves is 3×10^8 m/s. Calculate the wavelength of the waves. (1 MHz = 1 000 000 Hz, 3×10^8 = 300 000 000.)

Q3 The speed of sound is approximately 340 m/s. Calculate the wavelength of middle C, which has a frequency of 256 Hz.

Answers are on page 260.

REVISION SESSION 2 — The electromagnetic spectrum

☐ Electromagnetic waves

- The **electromagnetic spectrum** is a family of different kinds of waves. Electromagnetic waves all travel at the same speed in a vacuum, i.e. the speed of light, 300 000 000 m/s.

- **White light** is a mixture of different colours and can be split by a prism into the **visible spectrum**. All the different colours of light travel at the same speed in a vacuum but they have different frequencies and wavelengths. When they enter glass or perspex they all slow down, but by different amounts. The different colours are therefore refracted through different angles. Violet is refracted the most, red the least.

- The visible spectrum is only a small part of the full electromagnetic spectrum.

A prism splits white light into the colourful spectrum of visible light.

The complete electromagnetic spectrum.

Type of wave	gamma rays	X rays	ultraviolet	visible	infrared	microwaves	TV and radio waves
frequency	high						low
wavelength	low						high
use	killing cancer cells	to look at bones	sun tan beds	photography	TV remote controls	cooking	transmission of TV and radio

☐ The waves you can't see

- **X-rays** are produced when high-energy electrons are fired at a metal target. Bones absorb more X-rays than other body tissue. If a person is placed between the X-ray source and a photographic plate, the bones appear to be white on the developed photographic plate compared with the rest of the body. X-rays have very high energy and can damage or destroy body cells. They may also cause cancer. Cancer cells absorb X-rays more readily than normal healthy cells and so X-rays are also used to treat cancer.

- **Gamma rays** have even higher energy than X-rays. Gamma rays are frequently used in radiotherapy to kill cancer cells. Radioactive substances that emit gamma rays are used as **tracers** (see Unit 20).

- **Ultraviolet radiation** (UV) is the component of the Sun's rays that gives you a suntan. UV is also created in fluorescent light tubes by exciting the atoms in a mercury vapour. The UV radiation is then absorbed by the coating on the inside of the fluorescent tube and re-emitted as visible light. Fluorescent tubes are more efficient than light bulbs because they don't depend on heating and so more energy is available to produce light.

QUESTION SPOTTER

Questions often require you to remember which waves in the electromagnetic spectrum have the greatest frequency or greatest wavelength.

A* EXTRA

The energy associated with an electromagnetic wave depends on its frequency. The waves with the higher frequencies are potentially the more hazardous.

- All objects give out **infrared radiation** (IR). The hotter the object is, the more radiation it gives out. Thermograms are photographs taken to show the infrared radiation given out from objects. Infrared radiation grills and cooks our food in an ordinary oven and is used in remote controls to operate televisions and videos.

- **Microwaves** are high-frequency radio waves. They are used in radar in finding the position of aeroplanes and ships. Metal objects reflect the microwaves back to the transmitter, enabling the distance between the object and the transmitter to be calculated. Microwaves are also used for cooking. Water particles in food absorb the energy carried by microwaves. They vibrate more and get much hotter. Microwaves penetrate several centimetres into the food and so speed up the cooking process.

- **Radio waves** have the longest wavelengths and lowest frequencies. **UHF** (ultra-high frequency) waves are used to transmit television programmes to homes. **VHF** (very high frequency) waves are used to transmit local radio programmes. **Medium** and **long** radio waves are used to transmit over longer distances because their wavelengths allow them to diffract around obstacles such as buildings and hills. Communication satellites above the Earth receive signals carried by high-frequency (**short-wave**) radio waves. These signals are amplified and re-transmitted to other parts of the world.

CHECK YOURSELF QUESTIONS

Q1 This is a list of types of wave:

> gamma   infrared   light   microwaves
> radio   ultraviolet   X-rays

Choose from the list the type of wave that best fits each of these descriptions.

a Stimulates the sensitive cells at the back of the eye.

b Necessary for a suntan.

c Used for *rapid* cooking in an oven.

d Used to take a photograph of the bones in a broken arm.

e Emitted by a video remote control unit.

Q2 Gamma rays are part of the electromagnetic spectrum. Gamma rays are useful to us but can also be very dangerous.

a Explain how the properties of gamma rays make them useful to us.

b Explain why gamma rays can cause damage to people.

c Give one difference between microwaves and gamma rays.

d Microwaves travel at 300 000 000 m/s. What speed do gamma rays travel at?

Answers are on page 261.

Light reflection and refraction

⊡ Light reflects

- Light rays are reflected from mirrors in such a way that

   angle of incidence (*i*) = angle of reflection (*r*)

   The angles are measured to an imaginary line at 90° to the surface of the mirror. This line is called the **normal**. With a curved mirror it is difficult to measure the angle between the ray and the mirror.

- When you look in a plane mirror you see an **image** of yourself. The image is said to be **laterally inverted** because if you raise your right hand your image raises its left hand. The image is formed as far behind the mirror as you are in front of it and is the same size as you. The image cannot be projected onto a screen. It is known as a **virtual image**.

⊡ Uses of mirrors

- In a plane mirror the image is always the same size as the object. Examples of plane mirrors include household 'dressing' mirror, dental mirror for examining teeth, security mirror for checking under vehicles, periscope.

- Close to a **concave mirror** the image is **larger** than the object – these mirrors **magnify**. They are used in torches and car headlamps to produce a beam of light, make-up and shaving mirrors, satellite dishes.

- The image in a **convex mirror** is always **smaller** than the object Examples are a car driving mirror, shop security mirror.

⊡ Light refracts

- Light waves **slow down** when they travel from air into glass. If they are at an angle to the glass they bend towards the normal. When the light rays travel out of the glass into the air, their speed increases and they bend away from the normal.

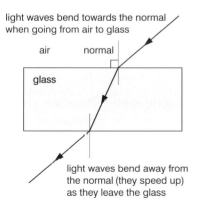

light waves bend towards the normal when going from air to glass

air   normal

glass

light waves bend away from the normal (they speed up) as they leave the glass

- Refraction is observed when a triangular prism (a glass or plastic block) is used to obtain the visible spectrum (see page 193). Lenses also refract light rays.

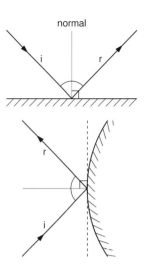

The angles of incidence and reflection are the same when a mirror reflects light. This type of curved mirror is known as a convex mirror.

A periscope uses reflection to allow you to see above your normal line of vision – or even round corners.

- **Convex (converging, positive) lenses** cause parallel rays of light to **converge** to the principal focus. They are used in magnifying glasses, cameras, telescopes, binoculars, microscopes, film projectors and spectacles.

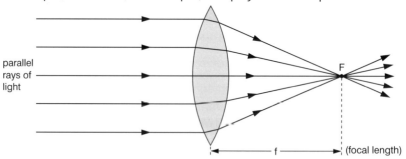

- **Concave (diverging, negative) lenses** make parallel rays of light **diverge** as if they were coming from the principal focus. You see concave lenses in spectacles, telescopes and correcting lenses in all optical equipment.

Total internal reflection occurs when a ray of light tries to leave the glass. If the angle of incidence equals or is greater than the critical angle the ray will be totally internally reflected.

⟳ Total internal reflection

- When rays of light pass from a **slow medium** to a **faster medium** they move **away** from the normal.

- As the angle of incidence increases, an angle is reached at which the light rays will have to leave with an angle of refraction greater than 90°! These rays cannot refract, so they are entirely reflected back inside the medium. This process is known as **total internal reflection**.

- The angle of incidence at which all refraction stops is known as the **critical angle** for the material. The critical angle of glass is 42°, the critical angle of water is 49°.

- Total internal reflection is used in **fibre–optic cables**. These are made up of large numbers of very thin, glass fibres. The light continues along the fibres by being constantly internally reflected. Fibre-optic cables are used in medical endoscopes for internal examination of the body.

- Telephone and TV communications systems are increasingly relying on fibre optics instead of the more traditional copper cables. Fibre-optic cables do not use electricity and the signals are carried by infrared rays. The signals are very clear as they don't suffer from electrical interference. Other advantages are that they are cheaper than the copper cables and can carry thousands of different signals down the same fibre at the same time.

Light does not escape from the fibre because it always hits it at an angle greater than the critical angle and is internally reflected.

QUESTION SPOTTER

Questions on total internal reflection are common. Typically you will have to draw or interpret simple ray diagrams in objects such as binoculars, periscopes, bicycle reflectors or endoscopes.

Optical fibres can transfer more information more quickly than copper cables. For example, they are used for broadband internet access. However, not everyone has access to broadband connections, often due to their location. For instance, it is easier and more economic to replace copper cables with optical fibres in built-up areas than in rural districts.

CHECK YOURSELF QUESTIONS

Q1 **a** Rays of light can be reflected and refracted. State one difference between reflection and refraction.

b The diagram shows a glass block and two rays of light.

glass block
X
a
Y
Ray 1   Ray 2

   i Complete the paths of the two rays as they pass into and then out of the glass block.
   ii What name is given to the angle marked a?
   iii What name is given to the line marked XY?

Q2 **a** Tom looks into the mirror. E is his eye and X an object.

E

   Complete the ray diagram to show clearly how Tom sees an image of X.
b Jane uses two mirrors to look at the back of her head. Explain how this works.

Q3 The diagram shows light entering a prism. Total internal reflection takes place at the inner surfaces of the prism.

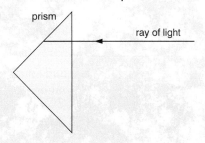

prism
ray of light

a Complete the path of the ray.
b Suggest one use for a prism like this.
c Complete the table about total internal reflection. Use T for total internal reflection or R for refraction.

angle of incidence/ degrees	total internal reflection (T) or refraction (R)
36	
42 (critical angle)	
46	

Answers are on page 261.

Sound waves

⟦⟧ Properties of sound waves

- Sound waves travel at about 340 m/s in the air – much slower than the speed of light. This explains why you almost always see the flash of lightning before hearing the crash of the thunder.

- Sound is caused by vibrations and travels as **longitudinal waves**. The compressions and rarefactions of sound waves result in small differences in air pressure.

- Sound waves travel faster through liquids than through air. Sound travels fastest through solids. This is because particles are linked most strongly in solids.

- High-**pitch** sounds have a high frequency whereas low-pitch sounds have a low frequency. The human ear can detect sounds with pitches ranging from 20 Hz to 20 000 Hz. Sound with frequencies above this range is known as **ultrasound**.

- Loud sounds have a high amplitude whereas quiet sounds have a low amplitude. Sound amplitude is measured in **decibels**.

⟦⟧ How do we use ultrasound?

- Ultrasound is used in echo sounding or SONAR (SOund NAvigation and Ranging). An echo sounder on a ship sends out ultrasonic waves which reflect off the bottom of the sea. The depth of the water can be calculated from the time taken for the echo to be received and the speed of sound in water.

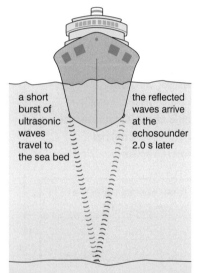

a short burst of ultrasonic waves travel to the sea bed

the reflected waves arrive at the echosounder 2.0 s later

WORKED EXAMPLE

A ship sends out an ultrasound wave and receives an echo in 2 seconds. If the speed of sound in water is 1500 m/s, how deep is the water?

Write down the formula:	speed = distance/time or $v = s/t$
Rearrange to make s the subject:	$s = v \times t$
Substitute the values for v and t:	$s = 1500 \times 2 = 3000$ m

This is the distance travelled by the sound wave.
Therefore the depth of the water must be half this. Depth = 1500 m.

- Ultrasound is used in medicine. Dense material, such as bone, reflects more ultrasound waves than less dense material, such as skin and tissue. Ultrasound waves have lower energy than X-rays and so are less likely to damage healthy cells.

⚡ A* EXTRA

▸ Ultrasound waves are reflected from the different layers of tissues in the body and so can produce quite clear images. They have lower energy than X-rays and so are less hazardous.

▸ However, they can be used to break down solid material such as kidney stones when they are highly focused.

The fetus reflects the ultrasound waves more than the surrounding amniotic fluids.

CHECK YOURSELF QUESTIONS

Q1 a i What causes a sound? **ii** Explain how sound travels through the air.

    b Astronauts in space cannot talk directly to each other. They have to speak to each other by radio. Explain why this is so.

    c Explain why sound travels faster through water than through air.

Q2 Ultrasonic waves are longitudinal waves.

    a What does the word 'ultrasonic' mean?

    b What does the word 'longitudinal' mean?

    c The waves travel through carbon dioxide more slowly than through air. How do the frequency and wavelength change when ultrasonic waves pass from air to carbon dioxide?

Q3 A fishing boat was using echo sounding to detect a shoal of fish. Short pulses of ultrasound were sent out from the boat. The echo from the shoal was detected 0.5 seconds later. How far away from the boat was the shoal of fish? (Sound waves travel through water at a speed of 1500 m/s.)

Answers are on page 262.

UNIT 19: THE EARTH AND BEYOND

REVISION SESSION 1

The solar system

⟲ What makes up the solar system?

■ The **solar system** is made up of the Sun and its planets. The planets are **satellites** of the Sun and are kept in **orbit** by the gravitational pull from the Sun. The orbits of the planets are slightly oval or elliptical.

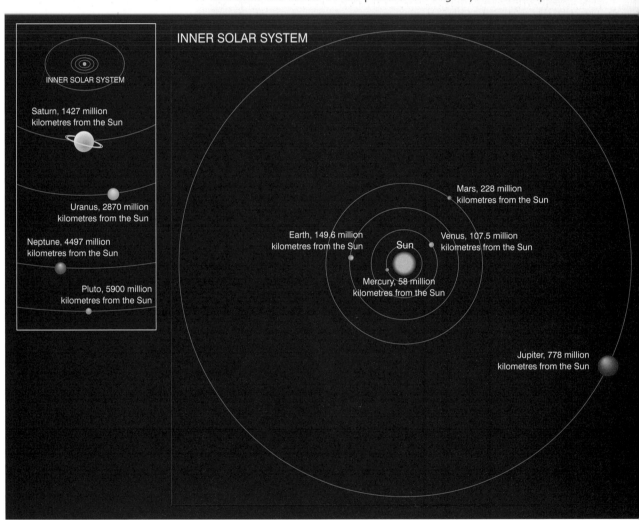

INNER SOLAR SYSTEM

INNER SOLAR SYSTEM

Saturn, 1427 million kilometres from the Sun

Uranus, 2870 million kilometres from the Sun

Neptune, 4497 million kilometres from the Sun

Pluto, 5900 million kilometres from the Sun

Mars, 228 million kilometres from the Sun

Earth, 149.6 million kilometres from the Sun

Sun

Venus, 107.5 million kilometres from the Sun

Mercury, 58 million kilometres from the Sun

Jupiter, 778 million kilometres from the Sun

Nine planets orbit the Sun.

■ **Asteroids** are fragments of rock, up to 1000 km in diameter, that orbit the Sun between the four inner planets and the five outer planets. The asteroids were formed at the same time as the Solar System.

■ **Comets** go round the Sun like planets but their orbits are much more elliptical. Comets spend much of their time too far away from the Sun to be seen. They are thought to be made from ice and rock. When they get close to the Sun some of the solid turns into gas, forming a 'tail' which points away from the Sun.

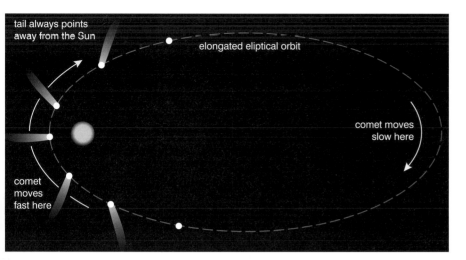

tail always points away from the Sun

elongated eliptical orbit

comet moves slow here

comet moves fast here

A comet moves round the Sun in an elliptical orbit.

⊡ Centripetal force

- Natural and artificial satellites orbit the Earth in a circle for the same reason that the planets orbit the Sun – **gravitational pull**.

- To keep an object moving in a circle, you have to constantly pull it towards the centre of that circle. A force that constantly pulls towards a centre is called a **centripetal force**.

- Near the Earth, gravity exerts a force that always acts towards its centre and keeps satellites like the Moon moving in a near-circular orbit around the Earth. Artificial satellites orbit the Earth for the same reason – and as they don't need motors or rockets to stay in such orbits, they can stay there for decades.

- At the right distance from the Earth, an unpowered orbit takes exactly 24 hours. This means that an artificial satellite orbiting above the Earth's equator and moving in the same direction as the Earth's spin, will appear to be flying over the same spot.

⊡ Galaxies

- The Sun is part of a group of stars called the Milky Way **galaxy**. The Milky Way is in the shape of a spiral.

- We can see other galaxies through telescopes. These other galaxies are so far away that it is difficult to see the individual stars, so earlier astronomers called them **nebulae** (singular: nebula) meaning 'a bright cloudy spot'. These days, we can see these galaxies properly, and the word nebula now usually means a cloud of gas where stars are being born. Many nebulae are formed by stars exploding.

Life-cycle of a star

Birth (thousands of millions of years)	Life (tens of millions of years)	Death (millions of years)
• The star starts as a huge cloud of hydrogen gas and dust. • Gravity pulls the hydrogen atoms closer together. • The gas gets hotter as the cloud gets smaller and more concentrated. • In the very high temperatures created, the hydrogen atoms join together to form helium atoms in a process called nuclear fusion. Large amounts of energy are released in this process. • The core sends out light and other radiation and the cool, outer layers are blown away, sometimes forming planets around the new star.	• Huge gravitational forces pull the outer parts of the star towards its core. • The energy produced by the nuclear fusion ensures that the gases on the outside are very hot. • The pressure exerted by the hot gases exactly balances the force of gravity. • This balance continues for millions of years until all the hydrogen has been used up and the nuclear reactions stop. • Some stars appear red-orange but hotter stars appear blue-white.	• The hydrogen in the star's core gets used up and the core starts to cool. • The star then starts to collapse and the core gets hotter again very quickly, enabling other nuclear fusion reactions to start. • A sudden surge of radiation is produced and the star expands to form a red giant or red supergiant. • In a medium-sized star like the Sun, the nuclear fusion reactions finish and the core collapses under gravity and the red giant forms a white dwarf star. • In a large star, when the core collapses there is a sudden explosion and the red supergiant forms a supernova. A supernova is brighter than a whole galaxy of stars. A very dense core is left behind becoming a neutron star and, if it is very small and dense, a black hole.

QUESTION SPOTTER

Questions on the life cycle of a star will usually require an extended written answer and be worth 3 marks or more. Divide your answer into three parts: birth, life and death. Remember that what happens at the death of the star will depend on its size.

IDEAS AND EVIDENCE

This whole section is about interpreting a limited amount of data – scientists cannot travel all over the universe to conduct experiments! Ideas change as new evidence is gathered, sometimes because a new technique is invented, such as using radio waves for observation as well as visible light. Sometimes the theory suggests new ideas that experimenters can use to guide their observations, such as searching for black holes.

CHECK YOURSELF QUESTIONS

Q1 How does a normal star produce energy?

Q2 The list contains the stages in the life cycle of a star. Arrange them in the correct order.
*supernova   clouds of hydrogen gas
red supergiant   blue star*

Q3 a A satellite moves around the Earth at a constant speed in a circular orbit.
i What force is acting on the satellite and
ii what is the direction of the force?
b Some satellites travel in geostationary orbits. Explain what is meant by a geostationary orbit.

Answers are on page 263.

REVISION SESSION 2 — How did the Universe begin?

⬚ Red shift

- If a star is moving away from the Earth, light waves will reach the Earth with a lower frequency than that emitted by the star. This change in frequency is called a **red shift**.

- Light from all the distant galaxies shows a red shift, so it follows that all these galaxies are moving away from us. In fact, **all galaxies are moving away from each other.** The Universe is expanding.

continuous light spectrum

hydrogen spectrum

light from a distant star

red-shifted hydrogen spectrum

⚡ A* EXTRA

One of the pieces of evidence that suggests the universe is expanding comes from examination of the emission spectra of hydrogen from distant stars. The lines in the spectra are at lower frequency than on Earth. This shift towards the red end of the spectrum ('red shift') indicates that the distant stars are moving away from the Earth.

The top picture shows the spectrum of white light. The second picture shows the spectrum produced by hydrogen when it glows. The bottom picture shows the spectrum of hydrogen from a star seen through a telescope. The pattern is shifted towards the red end. This red shift shows that the star is moving away from us.

⬚ The Big Bang theory

One explanation for the Universe expanding is that everything in the Universe originated from the same point, which exploded in the **Big Bang**. Since this explosion, the Universe has been expanding and cooling. Calculations suggest that the Big Bang could have occurred between 11 and 18 billion years ago. There are three main possibilities as to what will happen to the Universe:

1. **The Universe will keep on expanding.** The galaxies move fast enough to overcome the forces of gravity acting between them.

2. **The expansion will slow down and stop.** The galaxies will remain in a fixed position. The gravitational forces will exactly balance the 'expansion forces'.

3. **The Universe will start to contract.** The force of gravity between the galaxies will overcome the forces causing expansion and pull them back together again.

💡 QUESTION SPOTTER

Questions on the future of the Universe will usually require an extended answer. You should refer to the three possibilities and mention the importance of the differences between the competing forces acting on the galaxies.

❓ CHECK YOURSELF QUESTIONS

Q1 What is the red shift?

Q2 What is the evidence that supports the Big Bang theory?

Answers are on page 263.

UNIT 20: RADIOACTIVITY

  Unstable atoms

⌂ Inside the atom

■ Inside the atom the central **nucleus** of positively charged **protons** and neutral **neutrons** is surrounded by shells, or orbits, of **electrons**. Most nuclei are very stable, but some 'decay' and break apart into more stable nuclei. This breaking apart is called **nuclear fission**. Atoms whose nuclei do this are **radioactive**.

■ When a nucleus decays it emits:
- alpha (α) particles
- beta (β) particles
- gamma (γ) rays.

■ A stream of these rays is referred to as **ionising radiation** (often called nuclear radiation, or just 'radiation' for short).

QUESTION SPOTTER

You will often have to describe the differences between α, β and γ rays. You will be asked what the rays are, what materials they can penetrate and if they can be deflected.

alpha radiation

beta radiation

gamma radiation

skin or sheet of paper   2 mm of aluminium   thick lead or concrete

	alpha (α)	**beta (β)**	**gamma (γ)**
Description	A positively charged particle, identical to a helium nucleus (two protons and two neutrons)	A negatively charged particle, identical to an electron	Electromagnetic radiation. Uncharged
Penetration	4–10 cm of air. Stopped by a sheet of paper	About 1 m of air. Stopped by a few mm of aluminium	No limit in air. Stopped by several cm of lead or several metres of concrete
Effect of electric and magnetic fields	Deflected	Deflected considerably	Unaffected – not deflected

How was the 'nuclear' atom discovered?

IDEAS AND EVIDENCE

- In the 19th century, many scientists believed that atoms were just spheres of positive charge embedded with specks of negative charge (electrons).

- In a crucial experiment in 1911, a stream of alpha particles was aimed at a piece of gold foil a few atoms thick. Most of the alpha particles passed through the foil undeflected, showing that most of the atom is empty space. Some alpha particles passed through but were deflected and a few bounced back as if they had done a U-turn.

- The deflections meant that the atom's mass and charge isn't spread out but must be clustered together.

- The very small number of U-turns must have been caused by 'head-on' collisions with a concentration of mass and positive charge. This meant that such clusters were very small.

- Altogether, this showed that an atom has a tiny cluster of positive charge – a **nucleus**.

In this experiment, it is the *anomalous* results that hold the key to what happens. If the experimenters had just looked for the expected results and not checked *all* angles, this important discovery would not have been made.

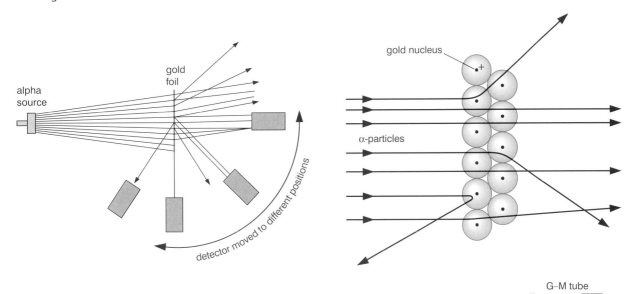

gold foil

alpha source

detector moved to different positions

gold nucleus

α-particles

Background radiation

- All ionising radiation is invisible to the naked eye, but it affects photographic plates. Individual particles of ionising radiation can be detected using a Geiger–Müller tube.

- There is *always* ionising radiation present. This is called **background radiation**. Background radiation is caused by radioactivity in soil, rocks and materials like concrete, radioactive gases in the atmosphere and cosmic rays from the Sun.

G–M tube

Radioactivity is measured using a Geiger–Muller tube linked to a counter.

Half-life

- The **activity** of a radioactive source is the number of ionising particles it emits each second. Over time, fewer nuclei are left in the source to decay, so the activity drops. The time taken for half the radioactive atoms to decay is called the **half-life**.

- Starting with a pure sample of radioactive atoms, after one half-life half the atoms will have decayed. The remaining undecayed atoms still have the same chance of decaying as before, so after a second half-life half of the remaining atoms will have decayed. After two half-lives a quarter of the atoms will remain undecayed.

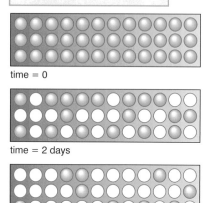

time = 0

time = 2 days

time = 4 days

The half-life is 2 days. Half the number of radioactive atoms decays in 2 days.

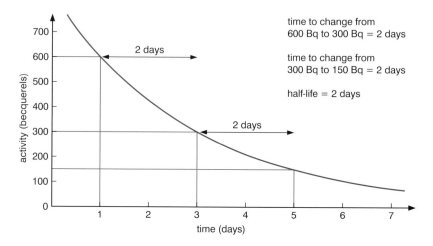

time to change from 600 Bq to 300 Bq = 2 days

time to change from 300 Bq to 150 Bq = 2 days

half-life = 2 days

WORKED EXAMPLE

A radioactive element is detected by a Geiger–Müller tube and counter as having an activity of 400 counts per minute. Three hours later the count is 50 counts per minute. What is the half-life of the radioactive element?

Write down the activity and progressively halve it.
Each halving of the activity is one half-life:

0	400 counts
1 half-life	200 counts
2 half-lives	100 counts
3 half-lives	50 counts

3 hours therefore corresponds to 3 half-lives and 1 hour therefore corresponds to 1 half-life.

Nuclear equations

- You can write down nuclear changes as **nuclear equations**. Each nucleus is represented by its chemical symbol with two extra numbers written before it. Here is the symbol for Radium-226:

the top number is the **mass number** (the total number of protons and neutrons)

$$^{226}_{88}\text{Ra}$$

the bottom number is the **atomic number** (the number of protons)

■ The mass numbers and atomic numbers must balance on both sides of a nuclear equation.

Alpha decay – the nucleus emits an α-particle (2 protons and 2 neutrons)

radium-226 (parent nucleus) → radon-222 (daughter nucleus)

alpha particle

$$^{226}_{88}\text{Ra} \rightarrow \,^{222}_{86}\text{Rn} + \,^{4}_{2}\alpha$$

Beta decay – a neutron changes into a proton in the the nucleus

polonium-218 (parent nucleus) → astatine-218 (daughter nucleus)

beta particle

$$^{218}_{84}\text{Po} \rightarrow \,^{218}_{85}\text{At} + \,^{0}_{-1}\beta$$

CHECK YOURSELF QUESTIONS

Q1 The diagram shows some of the results of an experiment using some very thin gold foil that was carried out by the scientist Sir Ernest Rutherford.

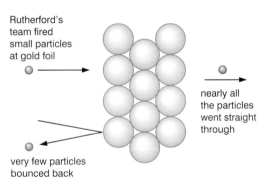

Rutherford's team fired small particles at gold foil

nearly all the particles went straight through

very few particles bounced back

a What type of radioactive particle did Rutherford use?
b What did Rutherford deduce from the observation that most of the particles passed straight through the foil?
c What did Rutherford deduce from the observation that some particles bounced back from the foil?

Q2 The graph shows how a the activity of a sample of sodium-24 changes with time. Activity is measured in becquerels (Bq).

a Sodium-24 has an atomic number of 11 and a mass number of 24. What is the composition of the nucleus of a sodium-24 atom?
b Use the graph to work out the half-life of the sodium 24.

Q3 The following equation shows what happens when a nucleus of sodium-24 decays.

$$^{24}_{11}\text{Na} \rightarrow \,^{x}_{y}\text{Mg} + \,^{0}_{-1}\beta$$

a What type of nuclear radiation is produced?
b What are the numerical values of x and y?

Answers are on page 263.

Uses and dangers of radioactivit

⬚ Radioactivity is dangerous

■ Alpha, beta and gamma radiation can all damage living cells. Alpha particles, due to their strong ability to ionise other particles, are particularly dangerous to human tissue. Gamma radiation is dangerous because of its high penetrating power. Nevertheless, radiation can be very useful – it just needs to be used *safely*.

⬚ Uses of radioactivity

■ Gamma rays can be used to kill bacteria. This is used in **sterilising** medical equipment and in preserving food. The food can be treated after it has been packaged.

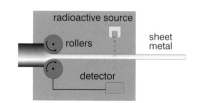

Sheet thickness control.

■ A **smoke alarm** includes a small radioactive source that emits alpha radiation. The radiation produces ions in the air which conduct a small electric current. If a smoke particle absorbs the alpha particles, it reduces the number of ions in the air, and the current drops. This sets off the alarm.

■ Beta particles are used to monitor the **thickness** of paper or metal. The number of beta particles passing through the material is related to the thickness of the material.

■ A gamma source is placed on one side of a weld and a photographic plate on the other side. Weaknesses in the weld will show up on the photographic plate.

■ In **radiotherapy** high doses of radiation are fired at cancer cells to kill them.

Tracers detect leaks.

■ **Tracers** are radioactive substances with half-lives and radiation types that suit the job they are used for. The half-life must be long enough for the tracer to spread out and to be detected after use but not so long that it stays in the system and causes damage.
  • **Medical tracers** are used to detect blockages in vital organs. A gamma camera is used to monitor the passage of the tracer through the body.
  • **Agricultural tracers** monitor the flow of nutrients through a plant.
  • **Industrial tracers** can measure the flow of liquid and gases through pipes to identify leakages.

★ IDEAS AND EVIDENCE

Using radiation to sterilise food has proved highly unpopular. People have the idea that the food would 'become radioactive'. How could a scientist demonstrate that this is not true? How could a scientist present the information to the public to help understanding? Is this a situation where what the public feels is more important than what a scientist would describe as 'the truth'? You should be able to give points on either side of the argument.

⬚ Radioactive dating

■ Igneous rock contains small quantities of uranium-238 – a type of uranium that decays with a half-life of 4500 million years, eventually forming lead. The ratio of lead to uranium in a rock sample can be used to calculate the age of the rock. For example, a piece of rock with equal numbers of uranium and lead atoms in it must be 4500 million years old – but this would be unlikely as the Earth is only 4000 million years old!

- Carbon in living material contains a constant, small amount of the radioactive isotope **carbon–14**, which has a half life of 5700 years. When the living material dies the carbon-14 atoms slowly decay. The ratio of carbon-14 atoms to the non-radioactive carbon-12 atoms can be used to calculate the age of the plant or animal material. This method is called **radioactive carbon dating**.

⎕ Nuclear fission

- In a nuclear power station atoms of **uranium–235** are bombarded with neutrons and split into two smaller atoms (barium and krypton). This fission of the atoms releases energy, other neutrons and gamma rays.

- The products of the fission are radioactive and so need to be disposed of very carefully.

- The amount of energy produced is considerable – a single kilogram of uranium-235 produces approximately the same amount of energy as 2 000 000 kg of coal!

- Don't confuse this process with the nuclear reactions taking place in the Sun. In the Sun, small atoms combine together to form larger atoms in a process known as **nuclear fusion**. This process also produces huge amounts of energy.

This woman's body was preserved in a bog in Denmark. Radioactive carbon-14 dating showed that she had been there for over 2000 years.

CHECK YOURSELF QUESTIONS

Q1 What type of radiation is used in
  a smoke detectors,
  b thickness measurement,
  c weld checking?

Q2 This question is about tracers.
  a What is a tracer?
  b The table below shows the half-life of some radioactive isotopes.

Radioactive isotope	Half-life
lawrencium-257	8 seconds
sodium-24	15 hours
sulphur-35	87 days
carbon-14	5700 years

Using the information in the table only, state which one of the isotopes is most suitable to be used as a tracer in medicine. Give a reason for your choice.

Q3 a When uranium-238 in a rock sample decays what element is eventually produced?
  b Explain how the production of this new element enables the age of the rock sample to be determined.

Answers are on page 264.

Exam tips

- **Read each question carefully**; this includes looking in detail at any **diagrams, graphs** or **tables**. Remember that any information you are given is there to help you to answer the question. Underline or circle the **key words** in the question and **make sure you answer the question that is being asked** rather than the one you wish had been asked!

- Make sure that you understand the meaning of the **'command words'** in the questions. For example:
  - **'Describe'** is used when you have to give the main feature(s) of, for example, a process or structure;
  - **'Explain'** is used when you have to give reasons, e.g. for some experimental results;
  - **'Suggest'** is used when there may be more than one possible answer, or when you will not have learnt the answer but have to use the knowledge you do have to come up with a sensible one;
  - **'Calculate'** means that you have to work out an answer in figures.

- Look at the **number of marks** allocated to each question and also the **space provided** to guide you as to the length of your answer. You need to make sure you include at least as many points in your answer as there are marks, and preferably more. If you really do need more space to answer than provided, then use the nearest available space, e.g. at the bottom of the page, making sure you write down which question you are answering. **Beware of continually writing too much because it probably means you are not really answering the questions.**

- Don't spend so long on some questions that you don't have time to finish the paper. You should spend approximately **one minute per mark**. If you are really stuck on a question, leave it, finish the rest of the paper and come back to it at the end. Even if you eventually have to guess at an answer, you stand a better chance of gaining some marks than if you leave it blank.

- In short answer questions, or multiple-choice type questions, **don't write more than you are asked for**. In some exams, examiners apply the rule that they only mark the first part of the answer written if there is too much. This means that the later part of the answer will not be looked at. In other exams you would not gain any marks, even if the first part of your answer is correct, if you've written down something incorrect in the later part of your answer. This just shows that you haven't really understood the question or are guessing.

- **In calculations always show your working.** Even if your final answer is incorrect you may still gain some marks if part of your attempt is correct. If you just write down the final answer and it is incorrect, you will get no marks at all. Also in calculations you should write down your answers to as many **significant figures** as are used in the question. You may also lose marks if you don't use the correct **units**.

- In some questions, particularly short answer questions, answers of only one or two words may be sufficient, but in longer questions you should aim to use **good English** and **scientific** language to make your answer as clear as possible.

- If it helps you to answer clearly, don't be afraid to also use **diagrams** or **flow charts** in your answers.

- When you've finished your exam, **check through** to make sure you've answered all the questions. Cover over your answers and read through the questions again and check your answers are as good as you can make them.

☐ Exam question and student's answers (Foundation Tier)

1 The diagram shows some blood cells.

red blood cells

cell **A**

a) Write down the name of cell **A**.

White blood cell. ✔ (1)

b) Red blood cells carry oxygen around the body.

i) Where do red blood cells **collect** oxygen?

From the lungs. ✔ (1)

ii) Red blood cells are adapted to collect and carry oxygen.
Write about **one** way that a red blood cell is adapted for its job.

It has a 'dip' on each side so it can carry more oxygen. ✔ ✗

(2)

c) Blood absorbs digested food from the small intestine.

i) Look at the diagram. It shows part of the digestive system.

Food passes from the mouth to the small intestine.
Describe the path it takes.
You can draw on the diagram to help you answer
Include the names of the parts that food passes through.

mouth

small intestine

Food travels down the oesophagus then into the stomach. ✔ ✔
It leaves the stomach and then goes into the small intestine. ✔ (2)

ii) Food moves through the small intestine by peristalsis.
   Explain what is meant by **peristalsis**.

   Peristalsis means that the muscles in the small intestine squeeze the food ✓

   along. _____ (1)

d) Food has to be physically and chemically digested before it can enter the blood.

   i) What happens to food when it is **physically digested**?

      It gets broken down into smaller pieces. ✓

      _____ (1)

   ii) Write about what happens to food when it is **chemically digested**.
       Include what causes chemical digestion and what happens to the food.

       ✓ Enzymes attack the food breaking it down. _____

       _____

       _____ (2)

                                                        (Total 10 marks)

                                        (8/10)

□ *How to score full marks*

a)   This is the correct answer for this straightforward start to the question.

b) i) This is an acceptable answer. More specific answers, such as 'alveoli', would also be correct.

   ii) There are two marks available, one for describing an adaptation of a red blood cell and one for explaining how this helps. One mark has been awarded here for the description of the biconcave shape. **Wherever possible use the correct scientific terms in examination questions but if you've forgotten the correct term, then you may still get the mark for a correct description.** The second mark has not been awarded. Many candidates have the misconception that oxygen is carried in the 'dip'. It is not; instead, the biconcave shape increases the surface area for oxygen absorption. Other acceptable answers include the lack of a nucleus allowing more room for haemoglobin or the cells being small or flexible to fit through small capillaries.

c) i) Both marks have been gained. The candidate could also have answered by a labelled drawing on the diagram. If other parts of the digestive system that are not between the mouth and small intestine, such as the large intestine, had been included in the answer then marks would have been lost.

   ii) The key idea here is that muscles are involved. The candidate has given a correct answer.

d) i) The candidate has answered correctly.

   ii) The candidate has gained one mark for explaining that enzymes cause chemical digestion. The second part of the answer, describing what happens to food, is too vague to gain a mark. The important difference between physical and chemical digestion is that in chemical digestion large molecules are broken down into smaller molecules. This is to make them soluble and able to move from the small intestine into the blood.

•   This candidate has gained 8 marks out of a possible 10. This corresponds to a grade C answer on this foundation tier question.

2 Read the following passage.

> In 1802 a book by William Paley was published called *Natural Theology*. Paley was a theologian, someone who studies religion. In his book he said that because living things are so complicated they must have had a designer. That designer was God.
>
> In 1859 Charles Darwin's book, *The Origin of Species by means of Natural Selection*, was published. In it he explained how animals and plants can change into new types. This can take a very long time and is called evolution.
>
> Darwin's ideas upset many people because he showed how new types of animals and plants could have appeared instead of God simply creating them.

Use information from the passage, as well as your own knowledge, to help you answer the questions.

a) William Paley said that organs like the eye are so complicated that they must have been designed by God.

If eyes were not designed but have evolved, why is it so difficult to find evidence of how they evolved?

<u>There aren't any fossils of eyes. ✓ Fossils only form from hard body parts like</u>
<u>bones, not soft parts like eyes. ✓</u>

_____ (2)

b) Darwin's book upset many people and caused a lot of argument. Why didn't Paley's book have the same effect?

<u>In those days lots of people believed in God so people weren't upset by Paley's</u>
<u>book. ✓</u> _____ (1)

c) More people accept Darwin's ideas about evolution today than did so one hundred years ago.
Suggest why.

<u>There have been lots of scientific discoveries that support the theory of evolution. ✓</u>
<u>Fewer people believe in God nowadays. ✓</u>

_____
_____
_____ (3)

(Total 6 marks)

(5/6)

This whole question is about 'ideas and evidence' in science. In these types of questions, sometimes you may be familiar with the subject matter but other times you may not be. **Make sure that you read the question, and any information you are given, very carefully. Remember that even if you are unfamiliar with the topic you should still be able to tackle the question.**

a) The candidate has given a detailed answer gaining both marks.

b) There are different ways of answering this

question but the important idea is that Paley's ideas were not controversial, unlike Darwin's.

c) The candidate has made two valid points, gaining two marks. Another possible answer could be the idea that evolution is no longer such a radical or shocking theory as more people are familiar with it, as it has been accepted and taught for many years.

● This candidate has gained 5 marks out of a possible 6. This corresponds to a grade A answer on this higher tier question.

⌐¬Questions to try

I This question is about hormones in plants and humans.

a) Look at the list of processes in plants.

FOUNDATION

  A absorbing light
  B absorbing water
  C flowering
  D fruit ripening
  E giving out oxygen
  F pollination

Which **two** processes are known to be controlled by hormones?

Choose **two** letters from the list. (2)

b) Jack puts some growing seedlings in a box.

The box has a hole in one side.

He leaves the seedlings for a week.

start

after a week

i) Look at the diagram. Describe **two** ways that the seedlings are different after a week.

ii) The seedlings are responding to a stimulus. (2)

Suggest what the stimulus is. (1)

iii) This response is controlled by a plant hormone.

Write down the name of the hormone. (1)

c) Plant hormones are used in selective weed killers.

They make the shoots of weeds grow faster than normal.

Explain how this can kill weeds. (1)

d) Hormones in humans are different from hormones in plants.

i)   Where are human hormones made? (1)

ii) How do human hormones travel around the body? (1)

e) Gemma has diabetes. This is because her pancreas does not produce enough insulin.

i)   Look at the list.

A Gemma's blood sugar level stays too high.
B Gemma's blood sugar level stays too low.
C Gemma's blood sugar level changes too much.

How does diabetes affect Gemma's blood sugar level?

Choose **A**, **B** or **C** from the list. (1)

ii) Gemma takes insulin to control her diabetes.

Describe how she takes insulin. (1)

(Total 11 marks)

2   Many people grow tomatoes in glasshouses.

Whiteflies are insect pests. They feed on tomato leaves.

They can be controlled by small wasps.

The wasps lay their eggs inside the young whiteflies.

When the wasp eggs hatch, the young wasps feed inside the young whiteflies, killing them.

HIGHER

wasp

whiteflies

a) Look at the pyramids of **numbers**.

A
B
C
D

□ whiteflies
■ tomatoes

Which pyramid shows the pyramid of numbers for the tomatoes
and whiteflies **before** the whiteflies are controlled?   (1)

b) The diagram shows a pyramid of **biomass** when the wasps are used.

wasps
whiteflies
tomatoes

Pyramids of biomass almost always get smaller as you go up the
food chain.

Write about pyramids of biomass.

Include in your answer:

● what they show
● why they get smaller as you go up
● ideas about energy in the food chain.   (4)

c) Another way to control the whiteflies is by using a chemical pesticide.

Write about the advantages and disadvantages of using chemical pesticides.   (3)

d) i) Cod are a type of fish.
        The number of cod in the waters around Britain is falling.

        Look at the list.

        A have fewer fishing boats
        B make the holes in fishing nets smaller
        C reduce the weight of fish any boat is allowed to catch
        D stop fishing boats going to sea on some days

        Which **one** of the changes would **not** help to protect the
        number of cod?   (1)

    ii) Some sea fish contain pesticides which have been used on farmland.
        The concentration of the pesticides in the fish is much greater than
        the concentration in sea water.
        Explain why.   (2)

                                                              (Total 11 marks)

Answers are on pages 265–266

I   Katie and Louise investigate the reaction between marble chips (calcium carbonate) and hydrochloric acid.

Carbon dioxide is given off during the reaction. They measure the mass of the reaction mixture every 30 seconds during the experiment.

Look at the diagram. It shows the apparatus they use.

After every reading, Katie works out the total mass of the carbon dioxide given off.

They do the experiment again.

They use the same amount of acid and marble.

This time they use **hot** hydrochloric acid instead of cold.

Look at the graph. It shows their results.

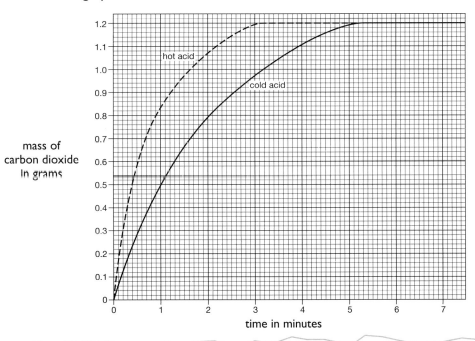

i) Look at the curve for the **cold acid**.

What mass of carbon dioxide is given off after 2 minutes?

_____ 0.8 ✔ _____ g (1)

ii) Look at the curve for the **hot acid.**

How long does it take for the reaction to finish?

_____ 3 ✔ _____ minutes (1)

b) i) The reaction with **hot** acid is faster than the reaction with **cold** acid.

How can you tell from the two curves?

The curve is steeper. ✔ _____

_____ (1)

ii) Explain why the reaction with hot acid is faster. Use ideas about particles.

The particles in the hot acid are moving faster so there will be more collisions. ∧

_____

_____ (2)

c) The reaction is slower with cold acid.

Write about other ways of making the reaction go **more slowly**.

Use acid of lower concentration. ✔∧ _____

_____

_____ (2)

d) Hot acid reacts faster than cold acid with marble.

Both reactions make 1.20 g of carbon dioxide.

Explain why.

They both have the same amount of marble and acid. ✔ _____

_____ (1)

e) Marble chips are left in the flask at the end of both experiments.

Why do both reactions stop?

The chemicals have been used up. ✗ _____ (1)

f) Look at the equation.

$$CaCO_3 + 2HCl \rightarrow CaCl_2 + CO_2 + H_2O$$

Write down the formula for one reactant.

<u>CaCO₃</u> ✓ _____ (1)

(Total 10 marks)

 7/10

 How to score full marks

a) i) The graph has been read correctly.

   ii) The graph has been read correctly. The candidate has not mixed up the two graphs which is a common mistake.

b) i) The candidate has correctly referred to the steepness (or gradient) of the curve.

b) ii) One mark has been missed. **The candidate has given two separate points to try to gain the two marks available.** One mark is gained for saying that the particles are moving faster in the hot acid. The second mark is either for saying that there will be more energy available in the collisions or that there will be more effective collisions.

c) **The question has asked for 'other ways' and two marks have been given. This suggests that you should give at least two ways.** Using acid of lower concentration is one way, using larger lumps of marble (lower surface area) would be another way.

d) The correct answer has been given. **This important piece of information is given in the question and the candidate has spotted this. Remember the information you are given is there for a reason.**

e) Reactions stop when one or other of the reactants gets used up. In this case the question says that some of the marble chips are left in the flask so it must be the acid that has been used up.

f) The candidate has answered this correctly. The other possibility would be the hydrochloric acid with formula HCl.

● A mark of 7/10 corresponds to a grade C on this foundation tier question.

2 This question is about compounds that contain carbon.

Look at the displayed formulae of ethene and ethanol.

ethene   ethanol

a) Ethanol is an alcohol made by fermentation.

Write about fermentation.

Include in your answer

- the chemical equation for fermentation
- the conditions needed for fermentation
- why fermentation cannot take place at high temperatures.

$C_6H_{12}O_6 \rightarrow 2C_2H_5OH + 2CO_2$ ✔

Fermentation of glucose ($C_6H_{12}O_6$) occurs in solution in the presence of yeast ✔

which provides a source of enzymes. The optimum temperature is about 35°C. ∧

_____

_____

_____

_____ (4)

b) The atoms in ethene are held together by covalent bonds.

Draw the 'dot and cross' diagram for ethene.

You only need to include the electrons in the outer shell of carbon and hydrogen.

(2)

c) Ethene has a simple molecular structure.

Ethene does not dissolve in water.

Write down **two other** physical properties of a substance with a simple molecular structure.

1. It has a low boiling point. ✔

2. It is inflammable. ✗ (2)

d) On analysis, 8.4 g of a hydrocarbon was found to contain 7.2 g of carbon.

i) What is the mass of hydrogen in the hydrocarbon analysed?

1.2 g ✔ (1)

ii) How many moles of hydrogen atoms, H, are present?

The relative atomic mass, A_r, of H is 1.

$\frac{1.2}{1} = 1.2$ moles ✔

(1)

iii) How many moles of carbon atoms, C, are present in the hydrocarbon?

The relative atomic mass, A_r, of C is 12.

$\frac{7.2}{12} = 0.6$ moles ✔

(1)

iv) The hydrocarbon has a relative formula mass, M_r, of 42.

The hydrocarbon has the formula C_xH_y.

What are the values of **x** and **y**?

C   0.6 moles   H   1.2 moles

Simplest formula is CH_2 (mass = 14)

42/14 = 3 ∴ formula must be C_3H_6

x = 3   and **y** = 6 ✔ (1)

(Total 12 marks)

10/12

a) The candidate has given a good answer. The chemical equation is correct. Three conditions have been given for fermentation: it occurs in solution; in the presence of yeast (which provides enzymes) and at a temperature of about 35°C. However, a maximum of 2 marks is given for this section. **The candidate has missed the last mark by not responding to the third bullet point. This is a common error in questions like this.** At high temperatures the enzymes in the yeast become denatured and cease to operate.

b) The 'dot and cross' diagram has been drawn correctly. Note that the carbon atoms have 4 electrons in the outer shell and the hydrogen atoms have only one. The double bond involves sharing 4 electrons between the two carbon atoms; the single bonds involve the sharing of 2 electrons.

c) The candidate has dropped a mark here. Physical properties of simple molecular structures include: low melting point, low boiling point and non-electrolyte. Flammability is a chemical property and not a physical property.

d) i) The subtraction (8.4 − 7.2) has been done correctly. **The mark would not have been awarded if the unit had been missed.**

ii) The number of moles has been correctly calculated by dividing the mass by the relative atomic mass. **The candidate has been sensible and shown the working out.**

iii) Again, the calculation has been done correctly and the working shown.

iv) The candidate has worked out the correct values for x and y. The ratio of the moles of carbon to hydrogen is 1:2 and so the simplest formula must be CH_2 (formula mass = 14). Knowing that the relative formula mass is 42 means that there are 3 CH_2 units in the molecule and its formula must be C_3H_6.

- A mark of 10 out of 12 corresponds to a grade A on this higher tier question.

Questions to try

I This question is about polymerisation.

Polymerisation changes many small molecules into large molecules.

FOUNDATION

small molecules ——polymerisation——▶ large molecules

Look at the list

    alkane
    butane
    methane
    monomer
    polymer

a) i) Write down the name of the large molecule made by polymerisation. Choose from the list. (1)

ii) Write down the name of the small molecules used in polymerisation. Choose from the list. (1)

iii) What conditions are needed for polymerisation? (2)

b) Plastics are used for making things. For each plastic given below choose a use from the list.

adhesive
insulation
plastic bags

Plastic	Use
polythene	
epoxy resin	
polystyrene	

(2)

c) People throw away a lot of plastics. This causes problems.

Mark works for the council. He has to get rid of a lot of waste plastic.

One way is to recycle it. Write about one other way of getting rid of waste plastic.
You should include

● How plastics can be got rid of;
● The problems this can cause.

(1 mark for using correct scientific words.)

(2 + 1)
(Total 9 marks)

2 This question is about ideas and evidence in science.

The ancient Greeks first thought of the idea of atoms. They had no experimental evidence for atoms.

In 1808, John Dalton worked out his atomic theory. He used the results of his own experiments and those of another scientist called Lavoisier.

a) John Dalton's theory was more scientific than the ancient Greeks' theory.
Suggest why. (1)

b) John Dalton found out about Lavoisier's work from scientific journals.
Write down one other way that modern-day scientists find out about each other's work. (1)

c) 50 years later, some important scientists still did not accept Dalton's theory.
Suggest why. (1)

(Total 3 marks)

3   Nitrogen monoxide is a gas which is made inside a motor car
engine.
This gas pollutes the air.

HIGHER

a)   Nitrogen and oxygen react together to make nitrogen monoxide.

$$N_2 + O_2 \longrightarrow 2NO$$

   i)   The rate of this reaction increases as the temperature inside
a car engine increases.
Explain why. Use ideas about collisions between particles.   (2)

   ii)   The rate of this reaction increases as the concentration of
oxygen increases.
Explain why. Use ideas about collisions between particles.   (2)

b)   Look at the equation for the reaction between nitrogen and oxygen.
It shows the displayed formulae of the reactants and the product.

This reaction is endothermic.
Explain why. Use ideas about bond breaking and bond making.   (3)

c)   A catalytic converter removes nitrogen monoxide from the exhaust
gases of a motor car.
The nitrogen monoxide reacts with carbon monoxide inside the
converter.
Nitrogen and carbon dioxide are made.

   i)   Write down the balanced symbol equation for this reaction.   (2)

   ii)   A catalyst in the converter speeds up the reaction.
When the catalyst is a powder the reaction is even faster.
Explain why. Use ideas about collisions between particles.   (2)

(Total 11 marks)

Answers are on pages 266–267

⬚ Exam question and student's answers (Foundation Tier)

I a) Look at the diagram of the power station.

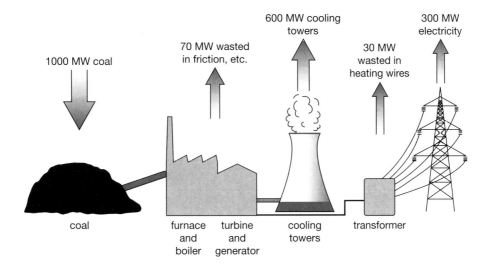

1000 MW coal

70 MW wasted in friction, etc.

600 MW cooling towers

30 MW wasted in heating wires

300 MW electricity

| coal | furnace and boiler | turbine and generator | cooling towers | transformer |

The power station uses coal and generates electricity.

i) The energy is transferred from coal to electricity.

Write about what happens in the

- furnace and boiler
- turbine and generator.

The coal is burnt in the furnace ✓ and the energy is used to boil the water in the ✓ boiler. The steam from the boiler turns the turbine ✓ which generates the electricity. Λ

────────────────────────────────────(4)

ii) Calculate the efficiency of the power station.

% efficiency = useful output x 100
                          input

$\frac{300}{1000}$ x 100 = 30

answer _____ 30 ✓✓ _____ % (2)

b) Power stations are often a long way from homes and factories.

Homes and factories need electricity.

The electricity is carried along a system of wires.

Write down the name of this system.

National Grid ✔

(1)

c) Electricity is transmitted from the power station at high voltage. Suggest why.

It is cheaper. ✘

(1)

d) Vicki uses electricity to heat her house.

Look at the diagram.

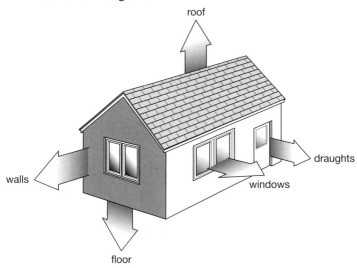

roof

draughts

walls

windows

floor

The diagram shows how heat escapes from her house.

Vicki wants to **insulate** her house.

Write about the different ways she could do this.

✔
Cavity foam insulation will stop heat escaping through the walls.
✔
Double glazing will stop heat escaping through the windows.

(3)

(Total 11 marks)

8/11

How to score full marks

a) i) **The candidate has followed the bullet point guidance** and has scored 3 of the 4 marks. Marks have been awarded for what happens in the furnace, boiler and turbine. The mark for the generator has been lost because it does not make it clear that it is the generator (when turned by the turbine) that generates the electricity.

   ii) Full marks have been gained. The candidate has **used the diagram accurately** to select 300 MW as the useful output and 1000 MW as the input.

b) The correct answer has been given.

c) The answer is too vague and scores no marks. The electricity is transmitted at high voltage, and hence low current, to reduce energy loss during the transmission.

d) The candidate has given two very good answers but the **three marks available should suggest that three ways should be given.** Additional ways include fitting loft insulation (prevents loss through the roof), draught excluders (prevents loss around doors and windows) and carpets (prevents loss through floors).

● A mark of 8 out of 11 corresponds to a grade C on this foundation tier question.

Exam question and student's answers (Higher Tier)

2 Tom cycles to school each morning along a straight flat road.

The graph shows his speed for the first 18 seconds of the journey.

a) During the first 8 seconds of the journey, Tom's acceleration was **constant**.

   i) How can you tell this from the graph?

     The line is straight ✓ or has a constant gradient during the first 8 seconds.

                                                                  (1)

   ii) Calculate his acceleration during this 8 s period.
      You **must** show how you work out your answer, including any equation used.

$$\text{Acceleration} = \frac{\text{change in speed}}{\text{time}} ✓$$

$$= \frac{(3 - 0)}{8} = \frac{\cancel{3}\,3.2}{8} = 0.375 \text{ ✓ t.e.}$$

                                      acceleration = _0.375_ unit _m/s²_. ✓ (4)

   iii) In the first 8 seconds, Tom travelled about 13 m.
      Describe how this could be worked out using the graph.

     This is the area under the graph. ✓

     $\frac{1}{2} \times 8 \times 3$ m

                                                               (1)

b) Tom and his bicycle have a combined mass of 60 kg.

   i) Calculate the total kinetic energy of Tom and his bicycle after 10 s.
     You **must** show how you work out your answer and any equation used.

$$\text{K.E.} = \frac{1}{2}mv^2 ✓ = \frac{1}{2} \times 60 \times 4 \times 4$$

$$= 480 ✓$$

                                      kinetic energy = _480_ ✓ ⌐ (3)

   ii) On another morning, Tom reaches a speed of 1.5 m/s after only 1 second of his journey.
      Calculate the average force needed for Tom to reach this speed after 1 second.
      You must show how you work out your answer, including any equation used.

     $F = 60 \times 1.5$ ✓

                                            force = _90_ ✓ N (3)

                                                 (Total 12 marks)

10/12

How to score full marks

a) i) The candidate has correctly answered the question and appreciates that a straight line with a positive gradient on a speed-time graph indicates constant acceleration.

ii) The candidate has used the correct equation and has worked through the calculation in an organised way. However, the intercept on the graph has been read incorrectly; it should have been 3.2 and not 3.0. **Always take great care when reading data from a graph.** As all the working has been shown, this error is only penalised once (the marker has used t.e. which stands for 'transmitted error'). **This is why it is really important to show your working. If only the answer had been written down, all 4 marks could have been lost as a result of one mistake.**

iii) This has been answered correctly. The distance travelled can be worked out from the area under the curve on a speed-time graph.

b) i) The answer is correct. **Again the equation has been given and the working shown.**

ii) The candidate has used the correct equation ($F = ma$) but has forgotten to write it down. As this was specifically asked for in the question one mark has been lost. **It is really important to read the question carefully so that you don't miss important instructions.**

● A mark of 10 out of 12 corresponds to a grade A on this higher tier question.

Questions to try

I This question is about electricity.

a) Look at the diagram of a plug.

FOUNDATION

13 A

i) What is the colour of the live wire? (1)

ii) There is a fuse in the plug.

What is the job of the fuse? (2)

b) The table shows information about different appliances in Samantha's house.

Look at the table.

appliance	voltage (V)	power (wattage) (W)
electric drill	12	60
heater	240	3000
kettle	240	2500
lamp	240	60
television	240	500

i) Which appliance costs the most to use for one hour?

   Choose from:

   electric drill
   heater
   kettle
   lamp
   television (1)

ii) Electricity costs 8 p per unit (kWh).

   The number of units (kWh) = number of kW x number of hours.

   Calculate the cost of using the 3 kW heater for 5 hours. (2)

iii) The television is double insulated.

   There are only two wires in the plug.

   Write down the names of these two wires. (1)

c) Electricity is a very good way of supplying energy to Samantha's house.

   i) Explain why. (2)

   ii) Write down **one disadvantage** of electricity compared to other ways of supplying energy to the home. (2)

(Total 11 marks)

2 This question is about waves.

a) Electromagnetic waves have different wavelengths and frequencies.

Look at the diagram of the electromagnetic spectrum.

gamma	X-ray	ultra-violet	visible	infra-red	microwaves	radio waves

(short wavelength)   (long wavelength)

   i)   Which waves have the **highest** frequency?

        Choose your answer from the diagram.   (1)

   ii) Write down one **danger** of ultra-violet waves.   (1)

   iii) X-rays are used in hospitals. They can be useful **or** dangerous.

        Write down **one use** and **one danger** of X-rays.   (2)

b) Gamma radiation is used in hospitals.

A tracer which gives off gamma rays is used by doctors to find a blockage in a patient's blood stream.

Explain how they use the tracer to find the blockage.   (3)

c) Scientists study the Earth. They make explosions and waves travel through the Earth.

The scientists transmit p and s waves. These waves travel through the Earth in different ways.

   i)   Describe how p waves are different to s waves.   (2)

   ii) Look at the diagram of the structure of the Earth. The diagram is not to scale.

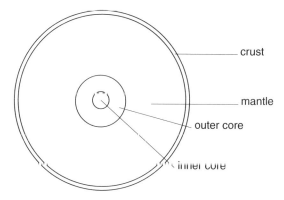

The crust is in the **solid** state.

Write about the **states** of the mantle, outer core and inner core.   (3)

(Total 12 marks)

Answers are on pages 267–268

UNIT 1: LIFE PROCESSES AND CELLS

1 Characteristics of living things (page 1)

Q1 a It does not contain any chloroplasts (and therefore no chlorophyll).

Comment Any green parts of a plant will contain chloroplasts.

Q1 b Onions grow underground, so they will not receive any light. There is no point in them having chloroplasts as they will not be able to photosynthesise.

Comment By going into detail and mentioning photosynthesis you show clearly that you understand the reason.

Q1 c It has a cell wall, a large vacuole and a regular shape.

Comment There are some exceptions, in that some plant cells may not have large vacuoles or a regular shape. But they all have a cell wall.

Q2 a Mitochondria.

Comment This is a better answer than simply saying cytoplasm.

Q2 b Cell membrane.

Comment Don't forget that everything that goes in or out of a cell goes through the membrane.

Q2 c Nucleus or chromosomes. Both are correct.

Comment Chromosomes is a more specific answer and shows more understanding.

Q2 d Vacuole.

Comment Don't forget that only plants have large vacuoles.

Q2 e Cell wall.

Comment The membrane would simply burst if the cell became too big. The cell wall is more rigid and resists this. You will find out more about this in Unit 4.

Q3 a Organism.

Q3 b Cell.

Q3 c System.

Q3 d Organ.

Q3 e Tissue.

Q3 f Organ.

Comment Organisms are whole animals or plants. (Don't forget that there are some organisms, like bacteria, which are only one cell big.) Organs are the separate parts of a body, each of which has its own job(s). Organs are usually made of different groups of cells (tissues).

2 Transport into and out of cells (page 3)

Q1 The salt forms a very concentrated solution on the slug's surface so water leaves its body by osmosis.

Comment This happens with slugs because their skin is partially permeable. It would not happen with us because our skin is not.

Q2 a Diffusion.

Comment There is a lower concentration of carbon dioxide inside the leaf as it is continually being used up.

Q2 b Neither.

Comment The food is squeezed along by muscles in the gullet.

Q2 c Neither.

Comment *Again, water is being forced out.*

Q2 d Osmosis.

Comment *As the celery is dried up the cells contain very concentrated solutions.*

Q3 To provide energy for the active transport of minerals like nitrates into the roots.

Comment *The concentration of minerals in soils is usually lower than the concentration of minerals in plant cells. Plants therefore can't rely on diffusion to get more of these minerals and must expend energy on actively 'pulling' them in.*

UNIT 2: HUMAN BODY SYSTEMS
1 Respiration (page 6)

Q1 To provide energy for life processes like movement and to generate warmth.

Comment *Don't give vague answers like 'to stay alive'. If a question in an examination has several marks then give the correct number of points in your answer.*

Q2 In every cell of the body.

Comment *You could be even more specific and point out that respiration occurs in the cytoplasm or in the mitochondria. Many examination candidates confuse respiration and breathing, and would have said 'lungs'.*

Q3 a Aerobic respiration provides more energy (for the same amount of glucose) and does not produce lactic acid (which will have to be broken down).

Comment *Given sufficient oxygen, respiration will be aerobic.*

Q3 b If more energy is needed and the oxygen necessary cannot be provided.

Comment *Anaerobic respiration is not as efficient as aerobic respiration. It is only used as a 'top up' to aerobic respiration.*

2 Blood and the circulatory system (page 8)

Q1 Substances, for example oxygen, will quickly diffuse into the centre of a small organism. For larger organisms, diffusion would take too long so a transport system is needed to ensure quick movement of substances from one part of the organism to another.

Comment *Another way of explaining this is to say that smaller organisms have a larger surface area to volume ratio (or a larger surface relative to their size).*

Q2 a In the lungs.

Comment *The blood arriving at the lungs contains little oxygen and is there to collect more.*

Q2 b In respiring tissues around the body.

Comment *Every cell will need oxygen. Active cells like those in muscles will need most.*

Q2 c To ensure that their bodies collect enough oxygen.

Comment *If the air contains less oxygen then less oxygen will enter the blood unless the body has some way of compensating.*

Q3 a The ventricles pump the blood but the atria simply receive the blood before it enters the ventricles.

Comment *The ventricle walls contract and relax to squeeze out blood and take more in. This takes a lot of muscle. The atria, by comparison, do not need to squeeze as hard and must be easily inflated by the incoming low-pressure blood.*

Q3 b The left ventricle has to pump blood around the whole body (apart from the lungs). The right ventricle 'only' sends blood to the lungs.

Comment This is why your heart sounds louder on your left side.

Q4 a Veins have valves, thinner walls and a larger lumen.

Comment The veins contain blood at a reduced pressure and are built so that they don't resist the flow of blood but rather help it on its way to the lungs.

Q4 b Capillary walls are permeable, allowing diffusion. Arteries and veins do not have permeable walls.

Comment The arteries carry blood quickly to each organ or part of the body and the veins bring it back. The capillaries form a branching network inside organs.

3 Breathing (page 13)

Q1 a Just two, the wall of the alveolus and the wall of the blood capillary.

Comment This short distance is important so gases can easily move between the alveoli and the blood. Another way of looking at it is that the short distance increases the concentration gradient.

Q1 b To ensure that oxygen rapidly diffuses from the area of high concentration, in the alveoli, to the area of low concentration, in the blood.

Comment Don't forget that there is also a concentration gradient for carbon dioxide.

Q2 The diaphragm lowers and the ribcage moves upwards and outwards.

Comment Both of these changes increase the volume of the thorax.

Q3 To keep them open to ensure that air can move freely.

Comment This is particularly important because when the air pressure drops to take in more air from the outside this could otherwise make the air passages close in on themselves.

4 Digestion (page 16)

Q1 a Proteins are too big to pass through the wall of the ileum, so they have to be broken down into the smaller amino acids.

Comment Only molecules that are already small do not need to be digested.

Q1 b Physical digestion is simply breaking food into smaller pieces. This is a physical change. Chemical digestion breaks down larger molecules into smaller ones. This is a chemical change because new substances are formed.

Comment Many candidates, if asked to describe digestion, lose marks because they do not describe the breakdown of **molecules**.

Q1 c They are denatured.

Comment This means they change their shape irreversibly, and can not work. In an examination **do not** say that they are 'killed' because they were never alive.

Q1 d To neutralise the acid from the stomach, because the enzymes in the small intestine can not work at an acidic pH.

Comment Many candidates think that stomach acid itself breaks down food. It is the fact that it allows enzymes in the stomach to work that is important.

Q2 a Ingestion is taking in food. Egestion is passing out the undigested remains. Excretion is getting rid of things we have made.

Comment *Many candidates lose marks because they confuse egestion and excretion. Passing out faeces is egestion. Getting rid of urea in urine or breathing out carbon dioxide are examples of excretion because these substances are made in the body.*

Q2 b Ingestion: mouth. Egestion: anus.

Comment *Excretion occurs in various places. You will find out more in Unit 3.*

Q3 They provide a large surface area. They have thin permeable walls. They have a good blood supply causing a concentration gradient. They are both moist.

Comment *The similarities are not a coincidence. These factors are vital to ensure the efficient absorption of the different substances.*

UNIT 3: BODY MAINTENANCE
I The nervous system (page 21)

Q1 a A change, either in the surroundings or inside the body, that is detected by the body.

Comment *For example, if you were crossing a road and noticed a bus approaching the stimuli would have been the sight and sound of the bus.*

Q1 b Receptors detect (sense) stimuli. The sense organs are receptors. Effectors are the parts of the body that respond. Effectors are usually muscles but can also be glands.

Comment *Some candidates get confused between effectors and the 'effects' that they produce.*

Q2 a Brain and spinal cord.

Comment *Many reflexes do not need the brain in order to function and the spinal cord is therefore not simply a nerve pathway to and from the brain but also processes some information itself.*

Q2 b Neurones are nerve cells. A nerve in the body is usually a bundle of neurones wrapped in connective tissue.

Comment *In exam questions you may pick up extra marks for using the correct terms.*

Q2 c Membrane, cytoplasm, nucleus.

Comment *Although neurones are specialised they are still cells and so share these features with other cells.*

Q2 d Cell body, nerve fibres (axons or dendrons), nerve endings or dendrites. Any two.

Comment *If you are asked for a certain number of answers in an exam only answer up to that number as any more will not be marked.*

Q3 a A and C.

Comment *The others do involve some kind of response, but reflexes happen **automatically** – without thought.*

Q3 b Since they do not have to be thought about, reflexes happen very quickly. This means that if there is some kind of danger you can respond very quickly to reduce or prevent any harm.

Comment *It is possible to override some reflexes by thinking about it, so you could hold on to something hot even though that is not usually a very wise thing to do.*

2 The endocrine system (page 26)

Q1 In the nervous system, signals are sent very quickly as electro-chemical impulses along neurones and the effects of the signal usually last a short time. In the endocrine system signals are sent more slowly as hormones through the blood and the effects usually last longer.

Comment *Both of these systems are involved in co-ordination (responding to stimuli). Both are needed because of the different nature of their effects.*

Q2 a Fighting and running away both need energy. This is released by respiration, which uses oxygen to release energy from glucose. So breathing increases to take in more oxygen, and glucose is released from stores in the liver and muscles. The blood is redirected and heart rate increased to carry the oxygen and glucose quickly to the muscles that need it. Sweating starts because the body will need cooling. Hairs stand up and pupils dilate to make an animal look larger and more fierce.

Comment *Although an exam question may be apparently about one particular topic, to gain full marks you might have to include ideas from other topics. In this example ideas about respiration are relevant. This is likely to happen in questions that require extended answers.*

Q2 b Otherwise all the effects caused by adrenaline would persist.

Comment *Where hormones are involved, constant fine adjustments need to be made – for example, in the amounts of insulin required in the blood. If hormones are not being constantly broken down and at the same time secreted this balance could not be maintained.*

Q3 Glucose and glycogen are both carbohydrates, but glucose is made of small molecules that dissolve in the blood whereas glycogen is made of larger molecules (lots of glucose molecules joined together) that are insoluble and do not travel through the blood. Glucagon is a hormone that converts glycogen back into glucose (i.e. it does the opposite of insulin).

Comment *It is very common for candidates to confuse these – especially glycogen and glucagon.*

3 Homeostasis (page 30)

Q1 The farmer will have been sweating to stay cool and so will have lost water this way. Unless the farmer has drunk a lot, his or her kidneys will have to reduce the amount of water that is lost as urine. This is why there is less. However, there will be just as much urea, so the urine is more concentrated and darker in colour.

Comment *The body has to lose extra water by sweating to maintain body temperature. Humans cannot reduce how much is lost in breathing as the lining of the alveoli in the lungs is always moist, nor can the amount lost in faeces be reduced greatly. The only way therefore to cut down on losses is to reduce urine output.*

Q2 They remove carbon dioxide and water from the body.

Comment *Excretion is the removal of substances that have been produced in the body. Carbon dioxide is a waste product of respiration, as is some of the water.*

Q3 The veins would have a lower concentration of salt and urea than the arteries. Also, as with any other organ, the oxygen level and blood pressure would be lower.

Comment *Although most other substances in the blood (e.g. glucose) are also initially filtered from the blood, most are the absorbed back before the blood leaves the kidneys. Also, don't forget that the arteries are carrying blood away from the heart into the kidneys, and the veins the reverse.*

4 Good health (page 34)

Q1 a Red blood cells are needed in large quantities to carry oxygen, whereas white blood cells are fighting infection and most of the time we are not recovering from diseases.

Q1 b When there is an infection to fight off.

Comment Even when we are making lots of white blood cells to fight an infection there are many times more red blood cells.

Q2 Your white blood cells remember how to make large quantities of the measles antibody quickly. If the measles virus ever entered your body again you would fight it off before it had a chance to multiply and cause the symptoms of measles.

Comment You only 'have a disease' when the micro-organism has had a chance to multiply and spread.

Q3 As reaction times are slower and judgement is impaired you are much more likely to have an accident.

Comment This does not just apply if you are 'drunk'. Drinking and driving is dangerous because the alcohol affects you to some extent, even after one drink. In exams a common shortcoming is to say drinking and driving is dangerous because you may have an accident, which is not wrong but might not get full marks. Always try to go beyond common-sense type answers and give a scientific reason.

UNIT 4: PLANTS
1 Photosynthesis (page 38)

Q1 Carbon dioxide from the air enters the leaves through the stomata. Water moves from the soil into the roots and up the stem to the leaves.

Comment As plants cannot move around, their raw materials have to be readily available. Note that sunlight is not a raw material. It is the energy source that drives the chemical reaction.

Q2 Starch is not soluble.

Comment Starch is a useful storage material but needs to be broken down into smaller molecules to be able to dissolve.

Q3 Being broad allows as much light as possible to be absorbed. Being thin allows carbon dioxide to quickly reach the photosynthesising cells.

Comment There are exceptions to this principle. See page 45 about cactus spines and pine needles.

2 Transport in plants (page 42)

Q1 Xylem is made of dead cells. It carries water and minerals from the roots, up the stem, to the leaves. Phloem is made of living cells. It carries dissolved food substances from the leaves to other parts of the plant.

Comment Make sure you can also identify the xylem and phloem in diagrams of sections of roots, stems and leaves.

Q2 On a sunny day the guard cells will fully open the stomata, allowing water vapour to pass out more easily. When it is hot, water evaporates more quickly into the air spaces inside the leaf, which causes the water vapour to diffuse more quickly out of the leaf.

Comment Don't forget that if the plant is losing more water than it is taking in it will start to wilt. In this case the stomata will start to close, so reducing transpiration.

Q3 In a turgid cell the cytoplasm presses hard against the cell wall because the cell contains as much water as it can. This gives the cell rigidity. In a plasmolysed cell so much water has been lost that the cytoplasm shrinks and comes away from the cell wall. A plasmolysed cell is flexible and can't keep a fixed shape.

Comment In a healthy plant none of the cells should be plasmolysed. Remember that when cells become plasmolysed, although the cytoplasm shrinks and the membrane with it, the cell wall does not.

3 Minerals (page 46)

Q1 a Nitrogen and sulphur.

Comment Plants do not take in and use the pure elements. For example, there is a lot of nitrogen in the air (79%), but in its pure form it is very unreactive and the plants cannot use it.

Q1 b Protein is used to make new cells. For example, cell membranes contain protein.

Comment This applies to animals as well as to plants.

Q2 Magnesium is found in chlorophyll, the green pigment that gives plants their colour. Without it they cannot be green.

Comment Chlorophyll is actually chemically similar to haemoglobin in the blood, but contains magnesium instead of iron.

Q3 Minerals are absorbed by active transport. This means that energy is required, which is provided by the mitochondria.

Comment Remember that although water and minerals both enter through the roots, water enters by osmosis, which is a 'passive' process – it does not require energy.

4 Plant hormones (page 47)

Q1 Plant hormones are not made in glands. Nor are they carried in the blood.

Comment It is because of these differences that many people refer to them as growth regulators instead. Look back at Unit 3 if you need to revise about animal hormones.

Q2 A, C and D.

Comment Plant hormones affect growth and development. Pollination is simply the transfer of pollen between flowers.

Q3 Auxin is no longer concentrated more on one side than the other, so one side does not grow more than the other.

Comment Remember that growth in tropisms is by cell elongation, not the formation of new cells by cell division.

UNIT 5: ECOLOGY AND THE ENVIRONMENT
I The study of ecology (page 49)

Q1 This is because the taller trees will be taking most of the light and with their roots taking most of the water and minerals from the soil.

Comment This is an example of **competition**, in which the trees are out-competing the smaller plants for these important resources.

Q2 If the numbers of rabbits went down, foxes would just concentrate their diet on other things. For example, many foxes live in towns, scavenging rubbish. If foxes died out, other things, including humans, would still kill rabbits.

Comment There are very few other large animals in northern Canada, which is why the example of lynxes and snowshoe hares is unusual in showing so clearly the way that predators and prey affect each other.

Q3 a The greenfly numbers would go down.

Q3 b There would have to be enough food to feed them and they would have already eaten most of their prey.

Comment Numbers of most species alter a little each year, but they are usually kept more or less constant because of factors like food supply and predation.

2 Relationships between organisms in an ecosystem (page 52)

Q1 a
ladybirds
aphids
rose bushes

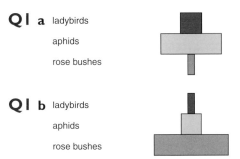

Q1 b
ladybirds
aphids
rose bushes

Comment In a food chain where the producers are much larger than their consumers the pyramid of numbers is inverted. However, the pyramid of biomass is always a normal pyramid shape.

Q2 It is more energy efficient to eat plant crops rather than to raise animals. This is because we are eating at a lower trophic level. At each transfer between trophic levels energy is transferred away from a food chain.

Comment Ecologically, therefore, it is much more efficient to be vegetarian.

Q3 Energy is lost at each stage of a food chain, so there is a limit as to how long a food chain can be.

Comment This is why pyramids of biomass are always a pyramid shape.

3 Natural recycling (page 56)

Q1 a Photosynthesis.

Comment Make sure you remember the details of photosynthesis from Unit 4.

Q1 b Respiration and combustion.

Comment Until the last few hundred years combustion played quite a small part in this. It is now playing a bigger role and this is the reason for the build up of carbon dioxide in the atmosphere.

Q2 This is the only way they can get the nitrogen they need.

Comment The nitrogen is made available by digesting the protein in the insects' bodies.

Q3 Nitrifying bacteria produce nitrates from decayed remains. Denitrifying bacteria convert nitrates and other nitrogen compounds into nitrogen gas.

Comment Denitrifying bacteria therefore have an opposite effect to nitrogen-fixing bacteria.

4 Human influences on the environment (page 59)

Q1 They do not easily break down and so remain in the bodies of organisms that have taken them in.

Comment This is the reason they accumulate in animals and are passed along food chains.

Q2 The greenhouse effect describes how some of the gases in the atmosphere restrict heat escaping from the Earth. Global warming is an increase in the Earth's temperature that may well be caused by an *increased* greenhouse effect.

Comment Remember that it is the **increased** greenhouse effect that people are concerned about. A greenhouse effect is not only normal but essential for life on Earth.

Q3 This would increase their costs, which would have to be passed on to their customers, who might not want to pay more.

Comment An added problem is that, unlike pollution into rivers, the problems caused by acid rain take place a long way from the source of the pollution.

5 Sampling techniques (page 66)

Q1 a Tullgren funnel.

Q1 b Pitfall trap.

Q1 c Beating tray and then a pooter.

Q1 d Pooter.

Comment Check with your teacher whether your science exam will ask you questions about these.

Q2 The average number of dandelions in 1 quadrat (1 m^2) was 25 ÷ 10 = 2.5. The field is 200 m^2 so the total number of dandelions is 2.5 × 200 = 500.

Comment You might have to do some maths so don't forget your calculator in your exam.

Q3 If the pupil in the previous question had only placed her quadrat where there were dandelions and had deliberately missed out those areas without any she would have calculated a much higher estimate.

Comment It is for the same reason, to get a more reliable average and total estimate, that you also need to take a reasonably large number of measurements before you work out your average.

UNIT 6: GENETICS AND EVOLUTION
1 Variation (page 68)

Q1 a A, C and E.

Q1 b B and D.

Comment If the features fall into distinct groups they are discontinuous. If they do not, they are continuous.

Q2 a Eye colour, height, shape of face (there are other examples). These are genetic features and as they are identical twins they will have the same genes.

Q2 b Skin colour, accent, how muscular they are (there are other examples). These features are affected by the environment. They are doing different jobs in different climates, so their environments are different.

Comment Some features like eye colour are purely genetically controlled and so will be identical. Some features like accent are purely environmentally controlled and so would probably differ. Many features, like skin colour, are controlled both by genes and the environment (i.e. tanning) so they would also show differences.

Q3 Chemical base, gene, chromosome, cell nucleus, cell.

Comment Look back at the diagram on page 69 if you're not sure.

2 Inheritance (page 72)

Q1 Let R be the dominant allele for tongue rolling and r the recessive allele for not being able to roll your tongue.

parents: **Rr**   **Rr**

gametes: **R**   r   **R**   r

F$_1$ generation: **RR**   **Rr**   **Rr**   **rr**
       (roller) (roller) (roller) (non-roller)

Comment If not being able to roll your tongue is a recessive condition then the 'non-roller' child must be rr. This means each parent must have at least one r allele. As the parents can roll their tongues they must therefore both be Rr.

Q2 Cross the spotted leopard with a known ss leopard. If there are any black cubs then they must be ss and have received one of the s alleles from the spotted parent, which must therefore be Ss. If there are no black cubs the spotted parent is likely to be an SS. The random nature of fertilisation means that an Ss leopard may still produce no ss cubs, but this is unlikely with a large litter.

Comment *Crossing with a homozygous recessive is known as a test cross or back cross. It is used because the homozygous recessive is the only genotype that can be identified by the phenotype alone.*

Q3 As neither has the condition both must be heterozygous carriers of the recessive allele if their child has two copies of the recessive allele. The probability of a child being homozygous recessive, i.e. having cystic fibrosis, is 1 in 4.

Comment *Look back at the monohybrid cross shown on page 73. You can see that the offspring showing the recessive condition are in the ratio 1:3 to those showing the dominant condition. Another way of saying this is that there is a 1 in 4 chance of a child being homozygous recessive and showing the recessive condition. The fact that the couple have one child with the condition is not a consideration.*

3 Applications (page 76)

Q1 Pick sheep with finer wool than the others. Breed these together. From the offspring pick those with the finest wool and breed these. Continue this over many generations.

Comment *The principle of selective breeding is the same whatever the example.*

Q2 *Advantages:* many roses with identical flowers can be produced relatively quickly. This would be useful if the roses on this particular plant sold well. *Disadvantages:* there is no variation, so if one rose was attacked by a plant disease then all the rest would be susceptible too.

Comment *The key point about cloning is that the new plants are genetically identical. This may or may not be an advantage.*

Q3 New combinations of genes can be produced quickly and reliably with genetic engineering. Genetic engineering allows genes to be taken from one species and given to another, which could not be done with selective breeding as different species cannot breed together.

Comment *The second answer is probably the more important. For example, a gene for resistance to a particular disease could be taken from one species and given to another.*

4 Evolution (page 79)

Q1 a Vertebrates have hard body parts, e.g. bones and teeth, which can leave fossil remains, whereas many invertebrates have only soft body parts which rarely leave fossils.

Comment *This does not apply to all invertebrates. There are many remains of the shells of marine invertebrates. Even so, these leave little evidence of what the soft tissues were like.*

Q1 b There are many reasons, such as: the remains of the animals did not lie undisturbed in the right environmental conditions to form fossils, fossils were formed but have been destroyed – e.g. by erosion – or the fossils have not been found yet.

Comment *Although the fossil record of evolution is incomplete and may not give detailed information about how all living things evolved it is still a very important source of evidence.*

Q2 Among the shorter-necked ancestors there would have been *variation* in height. A giraffe that was only slightly taller than others would have been able to reach and feed on some leaves that others would not have been able to. They would have had a slight *advantage* in the *competition* for food and so would be slightly better fed and slightly more healthy than shorter ones. They would therefore probably on average live a little longer and be able to successfully rear slightly more offspring. If they were able to pass on the longer neck to their offspring because it was a *genetic* feature, it would mean both that there would be more of their offspring than of the shorter-necked giraffes and that the overall average height of the giraffe population would have increased. If this continued for many, many generations it would lead to the giraffes we see today.

> **Comment** In an exam, questions about natural selection will often require extended answers and may carry four or more marks. To get full marks you will need to give a detailed response. Do not be put off if the example is unfamiliar. This is to test that you understand the **process**, which will be the same in each case. Note that natural selection favours features that give an advantage but will not always result in evolutionary change. In the example of the giraffe, being taller than they are today would pose disadvantages, e.g. the difficulty of pumping blood to the brain or problems of stability, which means that they will not just continue to get taller. Some animals alive today are known as 'living fossils' as they appear similar to ancient fossil remains. If an organism's environment has not changed significantly and it is well adapted to it, then natural selection would work to keep the animal's features the same.

UNIT 7: CHEMICAL FORMULAE AND EQUATIONS
I How are chemical formulae calculated? (page 82)

Q1 a NaCl

> **Comment** Na (group 1) combining power 1, Cl (group 7) combining power 1.

Q1 b MgF_2

> **Comment** Mg (group 2) combining power 2, F (group 7) combining power 1. 2, 1, cross over = Mg1 F2 = MgF_2.

Q1 c AlN

> **Comment** Al (group 3) combining power 3, N (group 5) combining power 3. 3, 3, cancel = Al1 N1 = AlN

Q1 d Li_2O

> **Comment** Li (group 1) combining power 1, O (group 6) combining power 2.

Q1 e CO_2

> **Comment** C (group 4) combining power 4, O (group 6) combining power 2. 4, 2, cancel = C1 O2 = CO_2.

Q2 a Fe_2O_3

> **Comment** Fe combining power 3, O (group 6) combining power 2.

Q2 b PCl_5

> **Comment** P combining power 5, Cl (group 7) combining power 1.

Q2 c $CrBr_3$

> **Comment** Cr combining power 3, Br (group 7) combining power 1.

Q2 d SO_3

Comment S combining power 6, 0 (group 6) combining power 2. 6, 2, cancel = S1 O3 = SO_3.

Q2 e SO_2

Comment S combining power 4, 0 (group 6) combining power 2. 4, 2, cancel = S1 O2 = SO_2.

Q3 a K_2CO_3

Comment K combining power 1, CO_3 combining power 2.

Q3 b NH_4Cl

Comment NH_4 combining power 1, Cl (group 7) combining power 1.

Q3 c H_2SO_4

Comment H combining power 1, SO_4 combining power 2.

Q3 d $Mg(OH)_2$

Comment Mg (group 2) combining power 2, OH combining power 1. Don't forget the brackets.

Q3 e $(NH_4)_2SO_4$

Comment NH_4 combining power 1, SO_4 combining power 2. Don't forget the brackets.

2 Chemical equations (page 85)

Q1 a $C + O_2 \rightarrow CO_2$

Comment This doesn't need balancing!

Q1 b $4Fe + 3O_2 \rightarrow 2Fe_2O_3$

Comment Remember that balancing numbers must always go in front of symbols and formulae.

Q1 c $2Fe_2O_3 + 3C \rightarrow 4Fe + 3CO_2$

Comment One maths trick to use here is to realise that the number of oxygen atoms on the right-hand side must be even. Putting a '2' in front of Fe_2O_3 makes the oxygen on the left-hand side even too.

Q1 d $CaCO_3 + 2HCl \rightarrow CaCl_2 + CO_2 + H_2O$

Comment Note that the carbonate radical does not appear on both sides of the equation.

Q2 a $Ca^{2+} + CO_3^{2-} \rightarrow CaCO_3$
Q2 b $Fe^{2+} + 2OH^- \rightarrow Fe(OH)_2$
Q2 c $Ag^+ + Br^- \rightarrow AgBr$

Comment The symbols and charges must balance on each side of the equation. State symbols could be used,
e.g. $Fe^{2+}(aq) + 2OH^-(aq) \rightarrow Fe(OH)_2(s)$
$Ag^+(aq) + Br^-(aq) \rightarrow AgBr(s)$.

Q3 a $Al^{3+} + 3e^- \rightarrow Al$
Q3 b $Na \rightarrow Na^+ + e^-$
Q3 c $2O^{2-} \rightarrow O_2 + 4e^-$
Q3 d $2Br^- \rightarrow Br_2 + 2e^-$

Comment At the cathode positive ions gain electrons. At the anode negative ions lose electrons. Remember that symbols and charges must balance.

UNIT 8: STRUCTURE AND BONDING
1 How are atoms put together? (page 89)

Q1 a The atomic number is the number of protons in an atom. (It is equal to the number of electrons.)

Comment Always define atomic number in terms of protons. However, as atoms are neutral there will always be equal numbers of protons and electrons.

Q1 b The mass number is the total number of protons and neutrons in an atom.

Comment Remember that electrons have very little mass and so mass number cannot refer to electrons.

Q2 Si 14 14 14 2,8,4

Mg 12 14 12 2,8,2

S 16 16 16 2,8,6

Ar 18 22 18 2,8,8

Comment The top number is the mass number and the bottom (smaller) number is the atomic number. The difference between the two numbers is the number of neutrons.

Q3 a (i) C; (ii) B; (iii) C or E or F; (iv) B; (v) C

Comment To have no overall charge the number of protons (positive charges) must equal the number of electrons (negative charges).
The atomic number (number of protons) is unique to a particular element. It is the atomic number that defines the element's position in the periodic table.

Q3 b

Comment Remember that an atomic diagram should show the number of protons and neutrons in the nucleus and the number and arrangement of electrons.

2 Chemical Bonding
(page 92)

Q1 a Covalent

Q1 b covalent

Q1 c ionic

Q1 d covalent

Q1 e ionic.

Comment Remember that ionic bonding involves a metal and a non-metal; covalent bonding involves two or more non-metals. Hydrogen, chlorine, carbon, oxygen and bromine are non-metals. Only sodium and calcium in the list are metals.

Q2 a K^+

Q2 b Al^{3+}

Q2 c S^{2-}

Q2 d F^-.

Comment These can be worked out from the position of the element in the periodic table. Look back in the unit for the rule if you have forgotten it. You will always be given a periodic table in the exam. Get used to using it: it will help you to gain marks in the exam.

Q3 a

Q3 b

$O{=}O$

Q3 c

$N{\equiv}N$

Q3 d

Q3 e

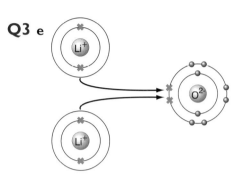

1 Remember that covalent compounds contain non-metals.
2 You can get the atomic number (needed to work out the number of electrons) from the periodic table.
3 With covalent compounds try drawing the displayed formula first. You will need to work out how many covalent bonds each atom can form. Again, the periodic table will help you. For example, oxygen is in Group 6 so it can form two covalent bonds. Once you have got the displayed formula, each bond corresponds to a shared pair of electrons. Don't forget the first electron shell can hold 2 electrons, others hold 8 electrons. So don't miss any electrons out.
4 In examples of ionic bonding don't forget to write the formulae of the ions that are formed.

3 Structures and properties (page 96)

Q1 a Potassium chloride exists as a giant ionic lattice. There are very strong electrostatic forces holding the ions together. A considerable amount of energy is needed to overcome the forces of attraction so the melting point is high.

Comment The key ideas relating to melting point are: strong forces between particles; large amounts of energy needed to overcome these forces.

Q1 b Potassium chloride is ionically bonded. When molten or dissolved in water the ions are free to move and carry an electric current.

Comment Remember that an electrolyte allows an electric current to flow through it when molten or dissolved in water – not when in the solid state.

Q2 a The carbon atoms are held by strong covalent bonds within the hexagonal layers. This can give a structure great strength.

Comment Have a look at the diagram of the structure of graphite. Remember that covalent bonds are strong bonds.

Q2 b Only three out of the four of carbon's outer shell electrons are used in forming covalent bonds. Each atom has an electron which is only loosely held to the atom. When a voltage is applied these electrons move, forming an electric current.

Comment Graphite has a structure similar to that of metals – there is a 'cloud' of electrons which are free to move. For more on metal structures see Unit 14.

Q3 The bonds within the molecule are strong (the intramolecular bonds) but the bonds holding the methane molecules together are weak (intermolecular bonds). Therefore methane molecules require very little energy to be separated from each other.

Comment This is one of the ideas candidates find very confusing. Always try to be precise. There are bonds within a molecule as well as bonds between molecules. You wouldn't be expected to use 'intramolecular' and 'intermolecular', but if you do be sure to get them the right way round!

UNIT 9: FUELS AND ENERGY
I How do we obtain fossil fuels? (page 98)

Q1 a Small sea creatures died, their bodies settled in the mud at the bottom of the oceans and decayed. They were compressed over a period of millions of years and slowly changed into crude oil.

Comment Remember the process involves compression and takes place over millions of years. Do not confuse crude oil with coal, which is formed from plant material.

Q1 b It takes millions of years to form. Once supplies have been used up they cannot be replaced.

Comment A common mistake is to say 'it cannot be used again'. No fuel can be used again but some, such as trees (wood), can be regrown quite quickly. Wood is therefore renewable.

Q2 a Fractional distillation.

Comment There is often a mark for 'fractional' and a mark for 'distillation'.

Q2 b The boiling point of the fractions decreases.

Comment Remember the column is hotter at the bottom than at the top.

Q2 c Components that have boiling points just above the temperature of X will condense to a liquid. Components which have boiling points below the temperature of X will remain as vapour and continue up the column.

Comment If a vapour is cooled below its boiling point it will condense.

Q2 d The component would be not very runny (viscous), very dark yellow/orange in colour, very difficult to light and very smoky when burning.

Comment Again the clues are in the table. A fuel needs to ignite easily and be 'clean'.

Q2 e It would not ignite easily. It would produce a lot of soot when burning.

Comment In a question like this, the clues to the answer will be in the table. Always give as full an answer as possible. Four points can be scored using the last three columns of the table.

Q3 a A compound containing carbon and hydrogen atoms only.

Comment Don't miss out the word 'only'. A lot of compounds contain carbon and hydrogen but are not hydrocarbons (e.g. glucose, $C_6H_{12}O_6$).

Q3 b High temperature, catalyst.

Comment 'Catalytic crackers' are used at oil refineries.

Q3 c C_8H_{18}.

Comment The equation must balance so the number of carbon atoms must be 10 − 2, the number of hydrogen atoms 22 − 4.

2 How are hydrocarbons used? (page 102)

Q1 a petrol + oxygen → carbon dioxide + water

Comment All hydrocarbons produce carbon dioxide and water when burnt in a plentiful supply of air. It is much better to use oxygen rather than air in the equation.

Q1 b Shortage of oxygen.

Comment Remember this is incomplete combustion.

Q1 c The carbon monoxide combines with the haemoglobin in the blood, preventing oxygen from doing so. Supply of oxygen to the body is reduced. Specifically this can quickly cause the death of brain cells.

Comment A much more detailed answer is required than 'it causes suffocation'.

Q2 a (i)

hexane

Q2 a (ii)

hexene

Comment Remember 'hex' means 6. The ending 'ane' means only single bonds whereas 'ene' means there is a carbon–carbon double bond.

Q2 b Add bromine water. It will be decolourised by hexene but not by hexane.

Comment This is the standard test for all alkenes. You should give the test reagent and what you would observe.

Q3 a

Comment 'Prop' means 3 carbon atoms.

Q3 b

Comment If you had problems here look back at how ethene polymerises. Then replace one H atom by a CH_3 group.

Q3 c Poly(propene).

Comment Just put 'poly' in front of the name of the monomer.

Q3 d Propane is saturated and doesn't have a carbon–carbon double bond to undergo addition reactions.

Comment The carbon–carbon double bond is the reactive part of the molecule.

3 Energy transfers (page 107)

Q1 a Energy = 40 × 4.2 × 32 = 5376 J.

Q1 b Energy = 5376/0.2 = 26 880 J/g.

Comment Use the formula energy = mass × 4.2 × temperature change.

Q2 a The reaction is exothermic.

Q2 b More energy is released when bonds are formed than is used to break the bonds in the first place.

Comment In an energy level diagram, if the products are lower in energy than the reactants the reaction change is exothermic. Remember that the overall energy change = energy needed to break bonds – energy released on forming bonds.

Q3 More energy is released when the H—Cl bonds are made than is needed to break the H—H and Cl—Cl bonds. The overall energy change is therefore exothermic.

Comment Again this refers to the balance between bond breaking and bond forming. Always refer to the specific bonds involved.

UNIT 10: ROCKS AND METALS
1 Plate tectonics and geological change (page 110)

Q1 a Earthquakes (or volcanoes).

Comment Remember that earthquakes occur when two plates rub together.

Q1 b As the two plates move apart a weakness forms in the crust. Magma from the mantle is forced up, cools and forms igneous rock.

Comment Igneous rocks are formed when the lava from a volcano cools. Volcanoes are not always formed – sometimes the magma doesn't break through the crust.

Q1 c High temperature and high pressure.

Comment As the oceanic plate is forced into the mantle the rocks are squashed and heated.

Q2 a Convection currents in the liquid mantle.

Comment Energy from the core is transferred to the mantle, causing convection currents.

Q2 b If two continental plates collide mountains form. If a continental plate collides with an oceanic plate then an ocean trench forms.

Comment You need to distinguish between the two types of plate.

Q3 *Weathering* – water gets into cracks in the rocks and then freezes and expands. As the ice melts, fragments of rock break away. *Erosion* – running water and strong winds carrying sand can wear rocks away. Acid rain dissolves limestone. *Transportation* – rain water carries particles into streams and rivers.

Comment It is important that you are clear about these three processes. If not, look back at the diagram on page 112. The differences between weathering and erosion are slight and so you shouldn't worry if you had trouble separating them. This is a very common examination question.

2 Extraction of metals (page 114)

Q1 a Iron oxide + carbon → iron + carbon dioxide

Comment In the blast furnace much of the reduction is done by carbon monoxide.

Q1 b Reduced. Reduction is the loss of oxygen. The iron oxide has lost oxygen, forming iron.

Comment Reduction and oxidation always occur together. In this reaction the carbon is oxidised.

Q1 c The limestone reacts with impurities, forming a slag that floats to the top and is removed from the furnace.

Comment Of the three raw materials in the blast furnace (coke, iron ore, limestone) this is the easiest one to forget.

Q2 a This is the breakdown (decomposition) of a compound using electricity.

Comment If you are still puzzled by electrolysis look back at page 116.

Q2 b This is a substance which when molten or dissolved in water allows an electric current to pass through it.

Comment Electrolytes must contain ions and the ions must be free to move before a current will flow.

Q2 c This is the substance which makes the electrical contact between the battery and the electrolyte.

Comment In a circuit there will always be two electrodes.

Q2 d This is the electrode connected to the positive terminal of the battery.

Comment Ions that travel to the anode are called anions (negatively charged ions).

Q2 e This is the electrode connected to the negative terminal of the battery.

Comment Ions that travel to the cathode are called cations (positively charged ions).

Q3 a The ions must be free to move. In a solid the ions are held in a giant lattice structure.

Comment Remember that the ions in a solid can be made free to move by either melting the solid or dissolving it in water. Aluminium oxide does not dissolve in water.

Q3 b Cathode.

Comment Aluminium ions are positively charged and so will be attracted to the negative electrode.

Q3 c Aluminium ions gain electrons and form aluminium atoms.

$$Al^{3+} + 3e^- \rightarrow Al$$

Comment The ionic equation must balance in terms of symbols and charges.

Q3 d The oxygen that is produced at the anode oxidises the hot carbon electrodes, forming carbon dioxide.

Comment This is one of the drawbacks of the method and also adds to the expense of producing aluminium.

UNIT 11: CHEMICAL REACTIONS
1 Chemical change (page 119)

Q1 Not all collisions provide enough energy for the reaction to take place.

Comment Energy is needed to break chemical bonds so that the atoms, molecules or ions can rearrange and form new bonds. Remember that collisions that do have sufficient energy are referred to as **effective collisions**.

Q2 Reaction A.

Comment Reaction A has a lower activation energy than reaction B. This means that there will be more effective collisions and so the rate of reaction will be higher. If you are still not clear about this idea of an 'energy barrier', look again at the explanation of activation energy in the **collision theory** section.

Q3 a Carbon dioxide

Comment Remember that marble has the chemical name calcium carbonate. The carbon dioxide is released from the carbonate ion.

Q3 b (i) 20 cm^3; (ii) 16 cm^3; (iii) 13 cm^3; (iv) 0 cm^3.

Comment 20 – 0 = 20; 36 – 20 = 16; 49 – 36 = 13; 70 – 70 = 0. Don't forget the units of volume.

Q3 c The volume of gas produced in each 10 second interval decreases as the reaction proceeds. This means the rate of production of gas decreases.

Comment The rate of reaction is measured in terms of the volume of gas produced in a certain amount of time. If you wanted to calculate rates in these time intervals you would need to divide the volume of gas produced by the time taken. So between 0 and 10 seconds 20 cm^3 of gas was collected giving a rate of 20/10 = 2 cm^3/s. Between 20 and 30 seconds the rate was 1.3 cm^3/s.

Q3 d As the reaction proceeds there are fewer particles of hydrochloric acid and calcium carbonate to collide with each other. Therefore there will be fewer collisions and hence fewer effective collisions.

Comment Don't forget to mention the idea of 'effective collisions' (see page 119). This is a key idea in this chapter. If you want to impress the examiner use the correct names for the particles – e.g. in this reaction collisions occur between hydrogen ions (H^+ ions) and carbonate ions (CO_3^{2-} ions).

Q3 e Measuring the change in mass as the reaction proceeds.

Comment The carbon dioxide gas will escape, causing a decrease in mass of the reaction container. The equipment you would need is shown on page 121.

2 Controlling the rate of reaction (page 123)

Q1 As the temperature increases, the kinetic energy of the reacting particles also increases. The particles will therefore be moving faster and will collide more frequently. In addition, there will be more energy transferred in the collisions and so more are likely to be effective and lead to a reaction.

Comment Don't forget to mention the energy of the collision. Many students only mention the increased number of collisions.

Q2 a (i) Experiment 1; (ii) the reaction finishes more quickly because the curve levels out soonest.

Comment A better answer would mention the gradient of the curve – e.g. the gradient of the curve at the beginning of the reaction is the steepest.

Q2 b (i) Experiment 3; (ii) the largest chips have the smallest surface area and so the lowest rate of reaction.

Comment The curve for experiment 3 has the lowest gradient at the beginning of the reaction. If you got this wrong check the section on **surface area** again.

Q2 c (i) 7.5 minutes (approximately); (ii) the reaction finished because the marble was used up.

Comment Try to read off the graph as accurately as you can. In an examination you will be allowed a small margin of error. In this example 7.3 to 7.7 minutes would be acceptable. The question says that the hydrochloric acid was 'an excess'. This means that there was more than would be needed. Therefore the reaction must have finished because the marble was used up. Always look for the phrase 'an excess' or 'in excess'.

Q2 d The same mass of marble was used in each experiment.

Comment As the acid is in excess the amount of marble will determine how much carbon dioxide is produced.

Q2 e The curve would be steeper (have a higher gradient) at the beginning of the reaction but would reach the same plateau height.

Comment Increasing the temperature will increase the rate of the reaction but will not change the amount of carbon dioxide produced. If you are still in doubt about this read the section on **temperature** again.

Q3 a A catalyst is a substance that alters the rate of a chemical reaction but does not change itself.

Comment Remember that whilst most catalysts speed up reactions some slow them down.

Q3 b A catalyst provides another route for the reaction with a different activation energy.

Comment Think of activation energy as an energy barrier that prevents reactants changing into products.

3 Making use of enzymes (page 127)

Q1 A biological catalyst.

Comment A really good answer would include the fact that they are protein molecules.

Q2 a Yeast.

Q2 b The brewing and baking industries.

Comment Remember that the ethanol is the more important product in the brewing industry and that the carbon dioxide is more important in the baking industry.

Q2 c At higher temperatures the enzymes present in the yeast are denatured and can no longer act as catalysts.

Comment A common mistake is to say that the 'enzymes are killed' at higher temperatures. Enzymes are not alive in the first place!

Q2 d glucose → ethanol + carbon dioxide

Q2 e $C_6H_{12}O_6 \rightarrow 2C_2H_5OH + 2CO_2$

Comment Remember when balancing an equation that the balancing numbers can only be placed in front of the formulae (see Unit 7).

Q3 a An active site is the part of an enzyme molecule in which reactant molecules are trapped.

Comment You can think of it as a hole or cavity.

Q3 b The arrangement and shape of the active site in an enzyme will only 'fit' one specific type of molecule.

Comment This is sometimes referred to as a 'lock and key' model – only one key fits the lock.

4 Reversible reactions (page 129)

Q1 A reaction is in equilibrium when the number of reactant and product molecules do not change.

Comment You might remember that at equilibrium the rate of the forward reaction equals the rate of the backward reaction.

Q2 a The rate changes (usually increases).

Comment Catalysts are usually used to increase reaction rate.

Q2 b No effect.

Comment A catalyst does not change the position of equilibrium.

Q3 The higher temperature is used to increase the rate of the reaction.

Comment The choice of temperature in industrial processes often balances how much can be formed (depends on the equilibrium position) and how fast it can be formed (depends on the rate of the reaction).

UNIT 12: THE PERIODIC TABLE
1 Organising the elements (page 132)

Q1 a b

Comment Group 4 is the fourth major column from the left.

Q1 b a

Comment This is the second row.

Q1 c d

Comment The noble gas family is group 0 or 8.

Q1 d c

Comment Transition elements are in the middle block.

Q1 e b

Comment Metalloids are found near the 'staircase' on the right side of the periodic table, which separates metals from non-metals.

Q1 f d and f

Comment These are on the right of the 'staircase'. If you included b you would not be penalised.

Q1 g d

Comment Gases are non-metals and so have to be on the right side. f is a possibility but in groups 5, 6 and 7 elements near the bottom of the group are solids.

Q2 They contain the same number of electrons in the outer electron shell.

Comment Remember that how an atom reacts depends on its outermost electrons.

Q3 a B. Its pH is less than 7.

Comment *Remember that the acidic oxide will also react with an alkali.*

Q3 b A and B. Both react with an acid.

Comment *'A' has a pH of 7 because it doesn't dissolve in water.*

Q3 c (i) Neutralisation

Comment *Copper oxide is a base. The reaction of a base with an acid is neutralisation.*

Q3 c (ii) Copper oxide + sulphuric acid → copper sulphate + water

Comment *Remember that acid + base → salt + water.*

Q3 c (iii) $CuO(s) + H_2SO_4(aq) \rightarrow CuSO_4(aq) + H_2O(l)$

Comment *No extra balancing is required here.*

Q3 c (iv) A.

Comment *Copper(II) oxide is insoluble in water and so the mixture will have a pH of 7.*

2 The metals (page 136)

Q1 a Caesium.

Comment *Remember that the reactivity of metals increases down a group.*

Q1 b To prevent the metal reacting with air and water.

Comment *These are highly reactive metals. They oxidise rapidly without heat being needed.*

Q1 c Caesium.

Comment *The melting point gives a measure of hardness. Melting point decreases down the group.*

Q1 d On cutting, the metal is exposed to the air and rapidly oxidises.

Comment *Tarnishing is another word for oxidation.*

Q1 e When added to water they react to produce an alkali.

Comment *The metal hydroxides formed in the reactions are alkalis.*

Q1 f Sodium is less dense than water.

Comment *Density increases down the group. The more reactive metals would not float but their reaction is so violent that the metal usually flies out of the water!*

Q1 g (i) rubidium + oxygen → rubidium oxide
$4Rb(s) + O_2(g) \rightarrow 2Rb_2O(s)$

Comment *Rubidium behaves in the same way as sodium but more violently.*

Q1 g (ii) caesium + water → caesium hydroxide + hydrogen
$2Cs(s) + 2H_2O(l) \rightarrow 2CsOH(aq) + H_2(g)$

Comment *The reaction of the group 1 metals with water produces the metal hydroxide (an alkali) and hydrogen.*

Q1 g (iii) potassium + chlorine → potassium chloride
$2K(s) + Cl_2(g) \rightarrow 2KCl(s)$

Comment *Potassium chloride is a salt with an appearance very similar to sodium chloride, common salt.*

Q2 a They are harder, have higher densities, higher melting points and are sonorous (any two).

Comment *If you couldn't answer this look back at the summary on page 133.*

Q2 b A catalyst is a substance that changes the speed of a chemical reaction without being changed itself.

Comment *Catalysts and their effects on rates of reaction are covered in Unit 11.*

Q2 c The alkali metals have only one electron in the outer electron shell. Transition metals have more than one electron in the outer electron shell.

Comment *Reactivity is principally related to the number of electrons in the outer electron shell. Metals lower down a group are also more reactive than those higher up, but this is of secondary importance.*

Q3 a A – sodium, B – copper, C – calcium.

Comment *The sodium and calcium can be identified from the flame test information. Only one of the compounds contains a transition metal (forms a coloured compound).*

Q3 b The hydroxides of the group 1 metals are soluble in water and would not form a precipitate.

Comment *Calcium is in group 2. Calcium hydroxide is only sparingly soluble in water and so a precipitate forms.*

Q3 c $Cu^{2+}(aq) + 2OH^-(aq) \rightarrow Cu(OH)_2(s)$

Comment *The important part of the compound is the copper ion. The non-metal ion or radical does not play a part in the reaction - it is a spectator ion.*

3 The non-metals (page 140)

Q1 a Fluorine

Comment *Unlike groups of metals, reactivity decreases down the group.*

Q1 b Bromine

Comment *Bromine is the only liquid non-metal.*

Q1 c Iodine

Comment *Astatine would be expected to be a solid but it is radioactive with a very short half-life so it is difficult to confirm this prediction.*

Q1 d They only need to gain one electron in order to have a full outer electron shell. Other non-metals need to gain more than one electron.

Comment *Remember that reactivity depends on the number of electrons in the outer electron shell.*

Q1 e (i) sodium + chlorine → sodium chloride
$2Na(s) + Cl_2(g) \rightarrow 2NaCl(s)$

Q1 e (ii) magnesium + bromine → magnesium bromide
$Mg(s) + Br_2(l) \rightarrow MgBr_2(s)$

Comment *The halogen elements react with all metals. They form salts, called fluorides, chlorides, bromides and iodides.*

Q1 e (iii) hydrogen + fluorine → hydrogen fluoride
$H_2(g) + F_2(g) \rightarrow 2HF(g)$

Comment *Hydrogen fluoride will have very similar properties to the more familiar hydrogen chloride. Its solution in water, hydrofluoric acid, is highly corrosive.*

Q2 a (i) Very pale yellow. **(ii)** Brown. **(iii)** Brown. **(iv)** Colourless.

Comment *Bromine is more soluble in water than iodine but it is very difficult to distinguish between dilute solutions of the two. Sometimes a solvent like cyclohexane is added. The bromine is brown in the cyclohexane, the iodine is violet.*

Q2 b On mixing the pale yellow solution with the colourless solution, a brown solution is formed.

Comment Observations are what you see, smell or hear. You don't see bromine; you see a brown solution.

Q2 c ✗ ✓ ✓
✗ ✗ ✓
✗ ✗ ✗

Comment The more reactive halogen will displace (take the place of) the less reactive halogen. Chlorine will displace bromine from sodium bromide because it is more reactive. Iodine cannot replace chlorine or bromine as it is less reactive than both of them.

Q2 d Bromine + sodium iodide → iodine + sodium bromide
$Br_2(aq) + 2NaI(aq) → I_2(aq) + 2NaBr(aq)$

Comment Bromine is more reactive than iodine and so will displace it from the solution. In this reaction it would be difficult to see a change as both the bromine and iodine solutions are brown. Using cyclohexane would confirm that a reaction had taken place.

Q3 Noble gases have full outer electron shells and so do not need to gain or lose electrons in a reaction.

Comment Remember that metals want to lose electrons and form positive ions, whereas non-metals often try to gain electrons and form negative ions. Details of ionic bonding are given in Unit 8.

UNIT 13: CHEMICAL CALCULATIONS
1 Atomic masses and the mole (page 143)

Q1 a 2 moles

Comment Moles = mass/RAM = 56/28 = 2

Q1 b 0.1 mole

Comment Moles = mass/RAM = 3.1/31 = 0.1

Q1 c 0.25 mole

Comment Moles = mass/RMM = 11/44 = 0.24

Q1 d 0.5 mole

Comment Moles = mass/RFM = 50/100 = 0.5
Note: Calcium carbonate is an ionic compound so the correct term is relative formula mass.

Q2 a 48 g

Comment Mass = moles × RAM = 2 × 24 = 48 g

Q2 b 4 g

Comment Mass = moles × RMM = 2 × 2 = 4 g

Q2 c 9.8 g

Comment Mass = moles × RMM = 0.1 × 98 = 9.8 g

Q3 $TiCl_4$

Comment	Ti	Cl
mass/RAM	25/48	75/35.5
moles	0.52	2.1
ratio	0.52/0.52 = 1	2.1/0.52 = 4.04
formula is $TiCl_4$		

2 Equations and reacting masses (page 147)

Q1 4 g

Comment $2Na$ = 2 moles = 46 g. $2NaOH$ = 2 moles = 80 g. The scaling factor is ÷ 20.

Q2 a 560 tonnes

Comment Fe_2O_3 = 1 mole → 160 tonnes. 2Fe = 2 moles → 112 tonnes. The scaling factor is × 5.

Q2 b 144 litres at room temperature and pressure

Comment Fe_2O_3 = 1 mole → 160 g. $3CO_2$ = 3 × 24 = 72 litres. The scaling factor is × 2.

Q3 2.33 g

Comment $BaCl_2$ = 1 mole = 1000 cm^3 (1 M). BaSO4 = 1 mole = 233 g.
First scale by ÷ 5. 1000 cm^3 (0.2 M) and 46.6 g.
Second scale by ÷ 20. 50 cm^3 (0.2 M) and 2.33 g.

UNIT 14: ELECTRICITY
1 Electric circuits (page 150)

Q1 a A_1 reading 0.2 A, A_2 reading 0.2 A.

Comment The current is always the same at any point in a series circuit.

Q1 b A_4 reading 0.30 A, A_5 reading 0.15 A.

Comment The ammeter A_6 has been placed on one branch of the parallel circuit. Ammeter A_5 is on the other branch. As the lamps are identical the current flowing through them must be the same. Ammeter A_4 gives the current before it 'splits' in half as it flows through the two parallel branches.

Q2 Reading on V_1 = 6 V.

Comment The potential difference across the battery is 9 V. This must equal the total p.d. in the circuit. Assuming there is no loss along the copper wiring the p.d. across the lamp must be 9 − 3 = 6 V.

Q3 a 0.33 A

Comment Use the equation $I = Q/t$, $I = 10/30 = 0.33$ A.

Q3 b (i) 10 C; (ii) 36 000 C.

Comment Rearranging the formula, $Q = It$, (i) $Q = 10 × 1 = 10$ C, (ii) $Q = 10 × 60 × 60 = 36 000$ C.

2 What affects resistance? (page 155)

Q1 a

The resistance is calculated using Ohm's law, $R = V/I$.

Comment Remember that the ammeter must be in series with the nichrome wire, but the voltmeter must be in parallel.

Q1 b (i) The resistance would double.
(ii) The resistance would be halved.

Comment Resistance is directly proportional to length. Resistance is inversely proportional to cross-sectional area. If necessary look back at the models on page 156.

Q2 a 24 V

Comment $V = IR = 2 × 12 = 24$ V

Q2 b 20 V

Comment $V = IR = 0.1 × 200 = 20$ V

Q2 c 0.12 A

Comment $I = V/R = 12/100 = 0.12$ A

Q2 d 23 A

Comment $I = V/R = 230/10 = 23$ A

Q2 e 60 Ω

Comment $R = V/I = 6/0.1 = 60$ Ω

Q2 f 23 Ω

Comment $R = V/I = 230/10 = 23$ Ω

Q3 a The resistance increases as the voltage increases.

Comment If the resistance were constant the line would be straight with a constant gradient. It curves in such a way that increasing voltage produces a smaller increase in the current, so resistance must be increasing.

Q3 b As the voltage increases the temperature of the wire must also be increasing.

Comment This is a common characteristic of non-ohmic resistors – that is, resistors that do not obey Ohm's law.

3 Power in electrical circuits (page 159)

Q1 920 W.

Comment Power = $V \times I$ = 230 × 4 = 920 W. Don't forget the unit. Power is measured in watts.

Q2 a 24p

Comment Cost = units × 8 = 1 × 3 × 8 = 24p. Remember that a unit is a kilowatt-hour so the 1000 W has to be converted into kilowatts, that is 1 kW.

Q2 b 8p.

Comment 200 W = 0.2 kW. Cost = units × 8 = 0.2 × 5 × 8 = 8p.

Q3 1800 kJ.

Comment Energy = power × time (s) = 3000 × 10 × 60 = 1 800 000 J or 1800 kJ. Remember that 1 watt is 1 joule/second.

4 Static electricity (page 162)

Q1 a Electrons are rubbed off the surface of the plastic onto the cloth.

Comment Static electricity is produced by removing electrons from one insulator to another. An excess of electrons leads to a negative charge.

Q1 b The positively charged rod induces a negative charge on the surface of the paper near to the rod. Opposite charges then attract. (A positive charge is therefore induces in the paper well away from the charged rod.)

Comment Electrostatic induction is a common phenomenon. Remember this is how you can make a balloon stick to the ceiling.

Q2 a The passenger is charged by friction as her clothes rub against the seat covers. The car is also charged by friction with the road and the air. Touching metal allows the charge to flow to earth.

Comment Remember static electricity is produced by friction.

Q2 b Touching a door handle after walking on a synthetic carpet, or removing clothing.

Comment Synthetic fibres are more likely to cause this effect than natural fibres. This must be due to the different atom arrangements.

Q3 Lightning, fuelling aircraft, in grain silos.

Comment Static electricity can cause explosions in any situations when there are fuels in the gaseous form or where there are very fine particles of solid material (dust).

UNIT 15: ELECTROMAGNETIC EFFECTS

1 Electromagnetism (page 164)

Q1 a No. Aluminium is not magnetic.

Comment Remember that very few metals are magnetic (e.g. iron, cobalt and nickel). The electromagnet would separate steel cans as steel is an alloy containing iron.

Q1 b Switch off the current to the electromagnet.

Comment The magnetic field is only present when the current is flowing. An electromagnet is a temporary magnet.

Q2 Increasing the current flowing through the coil. Increasing the number of coils. Adding a soft iron core inside the cardboard tube.

Comment These will produce a stronger magnetic field.

Q3 When the switch is pressed the electromagnet attracts the hammer support and the hammer hits the bell. The movement of the hammer support breaks the circuit and so the electromagnet ceases to operate. The hammer support then returns to its original position, forming the circuit again and the process is repeated.

Comment The electromagnet is constantly activated and then deactivated. This means that the hammer will continually hit the bell and then retract.

2 Electromagnetic induction (page 167)

Q1 If the rotation of the armature is producing electricity which is being withdrawn via A and B, then it is a generator. If, alternatively, electricity is being supplied via A and B to produce rotation then it is a motor.

Comment The same device can be used as either a motor or a generator. A motor needs an electrical supply in order to produce movement. In a generator the movement is used to generate electricity.

Q2 a Iron.

Comment The core must be a magnetic material. It concentrates the magnetic effect.

Q2 b A magnetic field is produced.

Comment Remember that a current flowing in a wire will produce a magnetic field around it.

Q2 c A current is induced.

Comment The varying magnetic field in the core induces a current in the secondary coil.

Q2 d 24 V.

Comment $V_p/V_s = N_p/N_s$; $V_p/14 = 12/7$; $V_p = 12/7 \times 14 = 24$ V.

Q3 An electric current produces a heating effect in a wire, thus transferring energy as heat. To reduce energy loss electricity is transmitted at as low a current as possible, which means transmitting at very high voltage.

Comment The heating effect of an electric current is considered in Unit 14.

UNIT 16: FORCES AND MOTION
I The effects of forces (page 171)

Q1 A – the wooden block would not move; B – the car would accelerate; C – the ice skater would maintain a constant speed.

Comment A – The forces are balanced and so the stationary wooden block would not move. B – The resultant force would be 4000 N. This unbalanced force will cause the car to accelerate. (As the car moves faster the resistive force caused by air resistance will increase and eventually reach 6000 N). C – The forces are balanced. As the skier is moving she will continue to do so at the same speed.

Q2 a

Comment Friction will always oppose motion and so the arrow points in the opposite direction to the direction of motion.

Q2 b The frictional forces slow the skier down.

Comment As the skier travels downhill the friction force opposes the motion.

Q2 c Using narrower skis, or using wax on the skis.

Comment Lubricant reduces frictional forces.

Q3 a *Stage 1* – The skydiver is accelerating. The downward force of gravity is greater than the upward force caused by air resistance. *Stage 2* – The sky diver is travelling at constant speed. The forces of gravity and air resistance are balanced. *Stage 3* – The sky diver is slowing down. The force caused by the air in the parachute is greater than the force of gravity. *Stage 4* – The sky diver is travelling at a constant speed. The forces are balanced again.

Comment In questions of this sort the first thing to do is to decide which forces will be acting on the object. The next thing is to decide whether the forces are balanced or unbalanced. If they are unbalanced the skydiver will be either accelerating or decelerating. If they are balanced the skydiver will either be travelling at constant speed or not moving. In stage 2 the skydiver will have reached the terminal speed and because the forces are balanced will not accelerate or decelerate.

Q3 b The force of gravity is balanced by the upward force of the ground on the sky diver.

Comment The upward force from the ground is equal to the skydiver's weight.

2 Velocity and acceleration (page 174)

Q1 a The speed remained constant.

Comment If the line on a distance–time graph has a constant gradient then the speed is constant.

Q1 b 600 m.

Comment This can be read off the graph: after 20 s the car had travelled 200 m, after 60 s it had travelled 800 m. So the distance travelled is 800 – 200 = 600 m.

Q1 c 15 m/s.

Comment Speed = distance/time, $v = 600/40 = 15$ m/s. Don't forget the units.

Q1 d It stopped.

Comment The line is horizontal during this time, indicating that the car was not moving (no distance was travelled).

Q2 a 2.0 m/s/s.

Comment Acceleration = change in velocity/time, $a = (1.5 - 0)/0.75 = 2$ m/s/s.

Q2 b 2.25 m.

Comment Total distance = area under the line = $(1/2 \times 0.75 \times 1.5) + (1/2 \times 2.25 \times 1.5) = 2.25$ m.
Note: the tractor showed constant acceleration from A to B and then constant deceleration from B to C.

Q3 a 2.5 m/s/s.

Comment Acceleration = change in speed/time, $a = (30 - 0)/12 = 2.5$ m/s/s. Don't forget the units!

Q3 b 2500 N.

Comment Force = mass × acceleration, $F = 1000 \times 2.5 = 2500$ N.

UNIT 17: ENERGY
1 Where does our energy come from? (page 180)

Q1 a A source that cannot be regenerated – it takes millions of years to form.

Comment A common mistake is to say that it is a source that 'cannot be used again'. Many energy sources cannot be used again but they can be regenerated (e.g. wood).

Q1 b Coal, oil and natural gas.

Comment These are the fossil fuels. Substances obtained from fossil fuels such as petrol and diesel are not strictly speaking fossil fuels.

Q1 c Coal.

Comment Coal is becoming increasingly more difficult to mine as more inaccessible coal seams are tackled. The 300 year estimate could be very optimistic.

Q2 a The total energy increased from 1955 to 1975 and then levelled out.

Comment Always describe a graphical trend carefully. Be as precise as you can.

Q2 b The amount of coal used has significantly reduced. The amounts of oil, gas and nuclear fuel used have significantly increased.

Comment It is important to refer to each of the energy sources given on the graph.

Q3 a Any two from: strength of the wind, high ground, constant supply of wind, open ground.

Comment Higher ground tends to be more windy than lower ground. However, the wind farm cannot be built too far away from the centres of population otherwise costs will be incurred in connecting to the National Grid.

Q3 b *Advantage:* renewable energy source, no air pollution. *Disadvantage:* unsightly, takes up too much space.

Comment Wind turbines can be very efficient. However, they need to be reasonably small and so a large number are needed to generate significant amounts of electricity. Environmentally, although they produce no air pollution they do take up a lot of land.

2 Transferring energy (page 182)

Q1 The thin layers will trap air between them. Air is an insulator and so will reduce thermal transfer from the body.

Comment Remember that air is a very good insulator. Trapping it between layers of clothing means that convection is inhibited as well as conduction.

Q2 The molecules that are able to leave the surface of the liquid are those that are moving the fastest, that is, the molecules with the most energy. The average energy of the remaining molecules is therefore reduced and so the liquid is cooler.

Comment The temperature of a liquid is related to the average speed of its molecules. If the temperature is reduced, on average, the molecules will move more slowly.

Q3 Energy from the hot water is transferred from the inner to the outer surface of the metal by conduction. Energy is transferred through the still air by radiation.

Comment In a question like this it is important to take the energy transfer stage by stage. Thermal transfer through a solid involves conduction. Thermal transfer through still air must involve radiation. In fact, convection would be occurring and it is very likely that the air behind the radiator would be moving (convention currents).

3 Work, power and energy (page 186)

Q1 12.5 m.

Comment Work done = $F s$
$F = 400 \times 10 = 4000$ N
$s = W/F = 50\,000/4000 = 12.5$ m

Q2 a 6000 J.

Comment Energy transferred = $30 \times 200 = 6000$ J

Q2 b 33.3 W.

Comment Power = work done/time taken = $6000/180 = 33.3$ W. Remember that a watt is 1 joule/s so the time must be in seconds.

Q3 a 10 500 J.

Comment P.E. = $m g h = 35 \times 10 \times 30 = 10\,5000$ J

Q3 b 24.5 m/s.

Comment Assuming all the potential energy is transferred to kinetic energy:
K.E. = $1/2\, mv^2$, so $v^2 = 2$ K.E./m
$= 2 \times 10\,500/35 = 600$, and $v = 24.5$ m/s

Q3 c Some of the gravitational potential energy will have been transferred to thermal energy due to the friction between the sledge and the snow.

Comment Energy must be conserved but friction is a very common cause of energy being wasted, that is, being transferred into less useful forms.

UNIT 18: WAVES
1 The properties of waves (page 189)

Q1 a D.

Comment The crest is the top of the wave.

Q1 b A and E.

Comment The wavelength is the length of the repeating pattern.

Q1 c B.

Comment The amplitude is half the distance between the crest and the trough. If you had difficulty with parts a to c look back at the diagram on page 190.

260 ANSWERS TO CHECK YOURSELF QUESTIONS

Q1 d 512.

Comment Frequency is measured in hertz and 1Hz = 1 cycle (or wave) per second.

Q2 0.33 m.

Comment $v = f \times \lambda$ or $\lambda = v/f$
$\lambda = 3 \times 10^8/9 \times 10^8 = 0.33$ m

Q3 1.33 m

Comment $v = f \times \lambda$ or $\lambda = v/f$
$\lambda = 340/256 = 1.33$ m

2 The electromagnetic spectrum (page 193)

Q1 a Light.

Comment The sensitive cells form a part of the eye called the retina.

Q1 b Ultraviolet.

Comment Suntan lotions contain chemicals that absorb some of the UV radiation from the Sun before it can act on the skin.

Q1 c Microwaves.

Comment The key word here was 'rapid'. Electric cookers make use of infrared radiation for cooking but microwaves produce much more rapid cooking.

Q1 d X-rays.

Comment A gamma camera would not be as good for this purpose as the gamma rays penetrate the bone as well as the flesh.

Q1 e Infrared.

Comment Remote car locking sometimes uses infrared beams.

Q2 a They can pass through soft tissue and kill cancer cells.

Comment Gamma rays are useful because of their great penetrating power. This is also their disadvantage. Consequently they have to be used extremely carefully. They are the highest energy waves in the electromagnetic spectrum.

Q2 b They can damage healthy cells and cause cancer because of their very high energy.

Comment All waves in the electromagnetic spectrum have different frequencies and wavelengths.

Q2 c They have different frequencies and wavelengths.

Comment All waves in the electromagnetic spectrum travel at the same speed in a vacuum – the speed of light.

Q2 d 300 000 000 m/s.

Comment As you might have guessed this is an important point and one that is often tested in exams!

3 Light reflection and refraction (page 195)

Q1 a In reflection light changes direction when it bounces off a surface. In refraction the light changes direction when it passes from one medium to another.

Comment In reflection the angle of incidence and the angle of reflection are the same. In refraction the angle of incidence does not equal the angle of refraction, as the ray of light bends towards or away from the normal.

Q1 b (I)

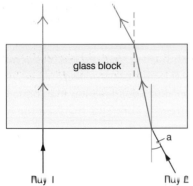

glass block

Ray 1   Ray 2

Q1 b (ii) The angle of incidence.

Q1 b (iii) The normal line.

Comment The ray of light will only be bent if it hits the block at an angle. In both cases the speed of the light in the block will be slower than in air.

Q2 a

Comment Remember that with a plane mirror the image is the same size as the object and will be the same distance behind the mirror as the object is in front. When drawing the ray diagram check that the angles of incidence and reflection are the same.

Q2 b Light will be reflected off the hair onto the first mirror. If the angle is correct the reflected ray will then travel to the second mirror. If the angle is correct it will then be reflected into the eye.

Comment Don't forget that the light travels from the object to the eye! In an examination you might find it easier to draw a diagram showing the passage of the ray of light. In this way you can show the correct angles on the mirrors.

Q3 a

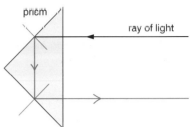

prism

ray of light

Comment You should draw a normal line to ensure that for each reflection the angles of incidence and reflection are the same.

Q3 b Binoculars, bicycle reflector, cat's eyes.

Comment Periscopes are also often made using prisms rather than mirrors.

Q3 c R, T, T.

Comment Total internal reflection occurs only when the angle of incidence is equal to or greater than the critical angle.

4 Sound waves (page 198)

Q1 a (i) Vibrations. (ii) Compressions and rarefactions travel through the air.

Comment These are both common questions, so don't forget. Sound is a longitudinal wave. The compressions and rarefactions are small differences in air pressure.

Q1 b Sound waves cannot travel through a vacuum. Radio waves don't require a medium.

Comment This is a big difference between sound waves and electromagnetic waves.

Q1 c Particles in water are closer together so the vibrations are passed on more quickly.

Comment The denser the material the greater the speed of sound. In concrete, for example, the speed of sound is 5000 m/s.

Q2 a Above the limit of audible sound.

Comment The frequency of ultrasonic waves is too high for the human ear to hear.

Q2 b The motion of the medium is parallel to the direction of movement of the wave.

Comment This contrasts with transverse waves where the medium moves at right angles to the movement of the wave.

Q2 c The wavelength decreases, the frequency remains the same.

Comment You should remember that $v = f \times \lambda$; v decreases, f stays the same so λ must decrease.

Q3 375 m.

Comment $s = v \times t \times 1/2 = 1500 \times 0.5 \times 0.5 = 375$ m

UNIT 19: THE EARTH AND BEYOND
I The Solar System (page 200)

Q1 Hydrogen nuclei join together to make helium nuclei in a process known as nuclear fusion.

Comment Don't get confused with nuclear fission, which is the process used to obtain energy in nuclear power stations. Very high temperatures are required before nuclear fusion will take place.

Q2 Clouds of hydrogen gas → blue star → red supergiant → supernova.

Comment The sequence is given in the table on page 202. A supernova is only produced from a very large star. A star such as our Sun will eventually form a white dwarf.

Q3 a (i) The force due to gravity, its weight, which (ii) acts towards the centre of the Earth.

Comment Gravity always pulls towards the centre of the Earth. The satellite's weight is providing the centripetal force required for it to move in a circle.

Q3 b The satellite is always at the same position above the surface of the Earth.

Comment The ring directly above the equator at the height of geostationary orbits is full of communication satellites.

2 How did the Universe begin? (page 203)

Q1 Light waves from a star near the Earth with a lower frequency than that emitted by the star.

Comment If the emitter is moving away from the observer the frequency is reduced. In the case of light waves, a reduction in frequency results in a shift to the lower frequency (red) end of the visible spectrum.

Q2 Red shift evidence shows that all galaxies are moving apart from each other. Reversing the direction of movement of the galaxies shows that they could all have come from the same starting point.

Comment It was the famous astronomer Edwin Hubble who first observed the red shift and then proposed the Big Bang theory.

UNIT 20: RADIOACTIVITY
I Unstable atoms (page 204)

Q1 a Alpha particles.

Comment Gamma particles would not have deflected at all as they are uncharged. Beta particles might work, but they deflect very easily because they have such a small mass.

Q1 b Most of the atom is empty space.

Comment The neutron wasn't discovered until 1932.

Q1 c The atom must have a very high concentration of mass and positive charge. Rutherford called this the nucleus.

Q2 a 11 protons, 13 neutrons.

Comment The atomic number gives the number of protons. The difference between the mass number and the atomic number equals the number of neutrons.

Q2 b 15 hours.

Comment The count falls from 100 Bq to 50 Bq in 15 hours. It also falls from 50 Bq to 25 Bq in 15 hours.

Q3 a Beta particle.

Comment A beta particle is an electron. The 'beta' symbol can also be written as an electron, 'e'. The electron is shown with an atomic number of −1 and a mass number of 0.

Q3 b $x = 24; y = 12$.

Comment The mass numbers must balance on the
left-hand and right-hand sides of the equation (24 = 24 + 0). The atomic numbers must balance on the left-hand and right-hand sides of the

2 Uses and dangers of radioactivity (page 208)

Q1 a Alpha particles.

Q1 b Beta particles.

Q1 c Gamma rays.

Comment Details of these uses are given on page 208. Alpha particles are the most ionising, gamma rays are the most penetrating.

Q2 a A tracer is a radioactive isotope used in detection.

Comment Tracers are widely used to detect leaks and blockages.

Q2 b Sodium-24. The lawrencium-257 has too short a half-life; the sulphur 35 and carbon 14 have half-lives which are too long.

Comment The tracer must be radioactive for long enough for it to be detected after injection into the body but must not remain radioactive in the body for longer than necessary.

Q3 a Lead.

Comment In fact the uranium-238 decays through a chain of short-lived intermediate elements before forming lead.

Q3 b The ratio of uranium-238 to lead-207 enables the age of the rock to be determined.

Comment In a similar way the carbon-14: carbon-12 ratio is important in finding out the age of previously living material.

ANSWERS TO QUESTIONS TO TRY

UNIT 21: EXAM PRACTICE
Biology (page 214)

Q1 a C (1).
   D (1).

Examiner's comments
One way of tackling multiple-choice type questions is to eliminate the answers you know are incorrect.

Q1 b (i) **One** from: taller / longer / bigger / have grown (1).
   One from: curved / bent (towards light) (1).
   (ii) Light / sun (1).
   (iii) Auxin (1).

Examiner's comments
Do not jump straight to the questions; make sure you look at all the information you are given first. Part i) is an easy starter that you can answer simply by using information from the diagram. The clue for part ii) is the hole in the box. Part iii) is an example of where spelling is important. **In most questions examiners will give the mark for the correct answer even if it is misspelt. However this does not apply if the misspelt word could be confused with another scientific term.** For example, in this case, if the answer given could be confused with the word 'axon' (part of a neurone) the mark would not be given.

Q1 c Weeds are too weak / collapse under own weight (1).

Examiner's comments
Although the mark can be gained for a straightforward answer, **if you give a more detailed answer than is required, but it is still correct, you will gain the mark.** For example, here you could explain that xylem vessels are constricted and that the plants dehydrate.

Q1 d i) In glands (1).
   ii) Through blood (1).

Examiner's comments
As mentioned above, answers that give more detail than necessary, but are still correct, gain marks. For example, if you said that hormones are carried by the blood plasma you would gain the mark for ii). **However, only be specific if you are sure of the answer.** For example, if you said that hormones are carried by red blood cells, which is incorrect, you would lose the mark.

Q1 e i) C (1).
   ii) Injections (1).

Examiner's comments
C is the answer to part i) because without insulin, the blood sugar level rises too high after a meal, but in between meals there are no reserves of glycogen to convert back into glucose, so the blood sugar level may fall too low.

Q2 a A (1).

Examiner's comments
Make sure you read any information and look at any diagrams you are given before you answer a question. If there are two whiteflies on a single leaf, then there will be a large number of whiteflies on a whole tomato plant.

Q2 b (Biomass is) the mass of organisms (1).
   Energy is lost between stages (1).
   Plus **two** from: as heat / from respiration / from movement; excretion / egestion; not all of each stage is eaten; other food chains are involved (2).

Examiner's comments
The only way to gain the maximum four marks in this question is to include in your answer all the points that are asked for. Not all high scoring questions will give as much guidance as this one but **make sure that if guidance is given you follow it.**

Q2 c A maximum of **two** advantages from: fast acting / can use at any time / might kill or harm more than one type of pest.
A maximum of **two** disadvantages from: might kill or harm other animals / pests may become resistant / expensive / may have to apply more than once / may cause pollution / pesticides may enter food chains.
The maximum for the whole question is **three** marks (3).

Examiner's comments
As the question asks about advantages and disadvantages you cannot get full marks unless you tackle both. In this example, an idea such as the fact that pesticides can kill more than one type of animal can be either an advantage (if the other animals are also pests) or a disadvantage (if the other animals are either useful or even harmless). You will only gain both marks if you clearly explain your answers.

Q2 d i) B (1).
ii) Pesticide taken in by small organisms / passed up food chain (1).
Pesticide is persistent / not excreted / not broken down (1).

Examiner's comments
The correct answer to i) is B because making the holes in nets smaller means that even younger (smaller) fish can be caught. As younger fish will have had less chance of reproducing than older ones, the population is likely to fall. You could also answer this question by eliminating incorrect answers as all the other options are likely to increase the number of cod.
To gain both marks in part ii) you do not have to give two answers but instead explain your answer fully.

Chemistry (page 222)

Q1 a i) polymer (1).
ii) monomer (1).
iii) high temperature (1) and high pressure (1).

Examiner's comments
A polymer ('poly' meaning many) is made up from a large number of monomers ('mono' meaning single). The reaction will only happen in a reasonable amount of time if the temperature and pressure are both high.

Q1 b polythene – plastic bags (1); epoxy resin – adhesive (1); polystyrene – insulation (1)

Examiner's comments
You will need to remember the uses of the more common plastics.

Q1 c Either

Landfill sites (1). Problems: any **one** from eyesore, plastic blows about, gets filled up quickly, takes up a lot of room, valuable resources wasted (1).
Or
Burning (1). Problems: any **one** from makes toxic gases, makes carbon dioxide, reference to the greenhouse effect, reference to global warming, valuable resources wasted (1).
Or
Develop new types of polymer (1) that are biodegradable or photodegradable (1).
Quality of written communication. Use at least one of the following scientific terms: Landfill, biodegradable, atmosphere, photodegradable, combustion, incinerate, toxic, poisonous, greenhouse effect, global warming, carbon monoxide, carbon dioxide, environment (1).

Examiner's comments
This question requires an extended answer. **Look at the number of marks available and the bullet point prompts you have been given.** Also, you should be aware that one mark is given for the quality of your written communication. Recycling is becoming more common but landfill sites are still the most common way of disposing of plastic materials.

Q2 a Based on experimental evidence (1).

Examiner's comments
This question is based on the ideas and evidence part of the syllabus. It is intended to test your knowledge about the nature of scientific enquiry and its development over time. Scientists are always trying to prove their theories by using experimental evidence.

Q2 b Any **one** from: books, speeches at conferences, the internet, TV, newspapers, telephone, talk (1).

Examiner's comments
There are numerous ways that scientists can communicate with each other in the modern world. Communication was much more difficult in Dalton's time.

Q2 c Any **one** from: atoms cannot be seen, could not be proved, no solid evidence, resistance to change, professional jealousy, religious, political or cultural pressure (1).

Examiner's comments
Even today scientists don't always agree on how information should be interpreted. Even with the same evidence, two scientists could draw very different conclusions.

Q3 a i) Any **two** from: as the temperature increases, there will be more collisions between the particles in a given time (1) and there will be more energy available (1) to ensure that more collisions are successful and lead to a reaction (1).
ii) The greater the concentration, the more collisions there will be in a given time (1) and so the more likelihood of successful collisions that lead to a reaction (1).

Examiner's comments
The key word in each part is 'explain'. Also note that there are two marks for each part suggesting that you need to make two different points. Not every collision leads to a reaction. For a collision to be successful there must be enough energy available to overcome the activation energy. If this is the case the collision is said to be effective or successful.

Q3 b The energy required to break bonds (nitrogen to nitrogen and oxygen to oxygen) (1) is greater (1) than the energy that is released when bonds are formed (nitrogen to oxygen) (1).

Examiner's comments
Again you must look for three separate points to gain the three marks. You could gain marks by drawing a diagram – in this case an energy level diagram. The clue is that the reaction is endothermic. This tells you that, overall, energy is absorbed by the reaction and so the energy needed for bond breaking must be greater than the energy released on bond making.

Q3 c i) $2NO + 2CO \longrightarrow N_2 + 2CO_2$
correct formulae (1) balancing (1).
ii) Greater surface area (1).
More collisions between reacting particles in a given time (1).

Examiner's comments
Remember that all symbol equations should be balanced. Read the question carefully as it tells you exactly what the reactants and products are. A powder has a much greater surface area than a lump of solid so there is more surface for the reacting molecules to collide with.

Physics (page 229)

Q1 a i) Brown (1).
ii) If there is a surge of current (1) the fuse burns out and breaks the circuit (1).

Examiner's comments
You need to know the colours of the wires in an electrical plug. **In part (ii) there are two marks so you must give two separate points.**

Q1 b i) heater (1).
ii) Cost = number of units x 8 p (1).
Cost = 3 x 5 x 8 = 120 p or £1.20 (1).
iii) Live and neutral (1).

Examiner's comments
The appliance with the greatest power will be the one which is the most expensive to use. **When doing the calculation always write down the equation you are going to use and show your working**. A double insulated appliance does not need an Earth wire. This is because it is made of plastic and so the outer casing cannot become live.

Q1 c i) Any **two** from: it does not need to be stored in the house (1), it can be turned on and off easily (1), it is a clean source of energy/no pollution in the home (1).

ii) Any **one** point from: it is more expensive than many other supplies of energy (1), economy 7 heaters are only switched on at night and so are less flexible (1), economy 7 heaters are harder to adjust quickly to outside weather conditions (1).

Examiner's comments
In part (i) there are two marks so you must mention two points. It is important to remember that whilst electricity is a 'clean' energy source in the home, much of the electricity we use is made by burning oil, coal or gas which cause pollution at the power stations.

Q2 a i) gamma (1)
ii) can cause (skin) cancer (1)
iii) use: detecting broken bones (1)
danger: can kill healthy cells (1)

Examiner's comments
The electromagnetic waves with the shortest wavelength have the highest frequency. UV waves from the Sun can cause skin cancer and hence it is recommended to use 'UV filter' suntan lotions. Radiologists always stand behind lead screens when using X-rays – this prevents them getting exposed to high doses.

Q2 b A solution containing a radioactive tracer is injected into the blood stream. (1)
The passage of the tracer round the body is monitored with a gamma camera. (1)
The tracer will accumulate at a blockage and produce a region of higher concentration of gamma rays. (1)

Examiner's comments
This requires an extended response for which 3 marks are available. **This type of question could be answered in bullet form. Always try to follow a logical sequence** – in this case starting from the injection of the tracer and finishing with finding the blockage.

Q2 c i) p waves are longitudinal waves whereas s waves are transverse waves. (1)
p waves can travel through solid and liquid rock; s waves can only travel through solid rock. (1)

ii) the mantle is in a liquid state (1)
the outer core is in a liquid state (1)
the inner core is in a solid state (1)

Examiner's comments
The different penetrating powers of the primary (p) and secondary (s) waves have helped scientists to understand the structure of the Earth. P waves can travel through the inner core and so from one side of the Earth to the other. S waves cannot pass through the inner core. **Again, part (ii) could be answered in bullet point format.**

Published by Collins
An imprint of HarperCollins*Publishers*
77–85 Fulham Palace Road
London W6 8JB

Browse the complete Collins catalogue at
www.collinseducation.com

© HarperCollins*Publishers* Limited 2005

First published 2001
This new edition published 2005

10 9 8 7 6 5 4 3 2 1

ISBN 0 00 719055 7

British Library Cataloguing in Publication Data
A catalogue record for this publication is available from the British Library.

Acknowledgements
The Authors and Publisher are grateful to the following for permission to reproduce copyright material:

OCR: pp. 211, 213, 214, 215, 217, 220, 222, 223, 224, 225, 227, 229, 231. All answers to questions taken from past examination papers are entirely the responsibiltiy of the authors.

Photographs
(T = Top, B = Bottom, C = Centre, L = Left, R = Right)
John Birdsall Photography 160T; Peter Gould 86; Holt Studios International 51, 61; Andrew Lambert 70T; 77T, 85B, 129L, C & R, 138, 158 160B; Natural History Museum 97 T & B; Natural History Photographic Agency 76L, T, B & R, 81; Science Photo Library 9, 68, 70B, 77B, 85T, 193, 199; Taxi/Getty Images 80.

Illustrations
Roger Bastow, Harvey Collins, Richard Deverell, Jerry Fowler, Gecko Ltd, Ian Law, Mike Parsons, Dave Poole, Chris Rothero and Tony Warne

Every effort has been made to contact the holders of copyright material, but if any have been inadvertently overlooked, the Publishers will be pleased to make the necessary arrangements at the first opportunity.

Series design by Sally Boothroyd
Book design by Sally Boothroyd and Wendi Watson
Production by Katie Butler
Index compiled by Julie Rimington
Printed and bound by Printing Express, Hong Kong

INDEX